THE EVERYTHING
PARENT'S GUIDE TO
RAISING MINDFUL CHILDREN

Dear Reader,

We are humbled by this opportunity to share our knowledge, experience, and practice with you. Raising children is extremely difficult, and we believe that parents need all the support they can get.

As educators we play a significant role in helping children grow and realize what they are capable of. Throughout our careers, we have intentionally studied information from diverse fields including developmental psychology, neuroscience, and mindfulness practice, and have integrated those lessons into how we teach. As a result, our understanding of children's behavior and how to support their development has deepened considerably.

It is critical for parents to have effective tools to care for themselves and work positively with their kids, regardless of the circumstances. We have found mindfulness practices to be profoundly helpful in meeting each moment head on. Ultimately, it has allowed us, and many others, the freedom to be more of who we would like to be in a world of both messiness and grace.

In this book, we try to share the best of what we have learned from our combined twenty years of experience in education. We hope you find it useful and practical.

Thank you for all that you do.

Jeremy and Maureen

WELCOME TO THE

EVERYTHING®

PARENT'S GUIDES

Everything® Parent's Guides are a part of the bestselling Everything® series and cover common parenting issues like childhood illnesses and tantrums, as well as medical conditions like asthma and juvenile diabetes. These family-friendly books are designed to be a one-stop guide for parents. If you want authoritative information on specific topics not fully covered in other books, Everything® Parent's Guides are your perfect solution.

 Alerts

Urgent warnings

 Facts

Important snippets of information

 Essentials

Quick handy tips

 Questions

Answers to common questions

When you're done reading, you can finally say you know **EVERYTHING®**!

PUBLISHER Karen Cooper

MANAGING EDITOR, EVERYTHING® SERIES Lisa Laing

COPY CHIEF Casey Ebert

ASSOCIATE PRODUCTION EDITOR Mary Beth Dolan

ACQUISITIONS EDITOR Eileen Mullan

DEVELOPMENT EDITOR Eileen Mullan

EVERYTHING® SERIES COVER DESIGNER Erin Alexander

Visit the entire Everything® series at *www.everything.com*

THE
EVERYTHING®

PARENT'S GUIDE TO

RAISING MINDFUL
CHILDREN

Giving parents the tools to teach
emotional awareness, coping skills,
and impulse control in children

Jeremy Wardle and Maureen Weinhardt

Avon, Massachusetts

This book is for loving parents everywhere:
Thank you for everything you do.

Contents

Acknowledgments

We would like to express our profound gratitude to the many people who have guided us along our path: To our many teachers in Buddhism and Zen, especially Melissa Blacker, David Rynick, James Ford, Josh Bartok, and the Boundless Way Zen community. To the Zen Peacemakers, Bernie Glassman, and Eve Marko. Thank you to Liz Gray and the Clonlara School community for supporting us in new approaches to classroom education. To the Mansfield Children's Center and the Jones family, particularly Aidan, Brian, and Sarah. Thank you to our many students who have taught us *so* much. And especially, thank you to our parents and families for your incredible love and support. You have made this all possible.

Mindfulness
The simple act of giving nonjudgmental attention, moment by moment, to one's internal and external environment and experience.

Introduction

BEING A PARENT IS one of the most important jobs a person can take on. Parents shape the future of the world as they shape their children, and to say it's demanding is a massive understatement. Unlike almost every other job on the planet, you don't get breaks. You don't get days off. You don't receive training. You often don't even get a full night's sleep. As a parent you are always on, which can be (and often is) completely exhausting and overwhelming.

When your child cries for no apparent reason, turns in disgust from the dinner you have prepared, behaves inappropriately, or ignores your repeated warnings or instructions, it is only natural to get frustrated (and even angry). This book has two significant tools to offer you:

First, there is a wealth of information here to help you better understand your child. Neuroscience and child development can help you gain insight into the why of your child's behavior. When you are aware of how his physical, cognitive, and social-emotional development affect what he is doing, it can be much easier to respond skillfully rather than to react emotionally.

Second, this book will help you teach your child to live a more mindful life, and will raise your self-awareness and show you different ways to deal directly with thoughts and feelings that emerge from your role as a parent. Mindfulness helps you to practice being present within your life, just as it is, and hopefully be more intentional about what you do as a result. As you learn new ways to pay attention, you can be more the parent you want to be.

These tools can help you have more positive and effective interactions with your child, but that is still only half the story. When you understand how your child experiences the world and how he learns, you can communicate in ways that really reach him. This largely happens through modeling, or teaching through example. Doing so allows you to pass on whatever values and lessons are important to you, regardless of your beliefs. By teaching your children to be mindful, you can help them develop the character and qualities that you want to see in them.

For example, the practice of paying attention is an important skill your children can use for the rest of their lives. Many children (and adults) get into trouble because they are not paying attention to the details of what is going on, both around them and inside them. Mindfulness is a powerful way to learn presence and awareness. More than that, it is a practical tool for working with thoughts or feeling instead of ignoring them or getting swept away by them.

In addition, mindfulness practice brings with it a host of other benefits. It has been a hot topic in scientific research for a number of years, and evidence continues to mount demonstrating that mindfulness does much more than simply help you to deal with stress and negative emotions. Research shows that it has very real impacts on the brain, including:

- Strengthening nerve cells
- Increasing overall gray matter density
- Improving connections throughout and across the brain
- Cooling the emotional centers of the brain
- Improving cognitive and executive functioning skills

No matter what goals you have for yourself or your children, having a mindfulness practice can improve how you navigate the landscape of life and relationships.

This book will give you a basic understanding of the brain and child development, the resources you need to begin practicing mindfulness in your life *right now*, and perhaps even more importantly, practical tools for teaching mindfulness to your children.

For parents, mindfulness can be a powerful tool in improving a family's communication, behavior management strategies, and appreciation of one another. In this way, the art of paying attention can actually strengthen your relationships. The more you practice mindfulness, the more open you will become to embracing every moment of experience as it comes without needing to control it.

So what are you waiting for? There's no time but the present.

CHAPTER 1

An Introduction to Mindfulness

Mindfulness is the practice of being attentive in every moment, and noticing what is taking place both inside and outside of you without judgment. It is the practice of purposefully seeing your thoughts, emotions, experiences, and surroundings as they arise. Simply put, mindfulness is the act of paying attention. This may seem easy, but the truth is, this is a difficult task for anyone, especially children. After all, there is so much to learn about this world for a child! But instilling mindful behavior in your children will give them the tools for emotional, academic, and social success now and in the future.

Being mindful cultivates awareness and concentration, two incredibly important traits for people of any age. The word *mindful* draws from three overlapping spheres: the physical, the emotional, and the environmental. These three areas are each processed in the same place, your mind. Together, they create the full realm of human experience. It is important to understand the basic parts of mindfulness, and how they can help both your child and yourself, before taking up this practice yourself or trying to teach it to your children.

Give Your Brain Something to Do!

You have been blessed with a fantastically powerful machine that resides between your ears. In fact, your brain is just about the most sophisticated, adaptable, and powerful machine ever developed. Not only does it control your body, interpret your senses, store your memories, and allow you to communicate through language, it can also learn new things and use what it already knows to create totally new ideas. The tricky thing about this machine is that it is always on and, if not attended to carefully, can easily run amok.

ALERT

Your brain has no off switch. No matter what you do, it keeps going. Sure, you can distract yourself in all sorts of ways, but your brain just keeps going. It is a biological Energizer Bunny. Even while you sleep, your brain remains busy.

Everyone has experienced this at one point or another: maybe you can't seem to shake a weird feeling, you can't get yourself to stop thinking an unpleasant thought, you can't stop daydreaming about the weekend or what you are going to have for dinner and do once out of work. Some of these thoughts are pleasant, and some of them can be downright scary. You never know what is going to pop into your head when you don't pay attention to what you are doing with your brain, and this is one of the keys to mindfulness.

Using Your Brain for Mindfulness

Mindfulness is the practice of paying attention to how you use and direct your brain. Think of your brain as a child with a toolbox. The tools give it enormous power to do useful and productive things, but if used improperly it can cause a lot of problems. You would never leave an unsupervised child to play with a bunch of tools, and this is exactly the attitude you need to take with your brain. Just like a child, your brain will wander and jump from thought to thought, even when you have given it something specific to focus on. You need to keep an eye on your brain and practice keeping it on task, lest you be at the mercy of its wanderings and storytelling. It might be helpful to understand mindfulness as the practice of making intentional choices about what you do with your brain, and taking responsibility for the power it has.

Mindfulness and Meditation

Mindfulness and meditation are two different (although complementary) things. Mindfulness is a state of paying attention to your inner and outer environments, which is something you can practice throughout each day and in the midst of any activity. Meditation is a special practice, a time you set aside to just sit still, breathe, and notice the activity of your mind. One way to think about it is that mindfulness is meditation in motion.

You do not need to meditate in order to practice mindfulness; however, it can help enormously to anchor and deepen your practice. When practicing meditation, you create a simplified environment that is ideally free from the distractions and busyness of life. This makes it much easier to focus and develop mindfulness skills, such as concentration and awareness, which you will need to use back in the chaos of the real world. Think of meditation practice as "going to the gym" for your mind. The foundation and intention that is cultivated during meditation is something you can carry with you everywhere and use in any situation, no matter how stressful.

Getting Started

Meditation is actually one of the simplest things in the world. It really is nothing more than sitting still and paying attention, but people can make it much more complicated than it needs to be. You might find yourself creating artificial roadblocks and barriers to meditation by saying that you need to set up a space first, then decorate it, buy some cushions, get a new pair of comfy pants to sit in, probably read a few books about meditation, maybe take a class . . . and only then, if you can "find the time," will you actually sit. In reality, you don't need any of those things to practice meditation. You can do it right now. Don't be shy, give it a shot! Here's how:

1. First you need a quiet room and a good chair. Choose a room that is comfortable and peaceful for you. The less clutter the better. Any old chair will do, but you will probably find that kitchen-type chairs work better than recliners. You need something supportive in which you can sit up straight.

2. Okay, do you have your room and your chair? Good. Now, before you sit down, stretch your body a little by reaching toward your toes and then reaching for the ceiling. Shake out your limbs just a bit to get the blood flowing. This helps get your circulation going before sitting down.

3. After moving a little, sit down in your chair. Put your feet flat on the ground, with your hands resting on top of your thighs. Now, imagine a string coming out of the top of your head. To find the proper posture, imagine the string pulling you up into position and holding you there. Your shoulders should be relaxed and lined up above your hips.

4. Relax your eyes and let them rest comfortably on a point on the floor a few feet in front of you. (Some people enjoy lighting a small candle to place on the floor, but it is not at all necessary). Don't stare or focus, just let your eyes *relax*. It is okay if they droop a little, but keep them ever so slightly open so that you stay awake.

5. Take a deep breath in through your nose. Pull the air down into your belly, filling up your lungs with fresh air. Gently but firmly, blow the breath out through your mouth. Good. Do this twice more.

6. After you take three deep abdominal breaths, relax and breathe normally through your nose, in and out. Keep your mind on your breath, counting silently in your mind with each inhalation and exhalation: "In,

one," "Out, one," "In, two," "Out, two." Stop after ten breaths. You're done. Congratulations! You just did your first meditation!

FACT

There are dozens of different ways to practice meditation. No one way is better than any other; the important thing is to find a form that works for you and meets your needs. If you are a physically active person and need to move, yoga or tai chi might work for you. If you like to sing, chanting meditation might be a good fit. Find what works for you!

Believe it or not, that's it. Meditation really is one of the simplest things in the world, but deceptively so. In reality, there is a lot happening! Reflect for a moment on the experience you just had: How do you feel? What did you notice? What (if any) thoughts or feelings came up while you were counting your breaths? Is anything different after meditating?

The Thoughts Haven't Stopped; Am I Doing It Wrong?

One of the biggest misconceptions about meditation is that when you meditate, your mind magically clears and you stop thinking. Ridiculous! Thinking is what the brain does. As long as you are alive, you will have thoughts. In fact, death is actually medically defined as the end of brain activity, so please don't stop thinking.

What is different about meditation practice is how you manage your thoughts. Normally, thoughts begin in the mind as individual neurological "sparks" that suddenly flash to life. You notice these flashes and, where they catch your interest or attention, you begin to think them, expanding out from that initial flash. You time-walk forward and backward with your thoughts; you make associations and jump around; you make predictions about the future, judgments about the past, set goals, make to-do lists, and so much more. As all of this happens, you are drawn away from the actual world and surroundings you are in and into a world created by your mind.

In meditation, this is the kind of mental activity that you will learn to redirect back to the present moment. Thoughts will continue to arise naturally with no effort on your part, even if you try not to think. This is not a problem. Going along with your thoughts or getting pulled by your thoughts is normal; the difference is that in meditation, you commit yourself to noticing these thoughts as they come up and then consciously returning to your breath.

Opening Up the House

A useful metaphor for meditation practice is that of a house with all the doors and windows wide open, allowing anyone or anything to come and go as it pleases. When practicing meditation, your mind is this house. You want to imagine that you, the host, are sitting quietly in your living room and noticing all the things that come and go. As a new guest arrives, you greet and acknowledge it, but nothing more. Then you return to sitting, breathing, and noticing. Your guests are all well acquainted with the house and will find their own way around, and their own way back out. You just greet and acknowledge each one as it arrives, notice what it does and how you feel in response, and come back to your breath.

Make Time to Meditate

Meditation works best when you practice it every day, but it can be awfully tricky to fit it in with all of the other demands on your time. You need to have a plan if you are going to fit it in. Here are some tips to help you make it happen.

- Start small: Dogen, the most revered Japanese Zen master of all time, recommended that practitioners meditate for five minutes each day. That is a great place to start. The key is to make your meditation practice manageable, something you can do easily, maybe even something so easy to do that it becomes hard not to do it.
- Pick a consistent time: If at all possible, meditate at the same time every day. This helps to establish a routine.
- Mornings work best: Meditating in the morning is usually easier than meditating later in the day. In the morning, your brain hasn't gotten up to full speed yet and you generally aren't as distracted as later in the day. That being said, if it is most convenient to meditate in the middle

of the day or in the evening, do it. The time of day you choose is less important than your commitment to sit for five minutes each day.

- Do something physical first: A few minutes of exercise or light stretching before meditation can help you to focus. Not only does it feel better to get your blood moving, but exercise actually helps improve concentration. Give yourself a boost, and warm up before you sit.
- Pick a spot: Most us don't have the space to designate as a "meditation room," and the truth is, you don't need to. It does, however, help to have a consistent space to use. You will find you develop a relationship with this space over time, so you want it to be comfortable, quiet, tidy, and easy to maintain.
- Chairs are fine: Meditation in a chair is just as good as meditation cross-legged on the floor. No need to buy fancy cushions and contort your body into a pretzel-like yoga pose. Just choose a sturdy chair, sit down, and count your breaths.

Meditating with Children

You can teach a child of almost any age how to meditate. The trick is keeping realistic expectations and tailoring the practice to your child. If you have your own meditation practice, your child has likely noticed. This can be a great starting point for a conversation. There is a natural curiosity about what parents do and a desire to participate in activities with parents, particularly with younger children.

When meditating with children, it is necessary to simplify the practice to make it accessible. Try to encourage your child's innate curiosity and invite her to turn this inward. What does she notice when she holds still? Guide your child to pay attention to her breath, the sensations of her body, and the activity of her mind. With children, it is particularly important to engage in dialogue about the practice. Always spend some time debriefing with your child after a sitting. Ask her what she noticed and what she experienced. Be supportive throughout. Remember, there is no such thing as doing it wrong!

Time

When meditating with children, you have to adjust the amount of time that you practice. Even five minutes might seem like an eternity to a child, so start small. Invite your child to sit still with you for one minute, breathing and listening. Keep it short and positive, even if your child moves around or breaks the silence.

Meditating with Very Young Children

If your child is an infant or toddler, it is not very realistic to try to get her to meditate on her own. However, it is totally appropriate to share your meditation with them: Simply hold your child in your lap while you practice your meditation. She will be comforted by the stillness and by the presence of your body.

History of Meditation

Meditation practices can be found in almost all of the world's spiritual traditions. In each, the instructions vary somewhat and the explanation of what is going on is different, but every religion from Hinduism to Christianity to Islam has at least one form of meditation.

Mother Teresa, the famous Christian nun and activist, used to describe her prayer practice as listening to God. When asked if God ever spoke to her, she said, "No, he just listens too." When asked by the interviewer to explain further, she replied, "If you don't understand that, I can't explain it to you."

Regardless of the form of the practice or its religious context, all meditation is about working directly with the human mind. What's more, you don't need any religious context at all if you don't want it. Some people come to meditation seeking spiritual guidance, while others come for the many benefits meditation can bring to the body and mind. Whatever draws you to meditation and whatever your goals, there is sure to be a good fit for you out there.

Is Mindfulness Meditation Religious?

Simply put, no. Mindfulness meditation is a secular practice that anyone can do without accepting any spiritual values or beliefs. It has been designed as such to make it accessible to as many people as possible. However, if you are a spiritual person, you can certainly practice in that way if you choose to.

Where Does Mindfulness Meditation Come From?

Mindfulness as it is taught today draws heavily from the Buddhist tradition. In traditional Buddhism, meditation is taught in two ways: mindfulness and concentration.

Buddhism is arguably the most diverse of all the world's religions. As it spread across Asia, it evolved into many different schools and sects as it encountered different cultures and was influenced by native beliefs. Today there are literally dozens of different sects, each with its own teachings, practices, and observances.

In concentration meditation, you focus your mind intently on one thing, traditionally a small clay disc, to the exclusion of all else. In mindfulness meditation, you open your awareness and watch the activity of your mind as it notices different things and different thoughts and emotions arise, moment by moment.

Who Was the Buddha?

The Buddha was born some 2,500 years ago as Siddhartha Gautama. As a prince of a northern-Indian village, he was raised in isolation from the rest of the world, as his father required him to remain within the walls surrounding the royal palace. The King wished to protect the young Siddhartha from the suffering of human existence and provided for his every want, wish, and desire.

As he grew in to a man, Siddhartha became discontented with his life within the palace and became more curious about the world beyond its walls. After many attempts, he eventually convinced his father to allow him out of the palace to see the city, and Siddhartha was taken on a tour of the city in a chariot. Of course, before the royal chariot made its rounds, an army of soldiers and janitors went along the chariot's route, clearing away all the trash, the old, and the sick. Despite these efforts, Siddhartha saw four things on his tour of the city: an old man, a sick person, a corpse, and finally an ascetic (a religious seeker living a life of poverty and austerity). These four things left an indelible impression on the young prince. It gradually dawned on Siddhartha that not only was everyone he loved subject to sickness, old age, and death, but so was he.

Siddhartha resolved to flee the palace one night, renouncing his throne and taking up with a group of ascetics and seeking release from suffering. For years, Siddhartha practiced the most extreme austerities, living out of doors and in total poverty, renouncing all comfort and pleasure, fasting and meditating. Siddhartha learned well what the ascetics taught him and he practiced their ways with great vigor and intensity, but he remained unsatisfied and unfulfilled: his mind continued to be consumed with doubt, confronted with the inevitability of his own death. Eventually Siddhartha left the ascetics and set out on his own, continuing to practice alone. He pushed his body to its very limits, starving himself and spending almost all of his waking hours practicing the austerities he had learned. But still, he suffered and despaired for his inability to overcome this suffering. One evening, a young girl stumbled upon Siddhartha, starved and near death. The prince was so frail that the girl mistook him for a ghost and made him an offering of milk and porridge. Siddhartha was deeply moved by the girl's compassion and, abandoning his austerities, consumed her offering and felt his strength return. Defeating his despair, he sat down beneath a near-by tree and resolved not to move from that spot until he achieved some insight into the suffering that seems to touch every aspect of human existence. He sat in deep meditation for days, eventually achieving his goal. From then on Buddha, or Enlightened One, would spend the rest of his life teaching his great realization to all who would listen.

Modern Mindfulness

The roots of the modern interest in mindfulness go back to the late nineteenth century. The first major contact Westerners had with Buddhism was at the Parliament of World Religions in 1893. Although this meeting had been planned to showcase the superiority of Western ideas and religions, the large Buddhist contingent stole the show. People were thoroughly impressed by speeches from great Buddhist teachers including Anagarika Dhamapala, Shoyen Saku, and D. T. Suzuki. This interest grew over the years as Westerners continued to find the ideas of Buddhism both intriguing and generally compatible with (if not complimentary to) modern scientific ideas.

Over the course of the twentieth century, this interest grew, particularly among psychologists who found Buddhist models of psychology and of the mind both rich and practical. Buddhism grew in popular culture in the West and meditation practices became more and more common. Starting in the 1970s, psychologists began research on the effects of meditation on the brain and found that there were real and substantial effects. One of these researchers, John Kabat-Zinn, wanted to separate the practices of mindfulness and meditation from their religious roots in order to make the practices more accessible to the general public. In 1979, he founded the Mindfulness-Based Stress Reduction Clinic at University of Massachusetts Medical Center in Worcester, MA and began teaching a secularized model of mindfulness practice. In more recent years, as meditation has become more popular, academic research about its beneficial effects has continued to mount, and mindfulness programs have spread broadly, including in the business world and in schools.

CHAPTER 2

The Benefits of Mindfulness

Practicing mindfulness brings with it a number of benefits including positive impacts on the brain and emotional health, improved communication, stronger relationships, and the feeling of greater happiness and satisfaction in life. Some of these benefits appear more immediately, while others take some time to emerge. Regardless, all of these benefits of mindfulness are a result of making it a part of your, or your child's, daily life. With practice, mindfulness becomes an integral part of who and how you are in the world, and will in turn become a central part of who your child is as well.

Impact of Mindfulness on the Brain

In recent years, there has been a wealth of scientific research on the effects of mindfulness on the brain. This research has shown the systemic impact that practicing mindfulness has on the brain, and specific benefits to both mental health and cognitive functioning. Mindfulness is particularly effective when working with anxiety and depression, and also has a positive impact on attention and executive functioning. Research has also shown that the brain is affected both structurally as well as functionally, meaning that mindfulness can actually stimulate further growth in existing brain cells in specific areas as well as enhance their existing functionality.

Mood and Emotional Regulation

One of the most powerful impacts of mindfulness practice is on mood. Your mood is influenced by a number of factors, including the amount of certain neurotransmitters circulating through your brain (particularly serotonin), as well as by patterns of brain activity. Much of the brain's serotonin is produced in the brain stem just above the spinal cord. A joint study by Britta Holzel and colleagues at University of Massachusetts Medical Center, Massachusetts General Hospital, and the Justus Liebig University in Germany showed that mindfulness meditation stimulates serotonin synthesis and release in the raphe nuclei. Seratonin has many functions in the body, but it is closely associated with mood and feelings of happiness and well-being. This may explain one of the ways in which mindfulness practice can enhance overall mood and well-being.

Another critical component of mood is the balance of activity between the right and left hemispheres in the region called the prefrontal cortex (PFC for short). Generally speaking, higher activity on the right side of the PFC is associated with stronger and more frequent negative emotions and a tendency toward avoidance and withdrawal. Conversely, high levels of activity on the left side of the PFC are associated with more positive emotional states and higher levels of flexibility. These patterns apply both to reactions to events and to baseline emotional states. A study by Richard Davidson and colleagues at the University of Wisconsin found that eight weeks of mindfulness training shifted activity in the prefrontal cortex toward the left side of the brain, both as a baseline and in response to stimuli. Participants in the study observed an overall reduction in anxiety, stress, and negative moods. Remarkably, this shift was maintained even when the participants were not actively meditating.

In the same study, Davidson also observed that mindfulness practice enhanced the ability of practitioners to cool down their emotions when they got stirred up. This is because the prefrontal cortex functions as the conscious control center of the brain, and has the ability to affect functioning in many other parts of the brain. The increase in emotional self-control observed by participants in Davidson's study was a result of a cooling of activity in the amygdala, a structure in the limbic system whose activity is closely correlated with negative emotions.

Mindfulness also has a strong impact on rumination, one of the most common and difficult to treat symptoms of depression. Clinically speaking, rumination is dwelling on negative emotions, thoughts, and memories. It is a passive mental task, one that occurs in the background of the mind and has a tendency to color a person's experiences, putting a negative slant on basically everything that happens. This often appears as withdrawal, where the person who cannot stop ruminating is loath to do much of anything. In a study released in January of 2012, Philip Keune and his team of researchers at Eberhard Karls University in Germany found that mindfulness is a powerful tool against rumination. It can help reduce rumination over time while also increasing the person's overall activity, which leads to an increased engagement in his life.

Increased Connectivity and Attention

In a study done by UCLA's Lisa Kilpatrick, she and her colleagues found that mindfulness meditation brought about measurable increases in brain connectivity, particularly in the auditory and visual networks of the brain. Participants who learned mindfulness improved their ability to maintain focus and block out distractions.

One of the strongest effects of mindfulness that Kilpatrick's study found was that not only does mindfulness help you to be less prone to distraction, it actually enhances your ability to focus on what you choose to give your attention to. This also correlates with improved cognitive functioning and perceptual learning, meaning that mindfulness can help you to be clearer, sharper, and more focused. When the brain can block out distractions and concentrate more steadfastly on what it is doing, it processes information much more efficiently. Imagine how your child could benefit from these effects.

Increased Gray Matter Density

"Gray matter" is composed of neuronal cell bodies, and is one of the two "traditional" components of the brain. Its counterpart, "white matter," is largely composed of the fatty sheath around nerve cell axons called myelin. In the joint study of Massachusetts General Hospital, University of Massachusetts Medical, and Justus Liebig University mentioned earlier, it was found that mindfulness meditation increases overall gray matter density in the brain. Areas most affected included the hippocampus, tempo-parietal junction, brainstem, and cerebellum. Another Massachusetts General Hospital study by Sara Lazar also found that mindfulness increases the thickness of the cortex, which is the outermost layer of the brain.

This research has numerous implications. First, the thickening of the cortex and increased gray matter density occurs *not* from the growth of new brain cells, but rather from stronger, more robust existing cells. We know that the relative size of gray matter correlates with its overall health and functionality, so it is fair to say that healthier gray matter leads to healthier and more functional brains.

Next, the specific areas of the brain most affected by mindfulness practice are the ones involved in a variety of functions that heavily influence mood, emotional regulation, learning, and memory. The hippocampus, part of the limbic system closely associated with emotional regulation, is known to decrease in both volume and density in people who suffer from posttraumatic stress disorder (PTSD) and serious depression. It is reasonable to infer that any activity that increases the density of the hippocampus will have a positive impact in these areas as well.

Another area that exhibited strong increases in gray matter density was the tempo-parietal (TP) junction, where the temporal lobe and parietal lobe of the cortex meet. This area of the brain is primarily associated with consciousness and social cognition. Your sense of where you are and how you are connected to your body are affected by the TP junction, and this is the area that gets most confused during out-of-body experiences. Even more interestingly, in terms of mindfulness, this is an area of the brain strongly associated with social cognition, that is, your ability to infer the feelings, desires, and intentions of others. An increase in gray matter density within the TP junction thus aids in a person's ability to "read" and empathize with others. This is a very important tool for your children to learn.

Surprisingly, this study also found a significant increase in gray matter density in the cerebellum, a part of the brain generally understood to be responsible for physical coordination. It was found that two specific subregions, which have recently been associated with emotional modulation and regulating the appropriateness of emotional responses, were most affected.

QUESTION

Does mindfulness meditation have an impact on the deterioration of the brain as we age?
Studies have shown that mindfulness meditation has a positive impact on age-related decreases in brain density. As we age, brain cells (much like other cells in our body) begin to lose mass and wither. This effect is closely correlated with diseases such as Alzheimer's and dementia. Mindfulness meditation may serve as a tool to decrease these effects over time.

Stress and Health

Stress is not just something we experience in our minds; it is a chemical and physiological reality, for both you and your children. Medical research has documented many effects of long-term chronic stress including decreases in memory and cognitive functioning; increased heart rate, blood pressure, and cortisol levels; increased susceptibility to overeating, obesity, alcoholism, and drug abuse; and ultimately a decreased life span.

Stress results from a combination of both physical and mental factors that increase levels of certain hormones in our body. Because one of the brain's primary roles is regulating the hormones in our body, stress can be reduced if you target the brain. When the mind is calm and soothed by a practice such as mindfulness, the production of cortisol and other stress hormones is reduced measurably. At the same time, mindfulness meditation has been proven to increase the activity of other hormones and neurotransmitters that reduce stress and promote feelings of relaxation. The net effect is an overall decrease in stress and an increase in feelings of well-being, happiness, and ease.

Imagine your child is nervous about a test. She notices that the anxiety she is having is a sign of stress, and instead of believing the thoughts about how badly she is going to do, she stops and takes a moment to breathe. She recognizes her stress as just thoughts, just something that is happening. Her brain calms and the stress cools and she is able to concentrate on the test despite her anxiety. Children and students who are able to self-soothe in this way are at a definite advantage when managing their stress inside or out of school.

Being More the Person You Want to Be

One of the most profound benefits of mindfulness is that it can help you to be more the person you would like to be in the world. One of the first benefits of mindfulness that you (and your child) will see is a heightened awareness of yourself and your inner life, including your emotions, thoughts, and feelings. As you become more aware of these various forces moving within you, you can begin to watch them rise without being at their mercy. For example, when you are aware that you are becoming angry, you have a choice about whether to act from that anger or attend to that feeling directly. Ultimately, mindfulness practice gives you more choice about who and how you want to be.

Self-Awareness

The first thing you learn to pay attention to is yourself and the rise of different thoughts and feelings in your own mind. The simple act of noticing that a feeling is coming on or that a particular idea has come up can be a powerfully liberating experience.

When you are first starting out, you may not notice that a thought or feeling has taken hold of you until you are in the middle of acting (or after the fact). That is no problem at all. As you become more acquainted with the practice, you will find it easier to notice the movements of your mind as they happen, rather than catching yourself "red-handed" in the middle of an emotional reaction or outburst (or once it has already passed). You will also start to notice the things that tend to set you off, your triggers, and you will begin to be able to anticipate your emotions before they have a hold on you.

ALERT

Most people come to mindfulness practice because they want to change something in their lives. Often, particularly in the early stages of practice, things can seem to get worse as you turn your attention inward and begin to see yourself more clearly. This is a normal part of the process and is actually a good sign!

Self-Control

As you become more skilled at noticing the thoughts and feelings that arise, you will begin to notice them more quickly, maybe even before they start to affect your actions. This awareness is itself a powerful tool. It opens up the possibility to say, "Hey, I'm pretty mad right now . . . " as opposed to yelling at somebody you care about because you were upset about something else. It can do exactly the same thing for your children, helping them learn to communicate about their feelings rather than just react from that place of emotion. As with most things, children learn this best by seeing it modeled by adults.

Often, you may notice that your emotions carry with them a sense of urgency. As you feel the impulse to do something arise within you, you will be able to see the forces driving that sense of "I need to do something." They could be, for example, the thoughts that come up as you watch your three-year-old put on his own shoes. Your mind might be buzzing with impatience, and the thought "I need to put his shoes on for him because he's taking forever" arises. When you notice this thought instead of immediately acting on it, you have some room to check in with yourself and act intentionally, instead of just reacting. This practice of noticing creates a certain amount of mental space in which you can deal with the thought or feeling itself rather than being moved to act by it.

FACT

Mindfulness acts directly on the parts of the brain that are most involved in self-control. By helping to raise your awareness of your emotions and to alter how you react, you will begin to see greater opportunities to respond in the ways you want to.

Inevitably, as you look inward, you will have opinions about the things you notice about yourself. This is totally normal. Recognize that these opinions and judgments are just another type of thought, and try to work with them like any other. Recognize them as they arise, acknowledge them, and give them space to breathe. Just because a judging thought arises (such as "Wow, I'm messed up," or "This is all *my* parents' fault!") does not mean it is true. Although you may not want to have these kinds of thoughts and tend to push them away, you cannot "let go" of these thoughts or force them to go away altogether. As they arise, acknowledge them for what they are (transient clouds passing across the sky of your mind), come back to your core practice, and these thoughts will let go of you when they are ready.

Choices

People who do not pay attention to their thoughts and feelings often react abruptly when a feeling takes hold of them. This is particularly true of children, whose prefrontal cortexes (the brain's center of reason, planning ahead, risk assessment, impulse control and emotional regulation) are still developing

Through the practice of mindfulness, you and your child can strengthen your emotional awareness and give yourselves space to choose how you want to respond. Regardless of the outcome, your ability to choose how you respond in any given situation presents you with the opportunity to be the kind of person you really want to be. This sets a powerful example for children.

Communication

As you become more aware of yourself and how you are responding to your environment, it becomes possible to apply this awareness to your communication with others. Noticing how your thoughts and feelings affect your speech can allow you to express yourself more intentionally, which can lead to more successful and satisfying communication with others. When applied to what you notice about others, mindfulness in communication can help you to express your perceptions or observations before reacting negatively (e.g., asking "You look/sound upset, is everything okay?" before reacting based on an assumption).

Saying What You Mean

Your words and particularly your tone of voice are hugely impacted by your feelings in any given moment. Even sensations in your body can have an effect on how you speak. When you are aware of these thoughts, feelings, and sensations, you can be more skillful in how you communicate and express yourself to make sure it comes across in the way that you intend.

Through mindful awareness, it also becomes possible to communicate about your feelings directly. It is not always possible to recognize an intense feeling like anger and still communicate in a positive way. If you are in pain, you are in pain! It can be difficult to speak with the kindness and care you might like to. However, if you are aware of this pain, whether it is physical or psychological, you can at least communicate that fact to others who then may not take the edge in your voice quite so personally. Just imagine what this skill could do for your child during a playground argument.

QUESTION

How can I communicate about a feeling when it really has a hold on me?
The simple answer is any way you can. Ideally, this would be something said with some restraint, like "I'm really mad right now," but sometimes it is hard to even muster that much control. Do the best you can in the moment and remember to give yourself credit for noticing how your feelings are affecting you. You will become more skillful with practice.

Listening

Communicating with other people is extremely difficult. Despite your best intentions to express yourself clearly, how other people understand and interpret your words is ultimately up to them and is in many ways beyond your control. You can do things that point them in one direction or another, but you can probably remember plenty of times when you have tried your best to get a point across and were misunderstood anyway.

It is funny to notice how quickly people forget about this when they are listening to others. It is easy to react to another person's words without checking with him about what he meant or intended. Through mindfulness, you can become aware of these reactions as they happen (and eventually before you react). In that awareness, you have the opportunity to check with the person you are talking to before taking offense or reacting negatively.

ESSENTIAL

Children are prone to leaving out important details in a story or exaggerating certain things. Like many adults, their stories are often loaded with emotion and can be confusing to hear. Whether you are listening to a child or an adult, it can be helpful to understand their words not as a description of what actually happened, but as their experience of what happened.

It is not always possible to talk to another person about how he is communicating or feeling, however. Sometimes the other person is not in the right frame of mind to be able to have that conversation, and sometimes it is just not the appropriate time or place to do so. You should be particularly sensitive to timing with children. Regardless, mindfulness can still be a powerful aid to you when listening to another person. When you notice yourself reacting to someone else's words, you can consider why he might be speaking with that edge in his voice or why he is being so curt. Ultimately you will only be able to guess at the reasons for his tone and attitude (until you can actually discuss it together); however, you do not have to take someone else's bad attitude personally. You should be particularly flexible about this with children, as they are much less aware of things like their tone of voice or body language and often convey emotions that they do not intend.

Remember that children learn through experimentation and have a conversation with them about how you respond to their behavior. Mindful listening can be a helpful tool for practicing compassion, and may allow you to respond to rudeness with kindness instead of reacting with mirrored rudeness or insensitivity.

In short, you never have to take anyone else's bad attitude personally, nor do you have to let their sourness ruin your mood. In fact, by responding with kindness, you might even have a positive effect on *them*. Keep in mind that responding with kindness is not about changing someone else's bad mood; it's about being the kind of person you want to be, regardless of the circumstances.

Relationships

Mindfulness practice can have a profound and positive impact on your relationships, not only with friends and family members, but also with total strangers. Through a heightened awareness of your own emotional state, you open up a multitude of options regarding how you navigate your interactions with others. This is equally true for your children. A mindful child is more likely to check-in and discuss a situation than react negatively to it.

Depersonalization

Mindfulness begins with looking at your feelings, thoughts, and emotions. As you begin to understand these forces better, you will come to see the many and often subtle ways in which they can affect your external behavior. The next extension of this lesson is to realize that all people are subject to the same forces, and that everyone's behavior is affected by how he or she feels. This creates more common ground between people, even those whom you've never met before.

When you are on the receiving end of somebody else's negative behavior, it is very easy to feel that it is personal or somehow about you. When practicing mindfulness, however, it is possible to realize that just as you are at the center of most of your own thoughts, the other person is likely at the center of most of her thoughts. Like you, her behavior is most often driven by her own feelings and experiences. What a person says or does almost never has anything to do with you; more often than not, it is about her. There is no need to take it personally. This is a great tool to teach your children, especially as they meet their peers at school or on the playground.

Empathy

The practice of mindfulness is an ongoing lesson in cause and effect. As you notice your own thoughts and feelings, moment by moment, you will come to better understand what gives rise to those feelings. Although there is rarely a concrete or simple answer as to why you feel a particular way, you will begin to understand the many complex factors that influence your feelings and your behavior. Because other people function much like you do, many of these lessons are readily transferable.

Any idea you have about why you (or anyone else for that matter) feels or acts a particular way is just that: an idea. Another way to think of our ideas is as stories. Some stories are simple, while others are considerably more involved and complex. When you notice that your thoughts about others are also stories, you can make the choice to tell a different story.

ESSENTIAL

Different stories can completely change our perspectives on other people's actions. What story do you tell when someone cuts you off in traffic? Is he an inconsiderate jerk? How does that story make you feel? How do you treat others after telling yourself that story? What if that person was rushing to the hospital for some reason? How would you feel then? Both stories are equally true and equally false. Ultimately, the choice is yours.

No story your mind comes up with about yourself or others is necessarily right or wrong. The important question is, "How useful is it?" If your story about that jerk cashier makes you treat someone poorly, ruins your mood, and puts you in a funk for an hour, it isn't a very useful story. Instead, you might look around the store and notice what a zoo it is and instead choose to tell a story about how tired the clerk must be, and how difficult it is dealing with all of these customers and chaos. Through that second story, you can choose to empathize instead of dehumanize.

Sympathetic Joy

One of the ways to experience closeness or intimacy with other people is to share in their emotional experiences. When you share in the happiness of others, it is called sympathetic joy. Not only is this one of the finest qualities cultivated through mindfulness, sympathetic joy is also the antidote to jealousy and envy, two of the most destructive forces in relationships with other people.

When you see another person receive cause for celebration, no matter what it is, it can be very easy to feel excluded from the experience. It is natural enough to see whatever made that person happy, and then to feel the absence of that thing in your life. This is both unfortunate and unnecessary. Mindfulness gives you a tool to work with any negative feelings that come up, and can also help you connect with the experience of others' happiness.

Happiness, Satisfaction, and Enjoying Your Life

Mindfulness is a powerful tool for working with what comes up in life, both in your own mind and in the world around you. By integrating mindfulness into your life it is possible to become more accepting of the things in life that you cannot change, experience less stress, and be more present in every moment of your life. The net result is greater satisfaction and enjoyment of whatever each day has to offer.

Acceptance

There are many things that happen in life that you have absolutely no control over. Sometimes these things are good and welcome, but sometimes they cause you suffering and distress. When you study how your reactions to these events arise through your practice of mindfulness, you will begin to see that it is not necessarily the events themselves that cause you to suffer, but rather the thoughts and feelings that come up that bring you pain.

For children, mindfulness can be a particularly powerful tool for cultivating acceptance. Children are regularly subjected to all sorts of stressors that they have no power over: Younger children are often entirely subject to the demands of their parents schedules and are transported back and forth on someone else's time table, put in groups to play with other kids, etc. School-age children and teenagers are famously trapped between childhood and adulthood. Regardless of age, a child's life is rife with circumstances they cannot control and may not like. Mindfulness can be a powerful tool to help children accept the circumstances of their life regardless of how they feel about it and give them a positive way of dealing with this stress. While you cannot control many of the things that happen to you in life, you *can* control how you respond to them. Mindfulness is a fantastic tool for working with the thoughts, feelings, and stories that arise in the face of challenging circumstances. By working directly with your reactions to events, it is possible to give yourself some breathing room. Just to be clear, mindfulness is not some silver bullet that can alleviate all the suffering in your life, but it can help you change your relationship to that suffering so that it does not completely eclipse the various joys that are available to you in each moment.

FACT

Accepting your lack of control over some situations can be a powerful practice. Research has shown that people who have developed ways of doing so generally experience less stress and are more emotionally stable than those who try to control everything. This can be achieved through spiritual belief or through logical reasoning. Whichever style suits you better, try talking to yourself when you identify something you are trying to control but can't. If you realistically can't do anything about it, why worry?

Being Here Now

One of the first things mindfulness practitioners learn is how to work with their own thoughts and emotions. Mindfulness does not stop these thoughts or feelings outright, but it does open up a certain amount of space around them. This space creates room to notice other things in the world and within you. While you may still feel whatever emotions are arising for you in that moment, they need not consume you. It becomes possible to enjoy other things you see or experience as well, even in the midst of difficult feelings.

CHAPTER 3

Welcome to Your Practice

Why, in a book about raising mindful children, is there a section about your practice as a parent? Great question. Mindfulness is a relatively simple concept that can be understood quite readily. Keep in mind, though, that understanding mindfulness is only part of the process; it is not mindfulness itself. To experience the full benefits of mindfulness practice, you have to make it a part of your daily life so you can learn how to use it creatively and spontaneously.

For Your Children

To be able to teach mindfulness to your children, you have to take up the practice yourself and learn how to apply it when you are angry or hurt or tired as well as when you are feeling good. Think of it this way: somebody can describe to you what it is like to ride a bicycle in fantastic detail, but you can't know what it takes to balance on two wheels or what the wind feels like in your hair until you get up and ride for yourself.

ESSENTIAL

Your children learn much more from what you do than from what you say. Ever notice how well-behaved parents tend to have well-behaved children? For your kids to realistically be able to make mindfulness practice a part of their lives, you will need to model it for them in your own life.

The other reason you need to take up this practice is because you can only be there for your kids if you take care of yourself. It is so tempting as a parent to neglect yourself, focus entirely on your kids and forget about your own (or your partner's) needs. This is a huge mistake. Not only is it completely impossible, because no matter how hard you push yourself you still need to sleep and eat, among other things, it sets a terrible example for your children. Remember, children learn most from what they see you do. If you do not model healthy self-care, how can they possibly learn it for themselves?

FACT

The Buddha taught that there is no difference between what we do for ourselves and what we do for others. If you think about it, you will see the wisdom in this for yourself. How do you treat others on days when you are tired and grumpy? What about on days when you are feeling good? To care for others, we must care for ourselves (and vice versa).

The Three Pillars of Mindfulness

Although mindfulness is a simple concept, applying it in daily life can be very challenging. When the world (and your mind) cooperate, it can be easy to enjoy the present moment. When things get complicated, however, it can become very difficult to navigate your life skillfully. It helps to have a reminder. The Three Pillars of Mindfulness offer a simple way to bring yourself back to center in the midst of chaos and confusion.

The Three Pillars of Mindfulness are:

1. Pay Attention
2. Receive Openly
3. Act with Intention

Pay Attention

The very core of mindfulness practice is to pay attention to whatever arises, moment to moment. This includes thoughts, feelings, and emotions; sensations in your body; and perceptions of others and of your environment. Obviously it is impossible to take in everything all the time, and that is not the goal. Your mind will naturally focus on things as it notices them; the challenge to you is to recognize what comes into your awareness as it does so. Notice how you move when you take physical action; notice the quality of your voice when you speak; notice not only what you think, but also how you react to the thoughts and feelings that come up. Paying attention is this simple act of noticing, and always looking deeper into the how of what you do.

Receive Openly

When you practice paying attention, you will notice many things both in your mind and in the world around you. No matter what form these things take, the next step in the practice of mindfulness is to receive them openly. Inevitably, judgments will arise in your mind; it is totally natural to have thoughts, feelings, and opinions about the things you see. Notice these too and accept them as well. It is not necessary to act on these thoughts, nor should you treat them in some way as "real," although some of them will inevitably feel that way. They are just thoughts. Try not to let yourself become distracted by anything that arises in your mind, just keep paying attention.

Act with Intention

When you receive your thoughts openly and do not judge them, you no longer have to be driven by them. Watching the workings of your mind creates a space in which you can pause and consider before you act. When anger arises, it may be tempting to lash out at a loved one, even if he had nothing to do with what has made you angry. If you notice this angry thought, you can take a moment before acting on it and choose to act differently.

Your Core Practice

While you may find the ideas in this book useful and interesting unto themselves, they take on a whole new meaning when you actually make these practices part of your daily life. This means practicing not only during the quiet and peaceful times, but amid the chaos and activity as well.

The first thing you need is a core practice. This is what you commit to doing throughout your day, every day, as often as you remember to do so. It anchors you and becomes the foundation of how you move through the world. Your core practice should be something that is simple and that has meaning for you. Ideally, it will be something you can practice intently during meditation and access during the activity of your life as well.

Core Practices

There are many different kinds of core practices, and each one is useful in different ways and for different people. No single core practice is better than another; they all lead to the same destination, which is the ability to be consciously present in this moment.

Ultimately, your core practice should be something that takes your focus away from fixating on thoughts or feelings and brings you back to your body and the present moment. Try out the following practices, and find the one that works best for you.

Breath

All meditation practices involve some awareness of the breath. Breath is the strongest bridge between your body and mind, and when the mind gets carried away the breath can help bring you back to the present reality.

To demonstrate how breath is a bridge between body and mind, consider this: hyperventilating can give you a panic attack, whereas breathing evenly and deeply increases oxygen flow throughout your body which helps you calm down, slow your heartbeat, and relax. Breath is a major point of leverage between your body and mind. Although you cannot force your mind to get rid of a thought or emotion, what you can do is intentionally set your mind's direction and pace. Breathing is one very effective way of doing so.

There are many ways to practice with your breath. Traditional Zen meditation begins with the instruction to count the breath in cycles of ten:

Inhale, one; exhale, one.

Inhale, two; exhale, two.

And so on.

When you lose count or notice that a thought has arisen and distracted you from counting your breath, notice the thought that took you away from your counting, acknowledge it, exhale, and begin again from zero. Should you actually make it all the way to ten without losing your focus, which is really more difficult than it sounds, just return to zero and continue.

Particularly for beginners, this is very helpful because it gives you something to do (counting) that is connected to a physical experience you can control (the breath), and gives you an easy way to check yourself when you start to drift. Be aware, you will certainly drift . . . everyone does. That's part of why it is called a practice.

FACT

Losing count in breath practice is not a mistake. Actually, you should think of it as a success. This is entirely the point of the practice: to notice when your mind drifts off, acknowledge what thought or feeling caused the drift, and consciously return to the present moment. Instead of thinking "Oops, there I go again . . . " when you lose count, say to yourself "Got one!" and keep it up.

You can carry this breath counting throughout many activities in your day. As you become more seasoned in counting your breath (you'll know because you routinely get to "ten" without drifting off into other thoughts), you can start counting only on the exhalation:

Inhale, exhale, "one."

Inhale, exhale, "two."

Mantra

Many practitioners of mindfulness find it helpful to use a mantra, which is a simple phrase you repeat to yourself over and over again to help guide your attention. The mantra can be anything at all that works for you: an affirmation, a reminder, words of encouragement, or something totally meaningless.

James Ford, a contemporary American Zen teacher, is fond of saying "Just" on the inhalation, and "This" on the exhalation. The Korean Zen teacher Seung Sahn taught students to say (think) "Clear mind, clear mind, clear mind" on the inhale, and "Don't know . . . " very slowly on the exhale. There was even once a monk who taught the mantra "Coca-Cola." "Om" is another popular mantra. It really doesn't matter what mantra you use. If it helps you connect your awareness to the present moment, it is a useful mantra.

Body Awareness

If you are a more kinesthetic person, you may find it useful to focus on your body as you practice. This can be particularly helpful if you find yourself physically restless or fidgety when you try to meditate. Some people just need to move! The key idea is to work with yourself as you naturally are, not to force yourself to do something awkward and uncomfortable. Mindfulness is about acceptance.

One of the reasons awareness of the sensations in the nostrils can be a powerful practice is that there are nerves in the nose that go directly into the brain. The sensation of cool air passing over these nerves has a natural, cooling effect on the mind.

One traditional form of body awareness is to focus your attention on the tip of your nose, cultivate an awareness of the physical sensation of breathing. You can attune to the rhythm of your breath, the cool sensation of the inhale and the warm sensation of the exhale. You can try this in combination with counting, or with a mantra, whatever you find works best for you.

Another powerful way to practice with the body is to focus your awareness on the soles of your feet and the sensation of the contact between your feet and the ground. This can be a very anchoring practice as it helps the body maintain a sense of itself in connection with the earth. As you become more aware of where you are in space, the mind naturally calms and becomes more centered, as if gravity were affecting your thoughts as well as your body.

ESSENTIAL

Awareness of the contact between your feet and the ground is a powerful practice to use while walking. Whether you are just walking from one room to another, going out for a stroll, going for a run, or working out at the gym, awareness of the contact between your feet and the ground can help you be more present. This can help prevent the mind from wandering off at times when it can be very tempting to do so.

Working with Thoughts and Emotions

The human brain is built to think and feel. Thoughts and feelings happen whether you want them to or not, and this is completely natural. Sometimes it can be exciting and other times quite stressful. If the thought or feeling is one you really don't want to have, it is all the more difficult to work with.

What you need to keep in mind is that thoughts are a natural product of the brain. There is a tendency for people to regard their thoughts and emotions as important and meaningful in some way, as if they were somehow indicative of one's character. Ultimately, it isn't your thoughts that determine the kind of person you are, it is what you *do* that really matters.

When you look closely at how thoughts arise in your mind, you will notice that there are really two types: some thoughts come about as the result of a deliberate action on your part. These are the thoughts you have when you are consciously thinking about something or trying to solve a problem. Then there is another way thoughts come about that is more passive: An idea comes up and you begin to ruminate on it. This in turn leads to a series of other thoughts that can go on and on. Thinking in this way is like riding a wild horse: you end up hanging on and going wherever the horse takes you. This kind of thinking can often lead to distraction and feelings of stress, anxiety, and fear. The difference between the two types of thinking is intention and bringing intention to your thoughts is what mindfulness is all about.

Unfortunately, most schools do not teach students how to manage their thoughts. People are generally at the mercy of their minds, subject to the whims of their thoughts and emotions, believing them to be in some way a true and accurate reflection of reality. This is not actually the case: thoughts are thoughts, nothing more. To be sure, thoughts come in many flavors; some are pleasant, others are not so pleasant, and can even be frightening or downright disturbing. Mindfulness practice gives you a set of tools that allow you to work with all of your thoughts constructively, and can help modulate their impact on both you and those around you.

Working with Emotions

Emotions shape your interpretation and understanding of the world. They are in some ways analogous to wearing different colored sunglasses. When you put on the blue pair, everything appears to be blue; when you put on the yellow pair, everything appears to be tinted yellow. In a similar way, your emotions change what you experience and how you respond (or react) to these experiences. When you are mindful of your emotions, you can recognize the "color of sunglasses" you are wearing at any given moment and perhaps even have an opportunity to take them off.

Imagine being awake all night with a sick child. In the morning, you have a nasty argument with your partner about cleaning up last night's dishes, and leave for work in an awful mood. You're exhausted, angry, and stressed out. To beat the Dunkin' Donuts drive-through line, you park and go inside. To your dismay there is a family with three kids in the line in front of you. The children are laughing loudly, and now you're angry with the parents for not making their children be quiet. It also seems like they are purposely taking forever to order. Time seems to slow down, and now you worry about being late for work. For some reason, all you want to do is scream and push that stupid happy family out of your way.

The expression "seeing red" is very fitting here. Emotions are the foundations of human experience; when you are swept away by feelings of frustration and stress, anything around you can fuel the fire of these emotions. When you're angry, you're at odds with whatever environment you are in; you can use anything as an excuse to remain angry or to escalate the intensity. Once you get to this point, it is very difficult to rein yourself in.

This same "colored sunglasses" phenomenon is true of any emotion, including joy. For example, imagine that you're about to go on a trip to see your best friend. You stayed up most of the night packing and preparing the house so your spouse can handle the kids alone. Despite the exhaustion, you can't help but be excited. On your way to the airport you stop at a Dunkin' Donuts for coffee and go inside. Just as in the previous example, there is a family with three children in the line in front of you. The kids are laughing loudly; watching the way they play with each other reminds you of your own children, and you can't help but smile. It takes some time for the family to get their order in, which you completely understand—you know that ordering breakfast with three happy, hyper kids at your feet can be like trying to herd kittens. You glance at your watch, and feel like there is plenty of time to get to the airport. *What a sweet family*, you might think.

ESSENTIAL

The issue is not about what thoughts come into your head. All sorts of ideas and emotions will arise for you as a parent, and many of them will not be helpful or pleasant. The question is, how do you handle them as they come up?

Mindfulness is a powerful tool for working with your emotions, and the first step is simply noticing what feelings come up under different circumstances. When you notice that you are getting frustrated, for example, this is an opportunity. Paying attention to the feeling as it arises means that you are not blindly swept away by the frustration. This moment of awareness gives you more control over what you say and do.

Working with Thoughts

We cannot ultimately control our thoughts. Thoughts come up no matter what, and often follow habitual paths in the brain that form over the course of a person's life. People have thoughts about the future, memories from the past, innovative ideas, small observations, violent fantasies, questions about existence—the range of human thought is incredible.

It's not merely the ability to think, reason, remember, and plan that sets our species apart; the fact that we can influence our minds in real time makes human beings truly unique. When a person chooses not to exercise that influence, their thoughts run amok.

ESSENTIAL

Thoughts have no substance unto themselves. They can make you feel things that are very real, and they may inspire action of some kind, but a thought itself is like a puff of smoke: here one moment and gone the next, leaving no trace except your memory of it. Thoughts exist only within your mind, and though some thoughts may recur, they are not permanent.

You do not have to be at the mercy of what you think or feel; however, trying to stop your brain from thinking is like trying to stop a frog from hopping. The goal of mindfulness is not to stop thoughts and emotions from coming up; mindfulness is about paying attention to the thoughts and emotions that come up, without being completely swept away by them.

CHAPTER 4

The Brain

The brain is the control center for your body. Everything you think, feel, or experience is the result of a chemical reaction in your brain, and everything you do begins as a signal in your brain that is then transmitted to another part of your body. The brain is intimately involved in all that you are and everything that you do, and the same is true for your children. A basic understanding of how the brain works is a powerful tool for better understanding yourself and your child.

Brain Growth and Development

The brain changes more than any other part of the body over the course of human life. These changes occur on two levels: The first type of change, the physical growth of the brain itself, occurs rapidly from birth through early adolescence and is largely complete by the age of ten. The second type of change comes from the growing connections between different parts of the brain. This kind of growth is ultimately even more important than the physical growth of the organ itself.

QUESTION

Which is more important in brain growth and development, genes (nature) or environment (nurture)?
Both genes and environment play critical roles in the development of the brain. While a child's genes determine the basic hardware that she has (think of it like a schematic or a set of blueprints), the stimulation a child gets from interactions with her environment as experienced through her senses determines how those plans get implemented. It is not a question of "nature or nurture," but rather the result of the combination of "nature and nurture" that really counts.

Physical Growth of the Brain

In utero, the brain develops from a tubelike structure of cells. Over the course of pregnancy, this tube grows very rapidly, twisting and turning in on itself to become the baby's brain and spinal cord. By birth, a newborn's brain closely resembles that of an adult, but it is much smaller, only about one quarter the size. Over the course of the first few years of the child's life, the brain will grow rapidly, reaching 80 percent of adult size by age three and 90 percent of adult size by age five.

ESSENTIAL

Remember that the physical growth of the brain is only half the story: just as important is the growth of connections between different parts of the brain and between the brain and the body. These connections develop and strengthen throughout life, so while a five-year-old's brain looks a lot like an adult brain, it only functions at a small fraction of the speed.

Brain Development

The brain develops from the bottom up and from the back to the front. This pattern closely mirrors the evolution of the brain, as the more primitive structures that control the autonomic functions of the body (things we do automatically and without thought such as breathing, the beating of the heart, and the release of different hormones) develop first. These are then followed by the development of structures associated with memory and emotion, then motor function (movement and physical control) and language. The last parts of the brain to develop are those associated with conscious thought. Each of these structures is reviewed later in more detail, but for now what is important is to be aware of the pattern of development.

FACT

Whenever our brain does something, whether it is a thought or feeling or sensation, it is the result of the transmission of signals along neurons, the special types of cell that make up our brain tissue.

Nerve Cells

Everything you feel or do is the result of the activity of nerve cells throughout your body. Feel cold? That is the result of a nerve signal between your body and brain. Hungry? Your stomach communicates with your brain along nerves that connect the two organs. Even when you turn a page in this book, the muscles in your arm and hand are being activated by signals carried by nerves connecting those muscles to your brain.

All organs are composed of different types of tissue and these tissues are composed of many individual cells. In the brain, tissues are composed of neurons, a unique and very special type of cell. The brain is almost entirely made up of different types of neurons (or nerve cells), and these cells also run throughout your body, connecting almost every part of your body to your brain. There are many different types of neurons, depending on where the cell is located in the body and exactly what it does. Luckily, all of these different types follow more or less the same basic structure, so you don't have to get lost in all of the details.

Neurons look a lot like trees and have three primary parts: a *cell body*, many branchlike extensions that grow off the cell body called *dendrites*, and a long trunklike extension of the cell called an *axon*. The cell body is responsible for keeping the cell alive and acts as its control center while the dendrites receive connections from other cells. The axon connects the neuron to other cells and can be very, very short, as in adjacent neurons in the brain, or extremely long, like the neuron that connects your big toe to your brain through your spinal cord. Neurons can connect to other nerve cells or to completely different cell types like muscles, glands, or organs.

FACT

The average adult brain weighs approximately 3 pounds and contains about 100 billion nerve cells!

Neuronal Cell Bodies

The body of the nerve cell, also called the soma, is the control center of the cell. It includes all of the structures responsible for the growth, development, and maintenance of the cell. Much like the body is composed of different organs, each with a specific function, cells are composed of different organelles, each of which has specific jobs. You don't need to know all of the different organelles, but you should know that the DNA of the cell is contained in the nucleus, which resides here in the cell body. These cell bodies constitute the so-called gray matter of the brain.

Dendrites

The dendrites of a neuron are the many branch-like extensions that emerge from the cell body. These branches allow the neuron to receive connections from other neurons. Nerve cells communicate by electro-chemical signals that are transmitted into the dendrites. Each different type of nerve cell has a unique pattern of dendrite growth and any one neuron can receive multiple connections from many other nerve cells.

Axons

The axon is an extension from the body of a nerve cell. While a single neuron can have many dendrites, each cell has only one axon. Axons vary quite a bit in length: the smallest are almost imperceptible while the longest run most of the length of your body. Most axons branch out into several terminals toward their end. The job of the axon is to transmit signals from the neuron to other cells. This may be through a motor neuron that activates a muscle or it may be a sensory neuron telling you that someone is tickling your foot.

FACT

Your spinal cord is largely made up of a giant bundle of nerve axons that connect your brain to the rest of your body. This is why people with broken backs or necks usually can't feel or move anything below the break: the nerves connecting those parts of the body to the brain have been severed.

Myelin: Greased Lightning

A special layer of fat, called myelin, develops along the axons of nerve cells. The myelin accelerates the speed at which a nerve signal travels along a cell. Unfortunately, there is a limit to how much myelin you can develop on any given nerve axon, but a nerve that is fully loaded with myelin can transmit its signal 100 times faster than a minimally myelinated nerve cell.

Myelin develops along a nerve axon in direct response to the use of that nerve: The more you activate that particular nerve, the more myelin it will develop. Much of brain development, particularly in adolescence and early adulthood, has to do with the growth of myelin on nerve axons. Myelin makes up the "white matter" of the brain.

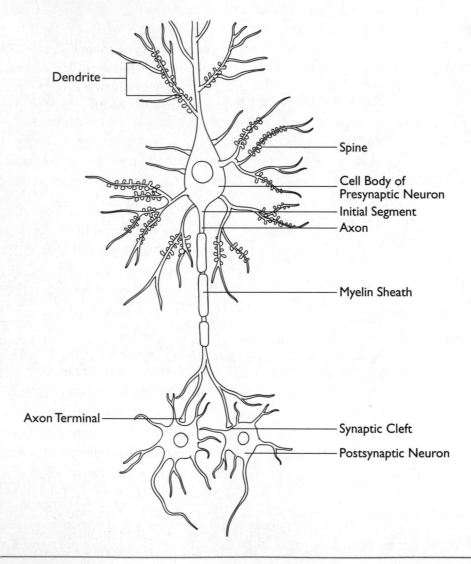

▲ Parts of a neuron

Some Things to Keep in Mind

Knowing the different parts of nerve cells is less than half the battle. It is even more important to understand how they function, grow, and develop. Doing so will help you better understand your own mind and your child's mind.

ESSENTIAL

One way to think of nerve cells is to imagine them like trees: The dendrites are the branches while the trunk is the axon. The cell body is at the top of the trunk where the branches originate and the bark along the trunk can be thought of as the myelin sheath.

Brain Function Is Localized

Different parts of our brain specialize in doing different things, as you will see when you look at the following section on brain structure.

This idea is very important because it allows different structures in the brain to specialize in certain functions. In order for you to get by out in the world, however, all of these different parts have to be able to communicate with each other to construct reality from what you perceive. It is actually a hugely complex task.

Let's try a small exercise to illustrate the point: Take a moment and look around the room you are in right now. What do you notice?

Likely, the room you are in is filled with various objects. One part of your brain sees those objects and notices their colors while another part of your brain calculates where each object is in space relative to your body so you can pick up a glass of water or walk around the couch without tripping over it. A different part of your brain recognizes those objects and finds the words used to refer to them. Still another part of your brain remembers the associations you have with those objects, where you got them, who gave them to you, your history with a particular item. If you can see any letters or numbers, there are very complex processes by which you decode those symbols to understand what they mean. If there are other people in the room (be they real people or just pictures of people) there is a whole part of your brain dedicated to recognizing their faces. That's quite a lot already, and we haven't even begun to scratch the surface of what is going on in your mind!

Other parts of your brain are busy processing information coming from each of your senses, particularly touch and sound. What you do with this information once your brain has interpreted it is entirely separate. This includes planning for the future, be it what you are going to do right now, later today, or twenty years from now; memories about the past; any feelings that come up, etc.

When you really start to look at it, the amount of work your brain does is just incredible! And this is all just for adult brains. For children, all of this is much more difficult because their brains are not yet fully developed. After the structural growth of the brain is completed, around age eight, it takes another twenty years for the brain to fully mature.

Connections

With all of those different things happening in different parts of your brain, it is no wonder that the connections across your brain are one of the most important parts of making you work.

The connections within the brain are so important that scientists have begun referring to them as the *connectome*, a play on genome, the map of human DNA. Researchers are currently in the process of mapping the connectome and estimate that there are more than 100,000,000,000,000 (that's 100 trillion!) connections in human brains.

Many of these connections develop before birth, but there are two large "blooms" of connections in life, one in infancy and the other at the onset of puberty. During these times, billions of new connections are formed across the brain, but they immediately begin to be pared down: connections that are used persist while ones that are not die off. Quite literally, our brains, much like our bodies, are "use it or lose it" systems.

Coordination

Coordinating between all the different parts of the brain is an extremely complex task. Most of this coordination is done by a very important part of the brain located above the eyes, called the prefrontal cortex. The prefrontal cortex is the seat of conscious thought and coordinates information from almost every other part of the brain. This is the part of our brain involved in self-control, calculating risk, and anticipating consequences, and it is also the last part of the brain to develop. This explains why even young adults in their twenties can struggle with decision making and poor choices. Remember, it isn't just about brain systems being "online," but also about being able to coordinate all of that processing power.

Brain Structure

The human brain is a complex system that is the result of millions of years of evolution. It developed in layers from the bottom up and from the back to the front, increasing in complexity as it went. Over the course of evolution, from reptiles to mammals to primates and finally to humans, the brain has vastly expanded its functionality and capacity.

There are many complex parts to the brain and they can be grouped in various ways based on anatomy and function. It is easier to think of the brain as being divided into three primary divisions or regions. The first, located at the base of the brain and connecting it to the spinal cord, is called the hindbrain. Above this sits the cerebrum, which includes the limbic system. This part of your brain is largely responsible for your emotions and memory. The cortex, the upper- and outermost layer, includes the four lobes: temporal, occipital, parietal, and frontal. These are the complex structures that process language, spatial relationships, and conscious thought, and are responsible for most of the human ability to think and reason.

The cerebrum is sometimes also called the forebrain. Astute readers may be wondering where the midbrain is in all of this. Indeed, there is a structure called the midbrain that rests on top of the hindbrain and connects it to the structures of the forebrain and limbic system. While the midbrain is very important to brain function, it is also one of the smallest structures in the brain.

The Hindbrain

The most primitive part of our brain is called the hindbrain and is located at the top of the spinal cord. The hindbrain includes structures such as the medulla oblongata, pons and cerebellum, and is largely responsible for your autonomic nervous functions (meaning the things you do automatically, such as your breathing and heartbeat). This region of the brain is also involved in regulating sleep cycles, the appetite, some motor functions, and the so-called fight-or-flight reaction.

FACT

The hindbrain plus a cerebral structure called the basal-ganglia are often referred to as the "reptile brain" because of how these brain structures function almost entirely on instinct. This derives from an evolutionary model called the triune brain developed by Paul MacLean and popularized by Carl Sagan's 1977 book *The Dragons of Eden*.

The Medulla Oblongata

Often referred to simply as the medulla, this part of the brain forms the lowest part of the brainstem and rests directly atop the spinal cord. The medulla controls many of the autonomic functions of your body, the things you do automatically and without conscious thought such as breathing, heart rate, blood pressure and reflexes such as sneezing, coughing, vomiting, and swallowing. It is also an important transfer station connecting the higher parts of the brain to the spinal cord.

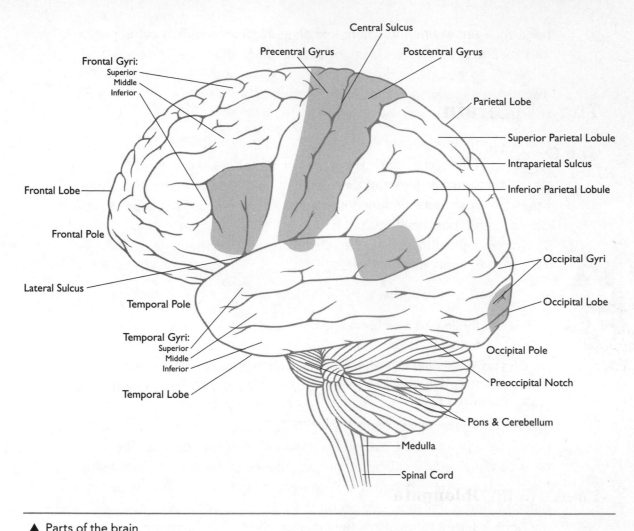

Central Sulcus

Precentral Gyrus   Postcentral Gyrus

Frontal Gyri:
Superior
Middle
Inferior

Parietal Lobe

Superior Parietal Lobule

Intraparietal Sulcus

Inferior Parietal Lobule

Frontal Lobe

Frontal Pole

Lateral Sulcus

Occipital Gyri

Occipital Lobe

Temporal Pole

Occipital Pole

Temporal Gyri:
Superior
Middle
Inferior

Preoccipital Notch

Temporal Lobe

Pons & Cerebellum

Medulla

Spinal Cord

▲ Parts of the brain

The Pons

The pons is a bulbous structure. It is about an inch long, and is located near the top of the brainstem and directly above the medulla. The name "pons" derives from the Latin word for "bridge." One of the most important roles of the pons is transmitting information between the cerebellum (which sits directly behind it), and the higher structures of the forebrain.

The pons is a very important structure that mediates between your conscious mind and your autonomic functions. It is involved in regulating sleep, the switch between inhaling and exhaling, bladder control, posture, equilibrium, and eye movement, among several other functions. The pons plays some role in generating dreams, although this is not well understood. It is also responsible for sleep paralysis, preventing brain signals from reaching your muscles while you sleep and dream.

The Cerebellum

By far the largest part of the hindbrain is the cerebellum. This "minibrain" hangs off of the bottom of the cortex and is attached to the brainstem directly behind the pons.

FACT

The word *cerebellum* literally means "little brain" in Latin.

The primary role of the cerebellum is in coordination of physical movement. The cerebellum does not tell your body to move (those commands come from the forebrain); rather, the cerebellum receives these commands and integrates them with data received from your body through your spinal cord. These functions of the cerebellum are the most understood because of research on individuals who have sustained damage to this part of their brain. Damage to the cerebellum consistently results in problems with coordination, timing, balance, and posture.

Recent research has also shown that the cerebellum has important roles in emotional regulation as well. It seems that the primary task has to do with regulation of emotional responses. Brain scans have shown that the cerebellum is active in attention, language, imagination, and learning, but research to determine exactly how it contributes to these functions is ongoing.

The Higher Brain

The part of our brain that makes humans distinct from other species is our cerebrum. It is the largest part of the brain and includes all of the structures that give us control of our bodies and minds and that are responsible for sensory processing, our memories and emotions, language and thought. Humans have the largest brains of all mammals relative to body mass.

Dolphins are the only other species whose brain size in relation to body size is comparable to humans'. Both the human and dolphin brain constitute more than 2 percent of total body mass, and the dolphin brain is actually 100 grams heavier than a human's on average.

Hemispheres

The cerebrum is divided into two hemispheres right down the middle, each half a mirror image of the other. Although apparently identical on a large scale, there are significant differences in the cellular composition of and processing performed by each side of the brain. The two hemispheres are bridged by a large structure called the corpus callosum and communication between the two sides is very important to overall functioning.

The difference in processing between the two hemispheres is called lateralization. Many brain functions are lateralized, such as perception, so a sensation from one side of the body is processed by the opposite side of the brain. This is also true of motor control and is related to hand preference, among other things.

Much discussion has occurred in popular psychology about cognitive differences between the sides of the brain. So-called left-brain people are said to be more concrete and procedural while right-brainers are more intuitive and creative. This is, at best, a gross oversimplification. Complex brain functions such as creativity and logical reasoning are distributed across both hemispheres and there is little neurological data to support these claims.

The Limbic System

The limbic system is made up of a group of structures located in the center of the cerebrum: If you think of a cross-section of the earth as a model for your brain, the limbic system would be the core. The limbic system is deeply involved in our emotions and memories, our sense of smell, and spatial navigation. You can think of it as the "feeling and reacting" part of the brain as opposed to the cortex above it, the "thinking" part of the brain. The limbic system is made up of many different structures, but the most important are the hypothalamus, amygdala, and hippocampus.

The Hypothalamus

The hypothalamus is an almond-sized brain structure located along the midline of the brain and directly above the pituitary gland. It is heavily connected to other parts of the brain and body, including the frontal lobe, brain stem, amygdala, and hippocampus. It also receives special connections from the nose and optic nerves.

FACT

The hypothalamus is very different between men and women. This is because one of the primary roles of the hypothalamus is in regulating sexual response and reproductive cycles.

The hypothalamus regulates many of our metabolic functions such as body temperature, hunger, thirst, tiredness, and circadian rhythms (our sleep/wake cycle based on exposure to sunlight). It is also the primary connection between the brain and the pituitary gland and plays a primary role in regulating our endocrine system.

The Amygdalae

You have two amygdalae, one on either side of your brain. They are both small, almond-shaped structures deep within the temporal lobe near the bottom of the cerebrum. The amygdalae are connected to both receive from and transmit to many other brain structures including the thalamus, hypothalamus, hippocampus, and brain stem. The olfactory bulb is connected to the amygdalae but does not receive a connection back from it.

The endocrine system is made up of the various glands throughout our bodies that secrete hormones. Hormones regulate many body processes including growth and physical development, sexual response, reproductive cycles, metabolism, and the experience of pain, as well as some emotions.

The amygdalae are some of the most important structures in our emotional reactions to our environment. They are directly involved in our stress response and play a very important role in fear and anxiety. In part, this is done by coordinating reaction in our behavior, autonomic nervous system, and endocrine system. (The amygdala helps get your heart rate up and helps trigger the release of adrenaline when you get scared. These physiological responses allow you to move more quickly whether you decide to run away or stand and fight.) Because the amygdalae can help to regulate these responses and is also connected to memory formation, it is a powerful tool in emotional learning as well. Generally speaking, the more you react emotionally to a situation, the more the amygdalae will be activated and the more you will remember from the experience.

The amygdala is at the heart of learning conditioned responses. Researchers have conducted conditioned learning experiments with rats and mice in which they have administered drugs that either increase or decrease the response in the amygdalae. It has consistently been found that rodents given drugs that increase amygdalae activity learn their conditioning faster and more successfully while those given drugs that inhibit amygdalae activity learn much more slowly.

The Hippocampus

The hippocampus is a brain structure located deep in the temporal lobe and shaped roughly like a seahorse. You have two hippocampi, one in each hemisphere of your brain. The hippocampus plays important roles in both short- and long-term memory and spatial navigation.

ALERT

The hippocampus is one of the first brain structures to be damaged by Alzheimer's disease.

Much of what is know about the hippocampus comes from research on people who have had theirs damaged. The most famous subject, Henry Molaison, had his hippocampus surgically destroyed in an attempt to relieve severe epileptic seizures. Molaison developed severe anterograde amnesia (the inability to form new memories) and lost some of his memories from the years preceding his surgery. However, his older memories, such as those of his childhood, remained almost entirely intact.

The hippocampus is also particularly susceptible to stress. Stress is the result of the release of certain hormones (corticosteroids, specifically) into the blood. For these hormones to affect a certain part of the body or brain, this part needs to have specific receptors to which the stress hormones can attach. The hippocampus has an unusually large number of these receptors, making it more vulnerable to long-term stress than most other brain structures. Recent research has shown that damage to the hippocampus is one of the effects of depression. This can be stopped easily with medication, even if that medication does not particularly alleviate the depression itself. The damage caused to the hippocampus by severe stress does seem to be at least partially reversible if the stress is treated.

The Cerebral Cortex

The part of your brain that makes you most uniquely human is the cerebral cortex. This is the wrinkly structure on the outer surface of the brain. It plays a critical role in complex thought, consciousness, language, perception, memory, and attention. The cerebral cortex is actually composed of six complex layers and can be divided into many different regions based on cell type and specific functions. To avoid confusion, it is best to talk about the cortex in terms of its four traditional divisions into lobes: occipital, temporal, parietal, and frontal. This is a good basic way to understand the functions of the cortex, but you should be clear that the four lobes are based on the physical appearance of the brain most of all. Through modern research techniques, scientists have been able to make finer distinctions of different parts of the cortex that are more specific as to what each part does.

The Occipital Lobe

The occipital lobe is located at the back of the brain and is the primary visual processing center. It receives information that is perceived by the retina of each eye and passed through the thalamus by the optic nerves. Interestingly, each hemisphere of the occipital lobe processes information received from the outside half of the same-side retina and information from the inside half of the opposite side: The left hemisphere of the occipital lobe processes information from the outside half of the left eye and the inside half of the right. This may play a role in depth perception and the evaluation of the distance of objects from the observer.

The information received by the occipital lobe from the retinas is based entirely on light and the movement of that light. There are cells toward the back of the occipital lobe that are arranged as an exact copy of the cells in the retina. Scientists have observed that these cells tend to activate at the same time as the retinal cells: When your eyes see a pattern, that pattern is based on activation of cells in the retina. The cells in this area of the occipital lobe duplicate that pattern of activation. Based on current research, the occipital lobe is not known to have significant functions beyond the processing of visual stimuli.

The Temporal Lobe

The temporal lobe is the primary auditory processing center of the brain and plays an important role in language and other brain functions. It contains many of the structures of the limbic system, including the hippocampus and amygdala, and contributes to memory and emotional response.

FACT

Interestingly, the temporal lobe is the part of the brain most responsible for facial recognition, a critical and complex brain function in humans. Damage to certain parts of the lobe can cause face blindness, or prosopagnosia.

The temporal lobe processes information received through the ears. In addition to constructing the meaning of words, the temporal lobe is responsible for understanding the name and purpose (meaning) of objects seen by the eyes. Evolutionary research has suggested that human capacity for language may have evolved by the temporal lobe co-opting resources from the visual cortex.

The Parietal Lobe

The parietal lobe is a complex structure with a variety of functions. Its primary purpose is to process sensations from the body and control fine motor functions. Additionally, it has important roles in the processing and manipulation of numbers, some language processing, and understanding of symbols and spatial relationships.

FACT

The parietal lobe, like all of the cerebral cortex, is divided into two hemispheres. The left hemisphere is primarily involved in processing numbers, language, and symbolic relationships (such as in reading and writing), while the right side is dedicated to spatial reasoning and mapping.

One of the most important functions of the parietal lobe has to do with spatial processing. This part of the brain tracks where different parts of your body are in space and controls hand, arm, and eye movement. The parietal lobe is also involved in understanding visual-spatial relationships and navigation.

The parietal lobe sits directly above the temporal lobe. The junction between the two lobes has been shown to play a role in your sense of being in your body and your social cognition. Recent research has shown this part of the brain to be of particular importance to certain empathetic functions, such as inferring the desires and intentions of others.

The Frontal Lobe

The frontal lobe is the seat of cognitive function in the brain. It is responsible for conscious movement, attention, short-term memory, planning, and motivation. The frontal lobe also governs the behavioral reward system. This is because the frontal lobe contains most of the dopamine-responsive neurons in the brain. Dopamine is an important neurotransmitter that is the foundation of the good feelings we experience in response to certain stimuli. This shapes our behavior and preferences. It supports learning, motivation, and aspects of cognition.

The Prefrontal Cortex

The prefrontal cortex is part of the frontal lobe, and is one of the most important parts of the brain. It is heavily connected to almost every other part of the brain and plays critical roles in cognitive behavior, decision making, self-control, and personality expression. It is the seat of executive function and one of the last brain areas to fully mature, not doing so until you are in your late twenties.

One of the unique qualities of the prefrontal cortex is its ability to act as a mental "clipboard." Most other areas of the brain only activate in response to (usually external) stimulation. The prefrontal cortex has the ability to retrieve and hold on to pieces of information stored in the memory or other parts of the brain. This allows it to consider a greater depth of information than what may be immediately confronting an individual. The slowness of this part of the brain to develop explains the observed risk taking and lack of self-control exhibited by adolescents and young adults.

What the Brain Does

The brain has two jobs: The first, and by far the most important, is to keep you alive. Everything about your brain has evolved over millions of years and is directed to this one purpose. All of the amazing things that the human brain is capable of achieving exist because they allow us to survive more effectively. When you think about it, this is a truly humbling thought. The human organism, for all of its strength, intelligence, and adaptation, is quite fragile, really. As a species, humans can move mountains and reshape the landscape, but they remain subject to sickness, old age, and, inevitably, death. No technology ever invented has been able to change that.

The second important function the brain serves is to make sense of the constant stream of information about the world that pours in through our senses. Far more than the classical five senses of smell, taste, touch, hearing, and sight, human beings have as many as eighteen different sensory capabilities, depending on how you define them. All of these sensory capabilities are bombarding your brain with information about everything around you. It is tempting to think that what you see, taste, or touch is in some absolute sense "real," but the scientific truth is that it is not. It is only a perception. Anything beyond a simple sensation is a construction, a story that you tell to organize and make greater sense out of what you perceive. That is how the brain handles all of the information it is constantly receiving: It systematizes it by creating meaning from raw data. What human beings believe is reality is really just one of a near infinite number of ways to imagine the world they inhabit.

ESSENTIAL

The senses a human being can have are: sight, taste, touch, pressure, itch, thermoception, sound, smell, proprioception, tension, nociception (pain), equilibrioception, stretch, chemoreception, thirst, hunger, magnetoception, time.

CHAPTER 5

How Children Learn

Children are great observers. Their capacity to absorb adult habits is largely underestimated; children are always watching, learning, and internalizing. It is important to be conscious of this because it will heighten your awareness of what you say and do around your kids. In addition, knowing that children are constantly learning from your words and actions can help you more actively consider which values you want to embody and model for their benefit.

Monkey-See, Monkey-Do

Animals, particularly mammals, learn chiefly through mimicry and imitation. Despite the abundant knowledge and technology of the human species, people still learn in the same instinctual ways. Children will see a parent, sibling, or family member do something and then they will want to try it themselves.

This phenomenon is seen across the animal kingdom, and although humans have a prefrontal cortex that allows for incredible powers of reasoning, self-awareness, and conscious thought, people are still subject to the same instinctual patterns of learning as other social mammals. This is most obvious in children, as their ability to learn in other ways (such as through reading or formal instruction) develops later in life.

So what does all this mean for a parent? It means that your child learns most directly from what you *do*. This isn't just about how to wash the dishes or change a light bulb; it also applies to how you behave and respond to different situations. If you regularly yell at your child for doing something wrong, for example, your child comes to learn that yelling is an appropriate and acceptable way to deal with mistakes or frustration. On the other hand if you consistently treat strangers with kindness, over time your child learns to do the same.

Of course it isn't quite this simple, as there are many factors that impact a child's behavior. Your being kind to strangers does not 100 percent guarantee that your child will behave the same way either now or in the future; however, it does lay a solid foundation of experience from which your child will draw as he matures. When a child consistently sees and/or experiences particular behaviors from his parents as he grows, these behavioral patterns are often internalized and become part of his value system.

The 90/10 Rule

Children learn roughly 10 percent from what you say and 90 percent from what you do. Though it is cliché, the saying "Actions speak louder than words" is a developmental reality. Among the most significant lessons that parents teach, how to handle one's emotions is at the top of the list. For better or worse, your child is always learning from how you express yourself.

For example, what do you model as appropriate ways to handle anger and frustration? This is an important question to consider. Your actions in these circumstances literally teach your child "This is how to behave when you are angry. This is how to behave when something goes wrong."

Again, none of this is about being perfect. There is no such thing. What this is about is setting constructive intentions, practicing mindfulness as best you can (realizing that your "best" changes with every passing moment), inevitably making mistakes, reflecting, setting constructive intentions, and continuing to practice.

Kids will naturally experiment with many different ways of handling their emotions. Even for adults, intense emotions are challenging to manage. All the more so for kids, whose capacity for self-control is developmentally limited. Do not fret if your child is not yet handling himself in the ways you are modeling; this takes time. As a parent, you have to take the long view of your child's growth. Rest assured that through repeated exposure to and direct experiences with your personality and way of being, many of those same patterns will be internalized and emerge as your child matures.

Think about Your Own Parents

Think back to your own parents and how their habits of speech, action, and emotional response (or reactivity) shaped your own development. What similar characteristics did you take on (or perhaps avoid)? What qualities of your parents do you now see in how you are with your own children?

The purpose of asking these questions is to help you reflect on how different qualities are passed on between generations, and to recognize which habits, values, or qualities you absorbed growing up. Each person is undeniably shaped by the people who raised them. Ideally, how would you like to shape your children?

If you've ever wondered about the most effective way to pass on your value system to your child, this is it: you have to live it. This can feel a bit intimidating, but in reality it is a great opportunity. You will never have better motivation to be the kind of person and the kind of parent you really want to be, and there is no greater gift to yourself or your kids than doing your best to mindfully live your values.

Give Your Child Your Attention

Plants need sunshine to grow, and so do children. For your child, however, their "sunshine" is your attention. She needs it to survive when she is little, and it continues to feed her throughout her life.

FACT

After World War I, orphanages across Europe were flooded with children. In England, it was standard practice to put all infants in cribs in large rooms. Despite having all of their nutritional and sanitary needs met, the infants were dying off in startling numbers. The nurses soon realized that none of the infants were being touched, and implemented a schedule to ensure that each infant was held for a few hours each day. With this new system of physical contact in place, the infants stopped dying.

Here is a strange twist to keep in mind: it doesn't actually matter whether the attention children receive is positive or negative. Children simply need attention any way they can get it. Some kids learn to get the attention they need through positive behaviors like helping out at home or working hard at school. Other children learn to get attention by acting out, disobeying rules, and taking unnecessary risks. (There is usually a combination and experimentation with both). As a parent, you have the huge opportunity to steer your child in one direction or the other.

Ask yourself, "What do I give my attention to?" Watch yourself as you interact with your child, regardless of his age. Do you mainly talk to him when something is wrong or when he didn't do what he was told? (This is a particularly common pattern between parents and adolescents).

Similarly, do you make a point of expressing gratitude for the things he does well? Even small things can make a big difference. However you behave with your child, you are constantly reinforcing patterns of behavior and thus patterns of feedback in the brain. Children habituate to seeking attention either positively or negatively over time, and the pattern you reinforce most will more often than not be the one they choose.

Attention and Behavior Management

Attention can be a powerful tool when addressing behavioral issues with your child. A classic case in point: children who bite. It is not uncommon for toddlers to develop the habit of biting others, adults as well as children. This behavior can be famously difficult to change. When a child bites, it is very tempting for parents (and teachers) to intervene and attempt to correct the behavior by talking to or sometimes raising their voices at the child who did the biting. While the intention is to logically explain why biting is inappropriate and unacceptable, the result is actually the opposite. What really happens?

How to React

First off, when it comes to toddlers, anything more than a couple of sentences amounts to a lecture. A logical conversation with an older child would yield different results; however, at this early stage in life, children will simply tune out. They cannot learn through words in the same ways that adults or older children can, especially when it comes to long multiclause sentences. On top of this, the child who did the biting ends up getting a *lot* of attention for her mistaken behavior. The fact that it is negative attention is irrelevant; any type of attention is sunshine, and this puts the wrong child (and the wrong behavior) in the spotlight.

So, what is a more skillful response in this situation? Of course you must quickly intervene to stop the unwanted behavior and it is perfectly appropriate to say "No," but try to leave it at that. Anything more is pointing your sunshine in the wrong direction. Instead, you should physically remove the biter from the group and sit her down outside the circle of attention (this could be just a foot or two behind you—it does not take much). From there, give all your attention to the child who was bitten. Ask if he is all right, give him a hug, and redirect him to a new activity. Although you want to be aware of what the child who did the biting is doing, it is completely acceptable to turn your back on her entirely. The biter may cry or pout for a time, but continue to ignore her. After a couple of minutes (it does not take long), if she is still sitting down and/or pouting, you should invite her to do something else. At most, say something like "Are you ready to play gently?" when inviting the child who bit into a new activity. Aside from that, let it go and refocus on the present moment with this child.

If you are dealing with a child who is a little older than a toddler, and more verbal, a short conversation about more appropriate ways to express anger or frustration is well warranted. Keep it brief, and in order to get the most out of the experience, ask the child, "What can you do next time if you get angry or frustrated? How else can you deal with those angry feelings?" This guides the child to come up with healthier, more constructive responses to her anger instead of just reacting blindly. It also gives her an opportunity to think of alternatives for herself (or to brainstorm with you), instead of you flat out telling her what she should do. This engages your child in a dialogue instead of turning the conversation into a mini-lecture. These brief two-way discussions with older, more verbal children will raise their emotional awareness and help them to find better ways of coping with the intense feelings that all people encounter from time to time. This is how children begin learning self-control.

To Cry or Not to Cry?

Children idolize their parents, pure and simple. Your kids look up to you, and rely on you to help them interpret the different circumstances they encounter. Children will often take their cues from you, teachers, and other relevant adults about how to react to whatever situations come up, and how you respond affects how they react. How and where you focus your attention makes all the difference when a child encounters physical pain or fear.

For example, there was once a three-year-old girl playing at a playground with her mom, who was watching from a nearby bench. At one point the little girl tripped and scraped her knees on the sidewalk, just enough to leave some dirt and red marks. As the little girl hopped up and began brushing her knees off without a second thought, her mom came rushing over to "help."

"Oh you poor little thing! Oh baby I'm so sorry, come here and let me take a look, my goodness that must have hurt so much . . ." and so on. When the little girl saw how much attention she was getting for scraping her knees, she hammed it up and immediately started crying. In response, her mother doted on her even more.

Now there's nothing wrong with attending to children when they get hurt. That is what responsible adults do. The question is: *how* do you attend to your child in that situation? In the previous example, because the mother overreacted and focused all her attention on a minor fall that did not even faze the little girl, she unknowingly encouraged her child to cry and become a helpless victim. How else might the mother have responded? How could she have lovingly encouraged her daughter's resilience instead?

Acknowledge Fear

It is possible to acknowledge a child's pain or fear without making it the focal point of your attention. For example, one winter day a preschool teacher took her students sledding. Despite the seemingly safe and gently sloping hill, one of the four-year-old boys somehow managed to do a complete flip on his way down and landed in a puff of powder. The teacher immediately ran over and checked to make sure he was okay, which he was. The boy stood up with tears in his eyes, shaken and unsure of how to react. He looked at his teacher, trying to decide whether or not he should cry.

"Oh my gosh, that was the craziest sled-flip I've ever seen! Up top," the teacher said, giving him a high-five. "How on earth did you do that? There's not even a scratch on you! That must have been pretty scary," she said, brushing snow off his coat. A huge smile spread across the boy's face. "I don't know, but that was wild!" the little boy said. Other students started giving him high-fives, and then he proudly dragged his sled back to the top of the hill for another run.

Fear is a powerful emotion. By acknowledging a child's fear and helping him realize that everything is okay, you give him permission to move beyond the fear. When you focus on a child's strengths and help him see that minor falls and such are no big deal, he will internalize that lesson over time and feel more confident.

How you focus your attention will also teach children helpful coping mechanisms in the face of fear or pain. For example, consider this story: one spring afternoon a kindergarten teacher came back from lunch to find the assistant teacher trying to pull a tick from the top of a little girl's head. The little girl was sobbing uncontrollably, and the assistant teacher was having a terrible time trying to help. The girl's sobbing made it impossible to find the tick hidden in her hair, and the two were feeding off of each other's frustration and anxiety. Needless to say, it was not going well.

Seeing that the assistant teacher needed some backup, the kindergarten teacher sat down in front of the little girl, held both her hands, and smiled. "Look at me Sarah," she said gently. Still sobbing, Sarah looked at her teacher. "Take a deep, slow breath." The two took a deep, slow breath together. "That's it Sarah, let's do it again. This is how you can calm yourself down." They took another few breaths, and after a minute Sarah was able to hold still. "No one likes having a tick on their head, but this is no big deal. Just keep breathing slowly with me, get yourself calm, and it'll be over before you know it." Sarah nodded, and although the tears kept coming she soon calmed herself down. Moments later the assistant teacher was able to pull out the tick with a pair of tweezers, and it didn't hurt at all. Within five minutes, Sarah was laughing about the whole situation.

When a child is in the throes of intense pain or fear, how you respond and what you focus on will make a significant difference. Children need to know that it is okay to feel whatever they are feeling in that moment, and then you can redirect their attention in ways that teach them how to manage these overwhelming feelings. By standing with a child, supporting him, and keeping your cool, you will heavily influence how he handles things like falling down or getting scared.

The Power of Relationships

The reality is that you cannot actually control your children, especially as they become older, bigger, and more independent. There are all sorts of things you can do to influence their behavior, but ultimately, your children are independent beings who will make their own choices in life. Often that choice will be about whether or not to listen to what you have to say. The power you have in getting your children to listen to you comes directly from the strength of your relationships with them; by putting the relationships ahead of your pride or ego, you can maximize the influence you have with your children as they mature.

Watch Out for Fear

Another way parents sometimes try to make their children do what they say is through fear. This can be a fear of punishment, a fear of getting hit, a fear of making Mom or Dad angry, etc. Although fear can arise naturally in children when they face the consequences of their actions or the possibility of disappointing their parents, it is not a very healthy strategy for controlling your child's behavior.

Cultivating a fear-based relationship with your child as a means of controlling him is bound to backfire as he grows, becomes more confident and independent, and also more desperate to assert control in his life. Standing beside your child as a guide, mentor, and ally as he matures is much more likely to cultivate an internal locus of control and a stronger relationship between you and your young adult.

A Challenging Truth

Your relationship with your child will inevitably evolve as he grows and the things he needs from you change. This is a crucial thing to be aware of: what your child needs from you changes over time. There are so many things to be treasured at every stage of his life, and you will get comfortable and attached to doing certain things with or for him. This is completely natural, and yet you must always remember that this constant change in the dynamics of your relationships is part of growing up. Try to remember that your child *always* needs you, at every age and stage—it's just that what he needs from you will be different at five than at fifteen.

The Ultimate Purpose of Parenting

It is also very helpful to keep the ultimate purpose of parenting in mind. Your primary goal is to raise an independent, healthy, and functional adult who is fully equipped to think for and take care of herself. You want the best for your child, and rightly so. Just keep in mind the context in which you make your choices, and the factors that are beyond your control.

It is not only inevitable that your child will grow up and move away one day, it is expressly the purpose of parenthood to prepare your child so she can live an independent, successful, and fulfilling life (however she defines it). You raise these birds so they can fly on their own. When you remain aware that this is the natural process, it becomes easier to accept whatever feelings come up (whether heartbreak, excitement, or a bit of both), and to work with them more effectively.

CHAPTER 6

Children's Learning Styles

As every parent knows, children have unique strengths. Some are wizards with logic puzzles and numbers; others can write stories that crack you up or touch your heart. People are not born with a cognitive capacity that is easily measured through standardized testing—intelligence is more complex than that. There are many avenues for learning, and children are naturally inclined to some styles over others. When you understand what learning styles speak to your child (and to yourself), you are in a much better position to guide their development and help them reach their potential.

You Are the Educator

As a parent, you are inherently an educator. Teaching and learning are intrinsic to the role you play in your child's life. When you are mindful of this role, both the content and the ways in which you teach will improve by leaps and bounds. When you live this role with intention, you can:

- Tailor the way you teach to fit your child's natural learning style.
- Connect with your child in more meaningful ways.
- Help him learn to master new skills and information.
- Seize on teachable moments.
- Make no distinction between living, teaching, and learning.
- Make learning more fun and interesting for yourself and your child.

Theory of Multiple Intelligences

The theory of multiple intelligences, proposed by Dr. Howard Gardner in 1983, is revolutionizing how educators think about teaching and learning. It is a different model for understanding how people learn. Dr. Gardner initially identified seven types of intelligence, and later added Naturalist as the eighth:

- Linguistic (word-smart)
- Logical-Mathematical (logic-smart)
- Naturalist (nature-smart)
- Spatial (picture-smart)
- Bodily-Kinesthetic (body-smart)
- Musical (music-smart)
- Interpersonal (people-smart)
- Intrapersonal (self-smart)

What Is Intelligence?

According to Dr. Gardner, intelligence is measured by an individual's ability to creatively solve problems, learn and integrate new information, and offer something of value in a culture. The theory contends that everyone is born with all eight of these intelligences to one degree or another. The question is, in what combination of strength and to what degree? Just like snowflakes, the shape these intelligences take in each person is unique. The important question for you is: To which intelligences is your child more naturally inclined?

Although many of the following activities are geared toward children and preadolescents, you can shape and change them as needed to complement whatever developmental stage your child is in. To cultivate your child's many types of intelligence, incorporate some of these ideas into your family life!

The Linguistic Intelligence

Does your child enjoy telling and hearing stories? Does he like to write? Is he sensitive to the musical qualities and rhythms of words? Does he enjoy saying, hearing, or seeing words? Is he skilled in the art of arguing and persuasion? What about explaining a concept, recounting an event, or remembering trivia?

If these questions describe you or your child, it probably means that linguistic intelligence is a major lens through which you learn and understand the world. In short, linguistic intelligence is the capacity to use language to express what's on your mind and to understand other people. Reading, writing, listening, and public speaking are characteristic activities of word-smart people. These learners often think in words instead of pictures, and have highly developed auditory skills. They are effective communicators who enjoy growing their vocabularies and using language as their canvas of expression.

Activities That Cultivate Your Child's Linguistic Intelligence

1. *Make up stories and tell them to someone else.* This can be done by having everyone in the family write a story and read it out loud, or by going around in a group with each person adding a sentence (written or aloud).

2. *Keep a journal.* If language is one of the primary ways you or your child understands the world, keeping a daily journal is very helpful in processing, organizing, and making sense of their emotions and experiences.

3. *Have regular debates and discussions.* This can be as simple as conversations at the dinner table, asking your child's opinions on different topics, or talking through current events.

4. *Create a magazine or newsletter.* A family or school magazine is a creative way to use writing skills to highlight recent events, opinion pieces, interviews, creative writing, pictures with captions, cartoons, and more.

5. *Have a word of the day.* Word-smart people enjoy learning new words and how to use them correctly, and often show interest in etymology (i.e., the source or origin of words). Finding new words to put on the fridge and play with in conversation is a fun way to build your child's vocabulary.

6. *Write poetry.* There are many different kinds of poetry to explore, including haiku or poems that rhyme. Rhyming in particular can be a great way to help word-smart learners remember new things.

7. *Write book reviews and/or have book discussions.* Word-smart learners love to read. Engaging in book discussions with others will animate stories in new ways, and will help to refine your child's communication skills, critical thinking, and analysis.

8. *Play word games.* Games like Scrabble, word searches, crossword puzzles, Apples to Apples, Boggle, and others are fun ways to engage the family and strengthen these skills.

9. *Sing!* Particularly with young children, opportunities to sing, rhyme, and play with language are major boons in cultivating linguistic intelligence. Keep it light and fun, and don't be afraid to be silly! Kids respond to silly. Even if they don't sing along with you, make no mistake that singing around your children will have a positive impact on their linguistic development. (Not to mention what you can teach through the message of each song…)

10. *Use the Play-Doh Snake.* This game has many variations, and is particularly fun for children who are learning how to read. Your child makes the head of a snake out of Play-Doh while you create different letters or words. When your child reads each letter or word correctly, their snake

gets to "eat" it and add it to the snake's body. How long can the snake get? Measure!

The Logical-Mathematical Intelligence

Logic-smart learners are good at reasoning, recognizing patterns, analyzing, and solving problems. They are conceptual thinkers who have a knack for precision, investigation, and scientific processes. They enjoy exploring and discussing abstract ideas, and have an affinity for the logic of math and numbers.

This intelligence looks slightly different in young children than it does in teenagers and adults, because young children do not yet have the neurological capacity for abstract thought. In the three-to-nine-year-old age range, kids are concrete thinkers. So how might logic-smarts emerge during this time?

Here are some characteristics to look for. Does your child:

- Draw or make patterns?
- Try to figure out how things work, possibly by taking them apart?
- Have good problem-solving skills?
- Enjoy doing science experiments?
- Have fun counting objects or doing math in her head?
- Organize things into categories?
- Enjoy playing strategy games?

If you answered yes to some or all of these questions, you are seeing the logical-mathematical aspect of your child's intelligence blossom.

Activities to Strengthen Your Child's Logic-Smarts

1. *Playing cards.* Interactive games that involve numbers and mental math are a great way to improve this intelligence. The games will vary depending on the skill level of your child; however, some classic card games to consider include blackjack (AKA 21), Crazy Eights, gin rummy and Go Fish (to name a few).

2. *Food math.* Any time you're sitting down to lunch or snack with the kids, try this improvisational game. Turn elements of the meal into word problems, and be creative! If your child is snacking on Goldfish, for example, you can turn it into Food Math by saying: "Imagine you're a hungry shark trying to catch these little fish. How many fish do you see? How many will be left if the shark eats 6?"

3. *Create mini-mysteries.* Kids love to solve mysteries. Create a scavenger hunt where the kids have to answer riddles and collect clues hidden around the house or outside to solve the mystery. If it can include some kind of treasure map—all the better.

4. *Create a maze or crossword puzzle.* Creating and solving these puzzles can be done as individuals or as teams. Trade your maze or crossword puzzle with someone else and try to solve theirs. You can also make these into reusable laminated placemats.

5. *Pattern games.* Take any opportunity to organize objects by color, size, shape, number, or type (mammals, reptiles, etc.). This can be done with toys, food, leaves, rocks, numbers, and more. Take advantage of any opportunity to point out patterns in the environment, and to ask your child what patterns *she* notices.

6. *Break or create secret codes.* Kids love breaking a secret code to read a secret message. A simple way to do this that also reinforces number and letter recognition is to equate each letter to a number (such that A=1, B=2, etc.). Write a joke, tongue twister, or riddle using the number code, and give them a cheat sheet so they know which letter each number represents.

7. *Debate night.* Logical thinking is strengthened through discussion and debate. Stating an opinion and supporting it with facts and reasoning is a great way to sharpen this skill. This may happen naturally during family dinners, or the family could play a debate game where two teams are given a position (e.g., Why bedtime should be 8 P.M., why dogs are better than cats) that they have to defend whether they agree with it or not.

8. *What happened in the story?* Sequencing events is a great way to cultivate the logical-mathematical intelligence. One way to do this is to choose a story, make some photocopies of various pictures throughout the story, and then after reading it, ask your child to arrange the pictures according to the order in which they happened.

9. *Jigsaw Puzzles.* Do puzzles as a family! You can even make your own puzzles using magazine photos, printed family photos, or a child's drawing.

10. *Measurements.* Measure things all over the house and outside and compare them. Create charts that show your results!

11. *Experiments.* Any and all science experiments will nurture the inquisitive mind, such as making homemade volcanoes, doing cooking experiments, playing with color. Remember to ask your child to predict the results.

ALERT

These activities offer great opportunities for the family to spend time with one another, so keep the mood light-hearted. Competition is not the purpose; having fun is. What your child learns is a powerfully quiet side effect of having a good time with you!

The Naturalist Intelligence

Almost all young children demonstrate a high naturalist intelligence. They often love playing outside (when given the opportunity), building forts, exploring the woods, and collecting leaves and bugs. The outdoors invites curiosity, play, and imagination. Here are some common characteristics of those with a high naturalist intelligence.

They:

- Are interested in animals, plants, and biology
- Are skilled at collecting, categorizing, and cataloging information
- Enjoy exploring the outdoors and doing activities like camping, hiking, and/or gardening
- Make shrewd observations
- Pick up on subtle changes to their environment
- Read books (both fiction and nonfiction) and watch shows related to the natural world

If this describes your child, the naturalist intelligence is an important lens through which she experiences and understands the world.

Activities That Nurture Your Child's Nature-Smarts

1. *Play outdoors.* It is important for children to have unstructured playtime outside. Imaginative play is improvisational; kids use elements from their immediate environment to create complex stories and explore social roles. When you encourage this to happen outdoors, the natural world becomes an intimate part of your child's growth.

2. *Go on short hikes and picnics.* Exploration and curiosity are driving forces in your child's life. Participate in exploring and simply *being* in the natural world with your child; your enthusiasm will fuel hers, and it establishes a meaningful way to bond.

3. *Keep a nature journal.* Nature journals are similar to scrapbooks, and are fun to bring on hikes, picnics, or any appropriate outdoor adventure. You can write personal reflections while sitting next to a waterfall, jot down factual information about birds, draw the flora and fauna around you, sketch a bug you have never seen before, etc.

4. *Grow something.* It is important for children to have responsibility for another living thing and to witness life cycles in action. The chance to care for a sunflower, tomato, or mint plant, for example, can be quite meaningful for kids, because it allows *them* to be the caregivers for once. This teaches your child responsibility and empathy, and forces her to balance the needs of others (watering the plant) with her own desires (running out to play).

5. *Create nature art.* When playing outside, collect interesting things like feathers, pinecones, twigs, and pebbles, and put them in a bag. When you get home, use these materials in an art project.

6. *Visit farms and petting zoos.* Contact with animals is essential for kids, as are opportunities to be involved with farms and food production. These experiences give your child a chance to bond with different kinds of living beings, understand what it means to live with the land, and experience the meaning of interdependence.

7. *Go camping.* Camping is an adventure. Sleeping outside, cooking food around a fire, singing and playing music, telling stories, stargazing, exploring new places—it is a chance for you to intentionally unplug

from the conveniences of modern technology and to experience something more elemental as a family.

8. *Read books and watch shows about the natural world.* Encourage your child's interest in any aspect of nature by supporting it through the books she reads and the shows she watches. Ask about the new things your child has learned each day, and keep a list of questions or curiosities that come up.

9. *Point out sensory experiences.* Drawing your child's attention to her different senses when you are outside together is an easy and experiential way to connect her (and yourself) with the immediate environment. Simple questions will do the trick. Close your eyes; what do you hear? What does it smell like?

The Spatial Intelligence

Picture-smart learners are skilled at visualization. They can recreate visual experiences of people, places, and objects that are no longer physically present. Not only that, but they can manipulate what they see in their mind's eye. This can mean zooming in or out, seeing from different angles, or somehow changing the mental picture by adding, subtracting, or transforming elements of it. These skills can also make it easier to give directions, follow directions, and read maps accurately.

This intelligence may or may not relate to a person's artistic abilities. Not all people who are spatially intelligent are artists, but most artists do possess this intelligence.

Activities to Strengthen Your Child's Spatial Intelligence

1. *Draw and paint.* Any opportunity to draw or paint pictures will help your child develop his spatial intelligence. This can mean drawing something that is physically present (like a teddy bear portrait), or painting an image from memory (like Grandma's garden).

2. *Take imagination journeys.* Tell your child that you want to take him on a journey through an imaginary world. Ask him to get comfortable, close his eyes, and relax. Describe a beautiful outdoor scene including sensory information (e.g., it smells like roses, you feel the warmth of the

sun). In this world, have your child find the most incredible tree. Start asking questions (What does the tree look like? Can you climb it?). Who knows what creatures might show up, or what might happen! When the journey is over, paint or draw different aspects of this imaginary world along with your child.

3. *Create 3-D art projects.* Pulling materials from the recycle bin, you and your child can have a lot of fun putting together three-dimensional projects. You can make castles, robots, dinosaurs, machines, costumes, and more. Clay and Play-Doh are other options for 3-D creations.

4. *Build.* Blocks, Legos, and Lincoln Logs are great examples of toys your child can use to strengthen his spatial skills.

5. *Play hide-and-seek.* A fun and self-explanatory game, hide-and-seek offers your child the chance to explore places in detail, exercise his memory, and imagine where others might be hiding.

6. *Play the "What's Different" game.* Ask your child to grab a certain number of toys and objects from around the room and put them on the floor. Ask him to arrange them so they are all in view, and to try and picture this arrangement when he closes his eyes. When he is not looking, you can add something, remove something, or move something. Tell him to open his eyes, and see if he can tell you what's different. Be sure to take turns!

7. *Practice make-believe.* Make-believe is all about projecting imagination onto the real world. Couches become boats, pets become fearsome beasts (or trusted allies), pillows become shields . . . you name it, it can happen. Dive into the world of make-believe with your child as often as possible.

8. *Practice sports.* Sports are physical activities that demand spatial and body awareness. They develop hand-eye coordination, balance, visualization, and planning ahead. Sports like soccer, gymnastics, baseball, swimming, and tennis are good examples.

9. *Treasure maps.* Making and following treasure maps will help your child translate a two-dimensional, bird's-eye view of the living room or backyard into the three-dimensional reality he actually experiences.

10. *Take pictures.* Encourage your child to take pictures of things that interest him, and to experiment with different angles and perspectives

The Bodily-Kinesthetic Intelligence

Is your child a good athlete? Does she enjoy dancing? Does she have a talent for gymnastics? Does she enjoy learning more when it involves physical activity? Body-smart learners are action-oriented people who love to move and are very engaged with their bodies.

Qualities of this intelligence often include:

- Great hand-eye coordination
- Balance, agility, grace
- A sense of timing
- Strong fine motor control
- A gift for using whole-body motions

Activities to Develop Your Child's Body-Smarts

1. *Play catch.* Help your child develop hand-eye coordination by throwing a ball back and forth. As her skills improve you can move farther apart, have her practice aiming when she throws, or use different types of balls (e.g., a beach ball or a baseball).
2. *Balance.* Balance beams are everywhere: fallen trees, curbs, short walls, a line of chalk on the driveway—be creative! Other balance-related activities include hopping on one foot, walking on tiptoes, doing headstands and handstands, and jumping from one spot to another.
3. *Perform gymnastics.* Even if you cannot join gymnastics classes, there are many gymnastics activities you can do safely from home. In addition to the balance activities, you can teach your child somersaults, cartwheels, and backbends.
4. *Practice yoga.* Yoga poses and postures stretch the body, increase blood and oxygen flow throughout the body, and help focus the mind. Invite your child to do one to three poses with you each day to help develop balance, concentration, and flexibility.
5. *Play kick.* Much like playing catch, playing kick is a fun and easy way to develop coordination and muscle control. As her skills improve, you can move farther apart, practice passing back and forth while running

across the yard, and eventually practice juggling the ball. (Playing with Hacky-Sacks is also very effective).

6. *Do martial arts.* Martial arts teaches self-discipline, balance, coordination, and accuracy. There are many different styles; aikido is a specifically nonviolent martial art that focuses on defusing situations without causing harm.

7. *Write descriptively.* Believe it or not, writing a descriptive paragraph with your child can strengthen this intelligence as well. Because writing about a sensory experience invokes the sensations you write about, the two are interlinked. This can also be done orally.

8. *Play charades.* This game is all about getting other people to guess a word or phrase without speaking, and requires lots of gestures and movement to give clues.

9. *Dance.* Make up a dance with your child, dance silly for fun, or teach her dances such as the macarena, the Twist, the Chicken Dance, or the Electric Slide.

10. *Perform fine motor activities.* Arts and crafts usually involve fine motor skills. You and your child can bead necklaces, write words as small as possible, use scissors to cut out shapes, trace pictures, play with chopsticks, pick things up using tweezers, etc.

The Musical Intelligence

Does your child retain new facts and concepts if they are sung? Does he enjoy having music on in the background, or have a sharp ear for other sounds in the environment? Are rhythms and melodies something he picks up easily? Does he play any instruments?

Music-smart learners are particularly attuned to patterns, rhythms, melodies, and song. Having a strong musical intelligence does not necessarily mean your child will become a musician; this intelligence also extends to the melodies of words. Poets and writers often love the song and rhythm of well-crafted sentences. They experience how the musical elements of great writing influence the nuanced meanings of poems and stories.

Activities to Develop Your Child's Music-Smarts

1. *Create songs or rhythms as memory aids.* Make a game of clapping, tapping, singing, or rhyming with your child when you or he learns something new. Use the tune of a familiar song, or make something up entirely.

2. *Listen visually.* Choose an interesting instrumental song, and explain to your child that you both are going to see a story in your minds based on a piece of music. Ask your child to close his eyes, lay back, and let his imagination follow the song. (You should do this too). When the song ends, talk about what you experienced: What did the song make you feel? What did you see in your mind's eye?

3. *Create musical art.* After having done the visual listening, paint or draw while listening to that same song. This can also be done without the visual listening: put on some different styles of music, and draw or paint with your child based on how you both experience or feel the songs.

4. *Play rhythm games.* Make your rhythm games fun and improvisational. Clap a short rhythm, and ask your child to repeat it. Get progressively trickier by adding stomps or snaps, and making the rhythms a little longer. Make sure to invite your child to make up a rhythm for you to try!

5. *Use background music.* When your child is reading, doing homework, or working on an art project, try putting different types of instrumental music on in the background.

6. *Give your child music lessons.* If possible, help your child develop his abilities with music lessons. Whether he plays piano, guitar, or the flute, practicing a little bit every day under the guidance of a good teacher will yield wonderful results.

7. *Play rhyming games.* This can be as simple as throwing out a word and going back and forth saying as many rhyming words as possible. (When you run out, choose a new word!) You can also do this with sentences— e.g., On top of the box . . . there was a fox.

8. *Draw what you hear.* This game is particularly fun when done in a natural setting; however, you can do it anywhere. Using a sketch pad, take ten to fifteen minutes to draw a picture of everything you hear. How many sounds did you each pick up on?

9. *Make up songs.* Although you can (and should) make up songs about anything at all, an easy place to start is focusing on whatever you and your child are doing, like a musical narration.

10. *Discover spoken-word poetry.* Read and write poetry with your child. Watch other poets' spoken-word performances, and set up your own family poetry time at home.

The Interpersonal Intelligence

Does your child notice how other people are feeling? Is she empathetic, and can she relate to others easily? Does she have strong communication skills?

People-smart learners are good at "reading" other people's emotions and understanding their motivations and desires. They are skilled at working and communicating with others, which gives them an advantage when it comes to mediation and conflict resolution. People with strong interpersonal skills have a knack for finding balanced compromises. They are good at interacting with, relating to, and getting along with others, and can become effective leaders.

Activities to Develop Your Child's People-Smarts

1. *Play "What are they feeling?"* Show your child pictures of people or characters. Ask her: "What do you think this person is feeling?" and "Why do you think they are feeling that way?" This can happen while reading a story, watching a show, or people-watching at the zoo.
2. *Build a fort.* Building forts should be a team effort between kids. You can supervise, give suggestions, and make sure everyone is being safe; however, the whole point is for your child to work together with others toward a common goal.
3. *Interview someone interesting.* What is your child interested in? Does she want to learn more about her grandfather's time in the war? Is there a neighbor who knows a lot about animals? Once your child decides on a person of interest, help her write down the questions she wants to ask ahead of time.
4. *Tutor a younger student.* Teaching something to someone else not only solidifies the information in your child's mind, it helps her learn to communicate what she knows. Reading buddies are a great way to do this.
5. *Create a puppet show.* Have your child and a couple of friends choose the puppets they want to make. Once the puppets are made, ask them to

make up a story to tell using their puppets. Give them time to sort it out, and then enjoy the puppet show!

6. *Solve a challenge.* Give your child a team-oriented challenge to do with one or two of her friends. This could be anything from raking the biggest leaf pile ever to putting together a puzzle.

7. *Play "Don't fall in!"* Create a very thin "bridge" of cardboard across the floor. Split your group of kids in two, and have them stand on either end of the bridge on "islands." To win the game, explain that they have to work together to switch islands by crossing the bridge, without letting anybody fall in. All the children take turns walking along the bridge to the other side without falling in.

8. *Play 2 on 1.* Your child and one of her friends work together, passing the soccer ball to each other to score a goal on you. Encourage them to try different strategies.

9. *Make a cardboard castle.* All you need is your child, some of her friends, and a bunch of cardboard boxes. Give them scissors, tape, markers, and construction paper for decorating. Before they can begin building, tell them they have to agree on what they want to build first (a fortress, rocket, boat, etc.). Once they've all agreed, let the building begin!

10. *Play "What would you do?"* Read or make up a story for your child that sets up a conflict between two friends and discuss. What would you do in that situation? Why? How might the characters handle things differently?

The Intrapersonal Intelligence

Self-smart learners have a strong awareness of their own thoughts, feelings, ideas, motivations, and goals. They are skilled at identifying their own strengths and weaknesses. They enjoy planning and setting goals, and often need time to be alone to process their experiences and/or for creative expression.

Activities to Develop Your Child's Self-Smarts

1. *Keep a journal.* Reflective journaling is a great way for children to give voice to their inner experiences and process their emotions. For this to fully work, your child needs to know that you will respect his privacy.

2. *Keep a scrapbook.* Scrapbooking can involve reflective journaling, drawing, collages, stickers, and more. It adds pictures and other visual elements that animate your child's reflective process.

3. *Set goals.* Help your child set a small number of daily or weekly goals, and have him write them down. Post the goals in a highly visible place and plan ways to achieve them. It helps if you set goals for yourself as well; when it is a shared activity, the two of you can encourage one another.

4. *Identify strengths.* It is empowering when children can self-identify their skills. They may need a bit of prompting and guidance to get started, but making a list of their strengths at school, at home, and with friends is a reflective and confidence-boosting activity.

5. *Analyze character motivations.* When reading stories or watching shows with your child, ask him why he thinks such-and-such character is doing what it is doing. What motivates Pooh Bear to get honey?

6. *Meditate.* A very real way for your child to notice his thoughts and emotions is through short periods of meditation. By anchoring himself to his breath and paying attention to whatever ideas and feelings come up, your child will come face to face with his own mind.

7. *Explore different ways of thinking.* Encourage books, shows, and activities that look at aspects of different cultures. For example, you can explore different types of toys children play with around the world, or what it means to be polite.

8. *Create a personal morning routine.* Ask and discuss with your child what he wants to do each morning to help prepare himself for a great day. This might include waking up to a particular song, having time to read, playing with toys once he's ready for school, or anything else that puts him in a good frame of mind at the start of each day.

9. *Keep a dream journal.* Give your child a dream journal to keep next to his bed. Encourage him to write or draw anything he remembers when he wakes up.

10. *Share gratitude.* Over dinner or near the end of the day, take a couple of minutes to share one thing you are grateful for and one thing you think you did well that day (and are proud of). Invite your child and other family members to share!

Intelligences as Entry Points

According to Dr. Gardner, everybody has all eight of these intelligences and each one is an entry point through which all sorts of content can be learned. For example, students with a high musical intelligence can make up songs to remember historical facts and events, and students with a strong bodily-kinesthetic intelligence can understand physics through numerous hands-on experiments.

The Benefits

One of the greatest benefits of this theory is seeing more parents and educators recognize, appreciate, and nurture the different skills children call upon when engaging the world. Understanding your child's multiple intelligences gives you insight into how you can more effectively communicate and interact with him, and help him learn and grow.

Understanding how our children are naturally inclined to learn is a gift. It allows you to create and seek out activities that complement your child's strengths and interests, and regardless of which intelligences are most prominent, your child can strengthen all of them, especially with mindfulness as a key tool.

CHAPTER 7

Child Development Basics

If you've ever wondered why infants enjoy games like peek-aboo, why toddlers want to be held one minute and then wiggle to be set free a moment later, or why teenagers always want to sleep in, you've come to the right place. The scientific study of how children grow offers answers to all of these questions and more.

What Is Child Development?

Child development is the science of understanding children through the development of their bodies, minds, and social relationships as they progress through life. It is a study of the subtle and overt changes in children as they age, the factors that influence these changes, and how these changes manifest in the child's daily life. There are three overlapping domains of development: physical, cognitive, and social-emotional, each of which is influenced by numerous other factors.

Child development offers a very helpful frame for parents who want to better understand the "why" behind their child's behavior. It offers insight into how children experience the world, and how parents can most effectively nurture their child's growth during each stage of development.

How Definitions Differ

It's important to note that the concept of "developmental stages" is just a model. It provides a useful way of thinking about how your child grows; however, the ages and stages are often grouped together based on the age ranges in which children tend to reach certain physical, cognitive, and social-emotional milestones. Ultimately, each child is unique and follows her own, similarly unique course of development.

What Everyone Agrees On

Despite the cultural subjectivity, there are a handful of fundamental points about development that everyone agrees on:

1. *All domains of development are interrelated.* Although it's convenient to talk about a child's body, mind, and social-emotional skills as separate categories, the truth is they all overlap and influence one another. There are no clear boundaries between them. For example, an infant who has just learned how to crawl will suddenly be exposed to new aspects of her environment due to her increased mobility. This will stimulate new cognitive growth, and will change the social-emotional dynamics between the baby and her caregivers now that the child is not as physically dependent on others to explore. To affect one domain of development is to affect them all.

2. *Normal development includes a wide range of individual differences.* Like snowflakes, each child develops differently and the definition of "normal" is quite broad. Some children start walking as early as eight or nine months, while others don't start until they are as old as eighteen months. Some children are outgoing and dive right into activities, while others are quiet and hesitant to try new things. These differences are the natural result of each child's combination of nature (i.e., their genes) and nurture (i.e., the influence of their environment). Nature and nurture work together in dynamic ways, and factors such as gender; family structure; social class; ethnicity; culture; and the presence or absence of physical, emotional, or learning disabilities all influence how children develop.

3. *Children help shape their own development and influence others' responses to them.* Children influence their environment as much as their environment influences them. For example, when a child begins to walk, she is usually met with enthusiasm and support from her parents. This encourages the child to walk more, which motivates her caregivers to establish more physically safe boundaries around the house. The influences go in both directions.

4. *Historical and cultural context strongly influence development.* All people are bound by the era and culture in which they are born. Both time and place are factors that play a major role in human development. For example, a child born in New York City today will have very different life experiences from a child born in New York during the Civil War.

5. *Early experience is important, and children can be remarkably resilient.* The early events in a person's life will have lasting influences that extend through adulthood. Issues such as malnutrition or traumatic stress can have serious, lifelong physical and emotional consequences. Luckily the human spirit is marked by a resilience that has helped countless people overcome such hardships. That said, the positive impact of experiencing a healthy, safe, and loving early childhood cannot be understated.

6. *Development continues throughout life.* Development is not a finite thing that simply comes to an end once children reach the age of eighteen or twenty-one. Child development is the early part of *human* development, and all humans continue to develop physically, neurologically, and emotionally in significant ways throughout their lives. There is no finish line!

What Influences a Child's Development?

There are many factors that shape children's development and contribute to how their values and personality form. The two you often hear about are "nature" and "nurture," or, in other words, the genetic blueprint a child is born with and the environment in which he grows up. There is still debate about which one plays a greater role in child development; however, this book understands nature and nurture as two sides of the same coin. In this section you will learn about the major environmental factors at play in your child's development, and where you as a parent have the greatest influence.

Nature vs. Nurture

The dilemma between nature and nurture comes from how these two concepts can be polarized and pitted against each other. In reality, it is not a matter of one dominating the other, but how the two are constantly interacting.

The interaction between the genetic hardwiring and the ever-changing environment is the dance that really shapes a child's development. Since you cannot alter your child's genes (nature), however, the most relevant point for you as parents is to understand the environmental factors (nurture) that shape your child's growth. This is where you have the most control.

Meta Environmental Factors

The meta factors that influence your child's development have to do with the time, place, and conditions under which he grows up. Parents have only partial control over these meta factors. The following list explores these factors in greater detail.

1. *Socioeconomic Status.* To be blunt, the term "socioeconomic status" (or SES) describes the primary differences between the upper, middle, and lower classes. A family's SES is based on three factors: income, education, and occupation.

   This is important, because families with a lower SES have different needs and abilities than families with a higher SES. For example, parents who have little education, do not make much money, and have to work multiple jobs to make ends meet have very different priorities than affluent, highly educated parents.

It is no secret that poverty has a negative impact on family dynamics and child development. In many ways, what a family's SES really describes is the level of opportunity available to them. To illustrate this, here are scenarios from both extremes.

Low SES

The Walker family rents a small apartment in Pontiac, Michigan. Father works two jobs, as a chef at Papa Vino's and as a mechanic at an auto-body repair shop. Mother is the assistant manager at the local Dollar Tree. They both graduated from high school and met while attending a nearby community college, but they had to drop out to make more money when Mother became pregnant. The Walkers now have three children ages one, four, and seven, and live paycheck to paycheck. Most of their money goes toward rent, food, gas, diapers, clothes, and other bills. They are responsible, hard-working parents who do everything in their power to keep food on the table and keep their apartment warm during the winter, but this comes at a cost. Neither parent has a set work schedule and they regularly have to work in the evenings. Because of this, their children are often shuffled between school, day care, and their grandparents' house. Mother and Father do not get enough quality time together, or with their children. They are often too tired or stressed out by the end of a workday to do much of anything except sit down and watch television, but they do their best.

High SES

The Pinot family owns a large house in Bloomfield Hills, Michigan. Father is the Chief Operational Officer of an automobile supply company, and Mother is a stay-at-home mom for their two children (ages two and five). They both graduated from college, and Father went on to earn a master's degree in mechanical engineering before asking Mother to marry him. They have more than enough money to cover their costs of living. They are responsible, hard-working parents who do everything in their power to provide the best for their kids. The Pinots can afford to take regular vacations, have multiple cars, and save for their family's future. Their children's college educations will be fully paid for. Father is home in time for a family dinner each night and enjoys playing and reading with the kids until their bedtime. Mother spends the majority of her days with the children. Mother and Father enjoy one evening a week together, and hire a babysitter to watch the kids. With complete job and financial security, their main priorities include happiness, saving money, planning for the future, and making sure that their children have the best educations possible.

The opportunities available to the Walker and Pinot families are vastly different. Factors like income, education, and occupation have a real influence on both the quantity and quality of time parents spend with their children. Consistent and meaningful contact with loving parents has a huge impact on children's cognitive and psychosocial development.

It is important to note that a family's love and support of one another transcends any socioeconomic limitations. Many families with a lower SES are strong, healthy, and nurturing; many families with a higher SES are cold, distant, and fractured.

2. *Neighborhood.* As you might imagine, a family's socioeconomic status is tied to the neighborhood in which they live. The community you live in influences what your child believes she is capable of achieving.

Children form ideas of what they can do as adults based on what is modeled by the world around them. In a neighborhood where the majority of adults are educated and employed, the local economy is more stable and kids are exposed to empowering examples of what is possible in their own lives. This kind of environment is also more likely to provide positive mentors in a child's life.

In a neighborhood rife with unemployment, substance abuse, and/or violence, positive mentors are fewer and farther between. This type of environment makes it more challenging for children to reach their potential, because they struggle to imagine what that might look like.

Though descriptions of these neighborhoods illustrate different socioeconomic extremes, one thing remains certain: Children will only reach for what they imagine is possible. The point is, wherever you live and whatever your family's circumstances, you have the power to nurture healthy definitions of success in your child and encourage him to work hard and dream big.

3. *Culture and ethnicity.* Culture is a group's total way of life, including customs, traditions, beliefs, values, language, and physical products, all learned behavior passed on from parents to children. Ethnic groups are united by ancestry, religion, language, and/or national origins, all of which contribute to a sense of shared identity.

4. *Historical context.* Certain experiences tied to time and place can affect the course of children's lives and create cohorts of shared experiences. For example, the children of New York City who survived the 2001 attack on the World Trade Center will be forever affected and united in a sense; much like every child in the United States who remembers seeing Apollo 11's moon landing on July 20th, 1969, has been in some way shaped by that event. The circumstances of time and place have, for better or worse, a collective impact on children's development by providing different influential stimuli that create a broader, richer historical context for their growth.

Immediate Environmental Factors

Immediate environmental factors are much closer to home and play a more significant role in shaping a child's development than the meta factors. The following list outlines the elements of a child's immediate environment that have the greatest impact on the quality, shape, and direction of his growth.

1. *Family relationships.* The closest relationships a child has are the ones that will influence him the most. Here are the characteristics of a nurturing family relationship:

   - Happiness and stability of parents
   - Child has regular contact with extended family
   - Child feeling loved and valued
   - Contribution and participation in family life
   - Family members regularly spend time together
   - Family has a culture of learning

2. *Safety of home.* A house that is safe for a child to explore relatively freely is important to healthy development.
3. *Communication and partnership between parents and teachers.* Parents and teachers work together to raise children. When they see one another as partners and communicate about a child's progress and needs, that child will receive better and more coordinated care.

Stages of Child Development

Although this book focuses primarily on the first three developmental stages, it divides child development into five overall stages: infants, toddlers, children, preadolescents, and adolescents. Each stage is characterized by certain physical, cognitive, and psycho-social milestones that children tend to reach during particular age ranges. These milestones reveal new ways for children to perceive and interact with the world.

Following Children Through Five Developmental Stages

To better understand the developmental stages, you can follow fictional newborns Jake and Allie as they grow up:

The infant stage is characterized by helplessness. Jake and Allie are completely dependent on their parents for food, mobility, protection, and more. Though learning to crawl gives them some independent movement, Jake and Allie are considered infants until they begin walking. Most babies will take their first steps between nine and twelve months old; however, some children begin walking closer to sixteen to eighteen months of age. Every baby is different!

Everything changes when they start walking: Jake and Allie have now graduated to toddlerhood (walking to three years old). As they build the muscles and coordination necessary to walk steadily, vast new worlds open to them. As anyone who has ever been around a toddler knows, this developmental stage is characterized by endless exploration and a constant testing of boundaries. Thus begins a new era of budding independence, where the primary question in life is "What will happen if I do *this?*"

Once in the child stage (three to nine years old), Jake and Allie become more social creatures. Their vocabularies and verbal skills improve by leaps and bounds, which allows them to communicate and express themselves more effectively with friends, siblings, and adults. Over time, Jake and Allie both come to understand that other people have thoughts and feelings just like they do. This growing awareness helps them to perceive and even empathize with the inner emotional lives of others, a connection that extends to animals and other natural beings as well. This stage provides a ripe opportunity to cultivate empathy.

As Jake and Allie grow into preadolescence (ten to twelve years old), they gradually go beyond concrete thinking and develop a capacity for abstract thought. Externally, however, they are increasingly occupied with resolving the demands placed on them by school, parents, peers, and society. As their academic and social responsibilities intensify, Jake and Allie sometimes long for the perceived freedoms of either childhood or adulthood. Thankfully their brains are now better equipped to process and organize new information, which helps them find ways to navigate issues such as social relationships, gender, and sexuality.

Adolescence (thirteen to twenty years old) is a time of major physical, emotional, and social change for Jake and Allie. This stage is characterized by growth and identity formation, which take place on both internal and external levels. The hormonal changes brought on by puberty trigger rapid and dramatic physical development, which has significant impacts on teenage psychology and social relationships. To their parents, Allie and Jake can seem like emotional roller coasters. They are more sensitive and reactive, and often take out their frustrations on immediate family members. This emotional volatility is normal for adolescents as they seek greater independence and try to figure out who they are and how they fit in.

Using Development to Teach Mindfulness

Understanding child development gives you an idea of your child's changing abilities as he grows, which will help you form appropriate expectations. This is necessary when teaching mindfulness, because you are looking for activities that will engage your child according to his abilities and interests. Just as you wouldn't try to talk politics with a toddler, you also wouldn't ask a child to sit still and meditate for fifteen minutes. It's simply not appropriate for where they are in life. What you really want to do is to set your child (and yourself) up for success.

The Mind

The changes that take place regarding a child's cognitive abilities as she grows are astonishing. Young children think in very concrete ways, and respond much more readily to the immediate physical world than to the conceptual realm of ideas. They also have short attention spans, which affects how long they can concentrate on any given topic. Having information like this will help you choose mindfulness activities that involve the concrete world, and that begin to help your child become aware of her own inner experiences.

Information about development also influences how you engage your child outside of specific mindfulness activities. For example, when you recognize that your child is a naturally high-energy creature who needs to move more often than adults, you will understand that she is not being disrespectful when fidgeting at the dinner table. Being mindful of this, you can suggest that she stretch or do ten pushups so that her body can be calm during dinner. This kind of mindfulness puts you in a better position to create an environment where you both get what you need without becoming frustrated or angry.

The Body

When it comes to the body's growth, it's easiest to teach mindfulness in synch with the skills children are naturally developing given the stage they are in. If you have a toddler, for example, you would want to help her concentrate on gross motor skills such as balance, running, jumping, etc. If you have an adolescent, you could help her learn breathing techniques that reduce anxiety and improve concentration before a big test. The point is to teach mindfulness in ways that are helpful and relevant given your child's needs and abilities.

Social-Emotional Skills

The term "social-emotional development" refers to the development of a child's internal and external environment. Specifically, the social aspect looks at how well a child can interact, cooperate, and contribute positively in group situations. The emotional aspect looks at how well a child can recognize, understand, and control her own emotions. When children interact with peers and adults, these complex and interwoven skill sets are continually put to use.

In some respects, the social and emotional aspects of development are sides of the same coin. For example, a preadolescent who has trouble controlling her temper (internal environment) will have a hard time interacting and cooperating with others (external environment). On the other hand, a teenager who is good at mediating conflict between friends (external) will simultaneously be strengthening her capacity to recognize, understand, and control her own emotions (internal) as a means of solving the problem at hand.

Understanding the developmental stage of your child includes knowing their social-emotional abilities. For example, four-year-olds have very little control over their emotions. They react emotionally to what's happening around them instead of responding constructively, and need to be taught how to identify and articulate what they (and others) are feeling. Books, games, and activities that help your child develop these skills are great ways to cultivate her emotional awareness.

Though there are general milestones for each stage, the degree of your child's social-emotional development depends on many factors. By paying attention to how your child plays and interacts with others, you will learn a lot about her particular strengths and weaknesses. This knowledge will help you determine the best ways to support her growth.

How you teach mindfulness to your child will vary depending on where she is on the developmental spectrum. When you have a solid understanding of what children are capable of and how they learn best at different developmental stages, you will have unique insights into how to teach mindfulness.

Spiral Model for Learning

Each child develops uniquely. Although children grow physically in a linear fashion, they do not develop cognitive and social-emotional skills in a linear way. Things that are easy for one child may be difficult for another, and children may return over and over again to skills that they previously appeared to have grasped. Just because a kid "got it" yesterday does not necessarily mean they will "get it" today.

What Does the Spiral Model Look Like?

A toddler who has learned how to use his words when he's frustrated instead of pushing or biting another child, for example, will inevitably backslide now and again. Just learning a new skill isn't enough; it takes time to successfully practice that skill often enough for a person to fully integrate it and use it dynamically in his life, regardless of age.

The same can be said for a teenager who has learned a new song on the guitar. One day he might nail the rhythm, notes, and dynamics; the next day could be a train wreck. Many factors affect a person's ability to use skills such as mindfulness in different situations, which is why it's called a *practice*.

Like it or not, learning is a process that requires patience, consistency, and encouragement. Children often revisit the same lessons over and over again as they seek to master new skills and refine old ones. Given this understanding of development, spirals are a more appropriate model for children's cognitive and social-emotional evolution.

Just like walking along a spiral path, children often return to skills they had (to varying degrees) acquired and cultivated during previous stages of their development. As they grow and circle back to various skills and concepts they had been exposed to in earlier stages, kids can understand things from a new perspective. In this way, children are continually revisiting and refining the skills they've acquired throughout each developmental stage.

Peeling Back the Layers

The spiraling process allows children to "peel back the layers," giving them an opportunity to integrate various skills and concepts in more mature and complete ways. This same spiraling process is true for adults as well: What you understood yesterday you know differently today, and what you know today you will understand differently tomorrow.

CHAPTER 8

Infants (Birth to Walking)

To infants, everything is fresh, brand-new, amazing, and scary at the same time. They are in the most fundamental stages of self-awareness, limited primarily to discovering their physical bodies and learning what happens when they cry, coo, and smile.

Infants initially perceive no difference between *self* and *other.* They are breaking in their bodies, getting comfortable and learning how to make their bodies do what they wish. They are entirely dependent on others to meet their survival needs, and use vocal and nonvocal communication to express interest and exert influence over their environment. In terms of their physical, cognitive, and social-emotional development, infants are purely absorbing, grasping, and testing the most basic of human learning blocks.

Through the Eyes of an Infant

A newborn's experience of the world is an intense intake of sensory stimulation. His mind has no filters yet, and his brain is just beginning to learn how to process everything he sees, hears, feels, tastes, and smells. He must adapt to life outside of his mother, learning how to breathe, eat, and respond to a wildly different environment.

People born in China often celebrate their birthday based on the estimated day of their conception instead of the day on which they were actually born. With this understanding, babies are considered to be one year old at the time of their birth.

Overview

Newborns have no language with which to categorize or understand the information they are flooded with at the time of birth. Over the course of their first few months of life, infants' brains are busy building neural connections that help them make sense of everything they experience, and allow them to develop more physical control.

The primary interests of infants revolve around meeting their basic needs and understanding their relationship with their surroundings. They perceive no difference between themselves and their mothers, and it takes time for them to adjust to the new physical demands of breathing, eating, and eliminating waste. The main way infants communicate their need for food, help, and security is to cry; when parents are responsive to these needs and also soothe their baby through contact, swaddling, rocking, and singing, the child feels safe and learns trust. Over time, babies come to understand the different ways they can affect their environment (e.g., cry and Mommy will appear; coo and adults will coo back).

FACT

The hair infants are born with is shed over the course of about six months, and the second head of hair that grows in tends to be darker and coarser. (A similar "shedding" takes place with the mother's hair as well.) This is completely normal, and happens because of a drop in hormone levels, particularly a drop in estrogen.

What Are Infants Learning about Themselves?

Of all an infant's senses, vision is the least developed at the time of birth. At first infants can only focus on objects about a foot away, which makes breastfeeding an even more intimate experience because an infant can see her mother's face. The other senses of sound, touch, smell, and taste develop quite rapidly, with their brains making more and more neural connections based on the form and frequency of sensory stimulation they experience.

Babies are born with basic motor skills such as grasping, sucking, moving their limbs, and turning their heads. Over the course of the next many months, their major muscle groups grow stronger through use. When given space, opportunity, and encouragement, babies are constantly attempting new physical feats. Their main preoccupations at this stage are learning what they can do and exploring their immediate environment to the extent they are able.

What Are Infants Learning about Others and Their Environment?

Over the course of their first year of life, an infant's understanding about the physical separation between herself and other people becomes apparent; emotionally, however, babies see their parents (primarily the mother) as an extension of themselves.

Babies are entirely wrapped up in their own physical and emotional experience of the world, and are not capable of logic, reasoning, or putting themselves into someone else's shoes. For the first few years of life, children assume that everyone else sees, thinks, and experiences the world in exactly the same way that they do. They have no concept of the inner emotional lives of others. When their physical and emotional needs are consistently met, babies learn that they are safe and protected. This gives them more confidence to explore and strengthen their physical capabilities.

Babies learn new ways to affect their environment through experimentation. Gravity, for example, is an endlessly fun concept to test: "When I drop my sippy cup, it falls down. Amazing!" They test this basic lesson in physics again, and again, and again. It becomes even more interesting if Mom or Dad picks up what they drop, push over, or throw.

Other examples might include: "When I smile and laugh, they smile and laugh! When my diaper gets heavy and smelly, they take care of it! When I cry at night, mommy or daddy appears! When I make noise, they make noise too! Can I make the same noises they do? Can they make the same noises as me? What happens if I do *this?*"

Of course babies don't have the language to think about things in quite this way, but language is not necessary to learn about cause and effect. Babies enjoy trying new things, and seeing what happens. Then repeat.

Developmental Markers

From the time they are born until they begin to walk, babies make huge developmental leaps. Their physical strength and control evolves from utter helplessness to new locomotion and independence; their language and communication skills begin blossoming; and their interactions with parents and other family members become increasingly complex and deliberate.

QUESTION

I've heard that older babies can be taught to communicate through sign language. Is there any truth to this?
This is absolutely true. Babies understand much more than they can verbally communicate, and by about six months of age they can begin learning how to sign. Research suggests that babies who sign develop a larger speaking vocabulary more quickly than their peers.

Milestones

Once certain simple skills are mastered, babies learn to combine these skills to undertake more complex actions. These systems of action increase in complexity over time. For example, infants begin with moving their arms and legs, and eventually build the strength to roll over by themselves. Once they can roll over and hold their heads up, babies are able to combine these previously mastered skills to begin crawling, and so on.

Early vocalization is also important. Since crying is the only way newborns can communicate, it helps to pay attention to their different pitches and patterns that indicate hunger, sleepiness, fear, or frustration. This evolves into babbling, where babies repeat consonant vowel strings such as "ma-ma-ma-ma" that actually have no meaning, and can be mistaken as their first word. A baby's actual first word, where she understands the connection between a sound and its meaning, tends to happen between ten to fourteen months.

It is important to note that all milestones have a wide age range in which they can be achieved, and that they vary depending on culture. This book focuses on the general milestones seen in Western families.

Birth to One Month

During her first month of life, an infant's motor skills are largely reflexive. She can suck and swallow, and if you touch her cheek, Baby will turn her head in the direction of your touch. This is known as the rooting reflex; it helps infants locate a nipple for feeding.

There is also the startle reflex: When Baby is surprised by a loud sound, for example, her arms and legs extend away from her body. One of the best known reflexes is the grasping reflex: put a finger (or some object) in Baby's hand, and she will clasp onto it.

Finally there is the stepping reflex: Hold Baby upright such that her feet can touch the ground, and she will make stepping motions with her feet. All of these reflexes fade within two to six months.

In addition to using inherent reflexes, by the end of this first month, Baby will probably:

- Make tight fists
- Lift her head a few seconds at a time while lying on her stomach
- Focus her eyes within about twelve inches
- Prefer the patterns of human faces
- Turn her head from side to side while lying on her back
- Begin watching moving objects
- Notice sharp contrasts in color, such as black/white

One to Three Months

This is a wonderful time when newborns begin to evolve from utterly helpless and dependent to more interactive and responsive beings. Baby's vision improves a great deal, which brings new interest in her surrounding environment. She begins recognizing more sounds and people from a distance, developing her hand-eye coordination, and smiles more frequently.

Baby also begins to make more cooing, babbling, and laughing noises. Her muscles strengthen to the point where she can hold up her head and upper body while lying on her stomach. Baby develops grabby hands, and explores things by holding them close to her face and putting them in her mouth.

By about three months, Baby will probably:

- Grab and shake toys
- Open and close hands
- Regularly follow moving objects with her eyes
- Try to hit or bat at dangling objects
- Stretch and kick her legs

- Look around to locate sounds
- Hold her head up (still wobbly)
- Smile at, respond to, and play with familiar people

Four to Seven Months

At this age, babies have increasing control over their bodies. Baby is learning to coordinate among his senses by integrating what he sees, hears, and touches with his physical movements. Rolling over, sitting up, and even crawling are all possible at this age.

Baby acquaints himself with toys and such by banging, shaking, and putting most things in his mouth, and is learning other ways to communicate his needs aside from simply crying. By this point Baby has developed a strong attachment to and preference for his caregivers, though he will usually smile and play with just about anyone.

By about seven months, Baby will probably:

- Roll over from stomach to back (and vice versa)
- Kick his legs and swim his arms
- Move toys and objects from hand to hand
- Sit without extra support
- Play with feet and toes
- Support his weight when held upright
- Laugh, giggle, and babble consonants
- Find objects that are only partially visible
- Distinguish emotions through people's tone of voice
- Hold his head up (controlled)
- Show signs of teething
- Discover other parts of his body
- Tell family apart from strangers
- Get upset if you take his toy away
- Prefer bright colors and complex patterns
- Begin noticing depth and space
- Respond to his name and "talk" when others are talking

Eight to Twelve Months

At this age, Baby can do more complex physical tasks such as rolling from his belly to a sitting position, and vice versa. He may well be in constant physical motion, grabbing his toys or feet and looking all around him. Baby will most likely learn to crawl (or scoot); this increased mobility requires extra attention from his parents, who will now have to create safe spaces for Baby to explore on his own. Childproofing is now a must!

Once Baby has mastered crawling, he will soon use nearby objects to pull himself up to a standing position. Walking will inevitably follow, and Baby will use furniture (such as couches and tables) to support his explorations. As Baby's balance improves, he may even take a few steps by himself. These first steps often happen around twelve months; however, it is completely normal for him to begin walking before or after that age.

Baby's fine motor skills have improved, and he learns to use a pincer grasp (his thumb and first or second finger) to pick up smaller objects. He loves manipulating toys with moving parts, ripping paper, and poking his finger through holes. Baby's language development is also in full bloom: he can make and combine different consonant sounds, perhaps say a handful of words, and can follow simple commands. Baby can understand much more than he can communicate verbally; however, he will communicate in nonverbal ways such as pointing, crawling, or gesturing.

This is usually the time when Baby learns about object permanence, meaning that just because an object is no longer in sight does *not* mean that the object has disappeared or ceased to exist. He enjoys and will initiate coordination games such as pat-a-cake and peekaboo, the latter of which reinforces her understanding of object permanence.

Separation anxiety typically manifests around this age, and is a completely normal part of Baby's social-emotional development. It is part of his evolving understanding of "self" and "other," and presents opportunities for Baby to begin self-soothing.

By twelve months, Baby can probably:

- Sit, crawl, and pull himself to a standing position without assistance
- Stand without support
- Walk while holding onto furniture or a hand

- Put objects into containers and take them out again
- Use a pincer grasp
- Say "mama" and "dada," referring to his parents
- Imitate words he hears
- Use simple gestures to communicate
- Initiate and play simple gesture games
- Find hidden toys and objects
- Get shy around strangers
- Cry when mommy or daddy leaves
- Demonstrate interest in pleasing his parents
- Repeat actions that draw attention to him
- Roll a ball
- Show excitement when he completes or masters a task
- Show frustration when his parents impose limitations
- Follow fast-moving objects
- Recognize objects by name

Supporting Your Baby's Development

The first year of a child's life is full of growth and change, and there are many ways that you can support your baby's physical, neurological, and social-emotional development. In fact, you probably don't even realize how much you are already doing!

QUESTION

There are lots of products in the market today claiming to make your baby smarter, including some types of videos and DVDs. Can they really improve your child's intelligence?
No, those programs are ineffective. Babies learn and grow from things in the environment that respond to them. If you want to stimulate your baby's neurological development, play with her!

Because babies develop in response to environmental stimuli, here are some things you can do to support that development.

1. Be responsive to Baby's needs

   - Feed, change diapers
   - Soothe when upset
   - Swaddle
   - Gently rock, swing, and bounce

2. Use music

   - Sing songs
   - Play classical music
   - Rhyme your words when you can
   - Dance to music

3. Read with Baby

   - Read and look at picture books together
   - Read and explore books with different textures (such as fur, ruffles, scales, etc.)

4. Talk to your baby

   - Interact as much as possible
   - Describe what you and Baby see, hear, taste, feel, and smell
   - Describe Baby's emotions
   - Encourage skills and behaviors you want to see

5. Provide plenty of sensory stimulation

   - Play with toys of different colors
   - Play with toys with different textures
   - Play barefoot on grass and sand
   - Provide dangling toys
   - Expose Baby to different smells

6. Play coordination and memory games

- Pat-a-cake
- Peekaboo
- High five, low five
- Say and touch body parts
- Clap
- Hide-and-seek with toys

7. Develop Baby's gross and fine motor skills

- Provide paper for Baby to rip
- Give Baby washable crayons to scribble on paper
- Finger paint together
- Crawl on floor together
- Help Baby walk and balance
- Play with nesting toys (e.g., cups that fit into one another)
- Play with blocks
- Provide small rings or objects Baby can grasp, pick up and drop

ESSENTIAL

Babies are still developing their sense of hearing. It can be difficult for infants and young children to distinguish between background noise and the voices around them, which in some cases inhibits their ability to pick up language. With this in mind, it is helpful to turn music into a focused activity instead of having it on constantly in the background (or at least keep the volume down).

Raising an Infant

Infants are also a source of abundant joy. When you and your partner gaze at your baby, it can be an overwhelmingly joyful and awe-inspiring experience.

The Joys

Infants can be thoroughly engaging. Your baby probably loves playing with you, clutching your fingers, smiling and laughing when you play peeka-boo or blow zerberts on her tummy. Infants invite you into the moment with joy and silliness, and when they do something cute, it can melt your heart.

Another great joy of caring for an infant is witnessing the astonishing rate at which she develops. Infants progress by leaps and bounds; as they develop more muscle tone and control and begin to move independently, each accomplishment big and small is cause for celebration. You may find yourself overjoyed when your baby first lifts her head, or you might be moved to tears when she rolls over on her own or reaches out and grasps something she wants for the first time.

The Challenges

The biggest challenge of caring for an infant is her total helplessness. Infants can do nothing for themselves and are completely dependent on you for their every need. Not only that, but they run on their own schedules, which invariably never coincide with yours. The sleep disruptions, constant crying, and perpetual need to feed her and change her diapers can really get to you after a while.

Infancy can also be a very scary time for parents. Infants are visibly frag-ile and prone to illness, yet they cannot really communicate beyond crying. When your baby cries, it is hard to tell whether she is hungry, is uncomfort-able, or has an ear infection. It is easy to imagine things that are even worse. Although this is true at all stages, parenting infants in particular can involve a lot of not knowing and insecurity.

Mindfulness with Infants

Babies have no sense of past or future; all that exists for them is the present. As a parent, you are invited to join them in the present moment, appreciate the little things, and create a safe space for them to experience the joys and challenges of early life. Doing so is easier at some times than at others.

How Mindfulness Can Help You Be Present with Your Infant

One of the hardest parts about parenting infants is the way that they need you pretty much all the time, regardless of how frustrated, totally exhausted, or burnt-out you may feel. You may sometimes feel ashamed when you catch yourself getting mad at your infant, but these kinds of negative responses are not only natural, they are inevitable given the enormous strain you are under. Feeling negatively toward your baby does not mean you are a bad parent, nor does it mean you are doing anything wrong. What really matters is how you handle it when these feelings come up within you. Remember that what your infant needs most is your contact and physical presence; he doesn't need you to be perfect all the time. Practicing mindful presence can help, especially when you are dealing with an abundance of stress, exhaustion, and frustration.

Begin by acknowledging the feelings that are coming up for you. Recognize what you are thinking or feeling and give it a name: "I am tired," "I am frustrated," "I wish this baby would just stop crying." You can do this as you attend to your baby, whether you are holding him, feeding him, or changing him.

After you identify and name what you are thinking or feeling, anchor yourself with three deep breaths, ideally in through your nose and out through your mouth. As you inhale, draw the breath deep into your belly. As you exhale, imagine that you are blowing out a candle a few feet in front of you. Notice the coolness of the air as it comes into your body, the warmth of the air as you exhale. You may find these sensations soothing.

The breaths should help you to return to the present moment with more awareness. You may already be feeling more spaciousness around your emotions, or they may still be gripping you tightly. Either way is fine; just notice how you are feeling. Maintain your breathing in an even rhythm as much as possible, and turn your attention inward. What is happening for you right now? What thoughts are coming up? Are you telling any stories about the future based on these feelings (e.g., "I am completely exhausted and now I'm not going to get any sleep and I am going to be a wreck tomorrow and I have so much to do . . . ")? Whatever you notice, identify it, name it, and return to your breath. This practice will help intense emotions pass through you instead of sweeping you away.

You may also find it helpful to scan your body after you identify a particularly strong feeling. What do you notice in your body? Is there tension, discomfort, or pain? If so, where? Bring your attention to these physical sensations and try to draw your breath into them. Imagine the cool, fresh air releasing the tension and healing the aches and pains. Continue breathing and noticing the thoughts as they arise in your mind as you hold your baby. This can be a particularly powerful practice to use when your baby is crying and nothing seems to make him stop.

How Mindfulness Can Help You Mirror Your Infant

The practice of mindful mirroring is a powerful way to positively interact with and engage your baby throughout infancy and beyond. Infants are constantly learning new things about the interconnectedness of the world: "When I do something, there is an effect! Something else happens!" Through these interactions, your infant gradually develops a sense of agency in the world; he learns that he can do things, interact with and affect his environment. In time, this will help your child to develop a sense of self and other. By directly engaging with your infant through mirroring, you help him develop a sense of his ability to interact with and affect the world around him.

ESSENTIAL

Talking to your baby and responding to your child's babbling and cooing is one of the best things you can do in supporting her neurological development. Doing this as a form of "dialogue," meaning to talk to your baby during the pauses in her vocalizations, is a wonderful way to encourage language development.

Mirroring Behavior

Mindful mirroring is really just a kind of mimic play; you probably already do this to some extent. The goal here is to bring more intention to it. Very simply, you engage your infant by entering into his physical space. This may mean putting your face close to his, holding him up in front of you, or lying on the ground with him. This can be done either facing him head-to-head or by lying beside him.

Engage your infant through eye contact whenever possible. Do this in a way that is responsive to him; don't force it. If your infant is looking for your eyes, then connect; if your infant is looking around the room, try to see what he sees and engage the same interest that he has.

As your baby moves and plays, imitate him. If he coos, coo back; if he grasps his (or your) hands, do the same. As you mirror your baby's behavior, pay careful attention to what he is doing and what he is interested in or looking at. Many thoughts may come into your mind; perhaps dinner plans for later, mulling over something you posted on Facebook, or even remembering something that happened last week. These are all time-traveling thoughts; as each idea comes up, notice it and then set it aside. The point here is about connecting to your baby, nothing else; this practice will help you maintain your full presence, just like your baby. For infants, there is no such thing as a time-traveling thought: nothing else exists but right now.

ALERT

You should only mindfully mirror your baby's behavior when she is happy and playful. It could be very unsettling for a crying infant if you were to cry back and flail your arms in her face!

Another benefit of this practice is that it helps to loosen you up, and sets a foundation for play with your child. All humans begin their lives as playful creatures. Indeed, play is one of the most important ways a person can learn. As people grow to be adults, however, many "forget" how to play. This is totally understandable: There are very strict norms of behavior that govern the adult world, but these norms generally do not apply to children, and certainly not to infants. By engaging in mindful mirroring with your baby, you can help loosen yourself up and get used to playing again.

How Mindfulness Can Help You Soothe Your Crying Baby

Babies cry. A lot. Sometimes infants cry for a reason, like being hungry or gassy or needing a diaper change. Other times, they cry for seemingly no reason at all. One of the hardest things about parenting infants is that they can never tell you why they are crying. A skillful thing to do when you hear your baby crying is to go through a simple checklist of possible reasons:

- Does her diaper need to be changed?
- When did she last eat? If it wasn't recently, could she be hungry?
- If she has eaten recently, could she be gassy?
- Is there anything about her environment that could be causing her discomfort or pain?
- Does she have a fever, or appear to be ill?

If any of the previous apply, obviously you should act to fix the problem. If you go through this checklist and can find no obvious reason for your baby's upset, then you can engage in the practice of mindful soothing.

The world is a big, intense, sometimes scary and overwhelming place for infants. One of the most important experiences that lays the foundation of their psychology and future development is learning how to deal with these qualities of the world. When you soothe your crying baby, this is exactly what she learns from the experience: she learns that the world is a safe and navigable place; it becomes something she learns to deal with.

Before you begin to soothe your child, prepare yourself mentally: First, recognize what feelings are present for you in this moment. If your baby is crying you may be worried, confused, frustrated, exhausted, or even angry. Name and acknowledge the feelings that you are experiencing. Next, take a deep breath. Your feelings don't have to go away (they likely won't), but preparing yourself in this way can make it easier to be with your baby as she cries herself out.

To practice mindful soothing, you must be in physical contact with your child. If she will let you hold her, do so; if not, lay beside her and if possible put a hand on her back. Feeling your presence is one of the most important parts of the practice, as infants are unable to control their feelings. A firm, steady pressure is most effective; you should try to have as much physical contact with your baby as possible. For very young infants, swaddling is a helpful option to make them feel safe, protected, and secure. It may be helpful to maintain a "Crying Journal," which can help you learn what to expect and identify different types of cries.

Understand that your presence alone is comforting. You may not be able to make her stop crying or make everything better, but you can support and love your baby simply by being present. It helps your child understand that she is not alone, even in her pain.

Things that might help your infant stop crying:

- Swaddling her
- Lay her on her side or stomach while awake
- Shushing, swinging, and giving her a binkie to suck on
- Singing songs or turning on a calming sound

FACT

Physical pressure is soothing to people of all ages. In fact, Temple Grandin, the autistic animal behaviorist, found that firm physical pressure helped her control herself when she became overwhelmed by other people. It is now standard practice in special education to use physical pressure as a soothing technique.

Remember that the point of mindful soothing is not to get your baby to stop crying. This will happen eventually, but on your baby's timetable, not your own. Soothing may help speed things up a little, but you cannot count on it. Part of this practice is to release yourself from expecting a particular result in a particular amount of time. It is also important to bear in mind that whether or not your baby stops crying, or how quickly she does so, is not a measure of how good you are as a parent. Sometimes babies just need to cry. The purpose of this practice is to be present with your baby when she is in distress, nothing more.

ALERT

If your baby is crying weakly and shows signs of illness, or is crying in a way you have not heard before (once you are accustomed to her regular cries regarding hunger or discomfort), make an appointment with your doctor as soon as possible.

CHAPTER 9

Toddlers
(Walking to Three Years)

The rate at which children grow and develop during their first three years of life is unparalleled, and often leaves parents dumbstruck by how quickly their child has gone from helpless to stubbornly independent. During this age, children begin to learn how to control their impulses and find new ways of getting what they want (e.g., talking instead of hitting, kicking, or biting).

Relative to infants, toddlers exhibit more self-control and problem-solving skills and demonstrate a stronger sense of self as an individual. A toddler's personality, interests, likes, and dislikes are at the forefront of his interactions with others. What he thinks and feels is exactly what you will see; toddlers are very reactive to their experiences, and are not capable of hiding what they think or feel.

Through the Eyes of a Toddler

A toddler's experience of the world is full of excitement, emotion, and exploration. His coordination has vastly improved since his days as an infant; his physical mobility and independence are light-years from where they were previously. His gross and fine motor controls are significantly more developed, and his ability to begin controlling bodily functions is another giant leap in the developmental process.

Overview

Cognitively speaking, toddlers are sponges for retaining new information (much like infants). The primary difference, however, is language. Toddlers are increasingly able to communicate with other children and adults through speech, and this fundamentally changes how they interact with others.

In terms of social-emotional skills, toddlers are developing a real awareness of other people and are ripe for beginning to learn and internalize empathy for other beings. Though toddlers are beginning to understand the benefits of cooperation, they are usually inclined to parallel play (meaning to play alongside other children without much interaction).

The primary interests of toddlers revolve around exploration, experimentation, and developing an identity separate from that of their parents. Now that they can move around independently and communicate through speech, they become clearer about their likes and dislikes and have new avenues to assert their will. Toddlers are empowered by the new ways they can affect their environment, and as a result will end up in power struggles with Mom and Dad as they test every boundary possible.

What Are Toddlers Learning about Themselves?

Toddlers are in a new phase of self-understanding as they explore their independence. There are many things they can now do for themselves that previously depended upon Mom and Dad (e.g., moving around, investigating new things, eating and drinking on their own, and much more). This also includes a fair amount of control over potty training, which happens on *their* timetable more often than their parents'.

Toddlers are learning how to meet some of their own needs without the help of adults. Their independent mobility and innate curiosity certainly keeps parents on their toes. As their brains synthesize and integrate new skills, toddlers are constantly learning and pushing themselves to see what else they are capable of. This is a major part of their identity formation—to see who they are aside from their parents.

This is sometimes a scary process for toddlers, however, which is why they constantly look for reassurance and affirmation from caregivers. They struggle between wanting the safety and comfort of being held one moment, and then fight to be put down the next. They boldly run off through the playground, seeing how far they can go and checking over their shoulder to see when Mommy will tell them to come back, and then hide behind Daddy's legs when they meet someone new. This flip-flopping between unabashed confidence and acute shyness is part of how they navigate the conflicting impulses of this age.

What Are Toddlers Learning about Others and Their Environment?

Just as toddlers test their personal boundaries, they are constantly testing the boundaries of the people and things in their environment.

To be clear, this not a precalculated endeavor. Toddlers do not plan ahead or say to themselves, "Maybe next time if I throw myself on the ground in the middle of the grocery store and make a huge embarrassing scene, mommy will buy me the candy I want!"

No. It does not work like that. Toddlers are very reactive creatures, and have no impulse control whatsoever. The parts of the brain that allow for conscious and reasoned thoughts are not yet developed, meaning that toddlers will react emotionally to anything and everything. This can be with delightful joy at a silly balloon, or a complete meltdown at having to wear shoes.

QUESTION

I'm worried that my child isn't eating enough. I've even tried to bribe her to eat, but nothing seems to work and I'm worried. What should I do?
Unless there is a medical problem, under normal conditions children only eat when they are hungry. A bigger concern is your child learning to "blackmail" you by either eating or not!

The latter situation will certainly test a parent's patience. It is how you respond to these more difficult situations that actually teaches your child the very boundaries he is unknowingly testing. Without intentionally doing so, what toddlers learn as they experiment, try new things, and push various limitations is "If I do *this,* they will do *this*" or "*that* will happen." Using the meltdown-in-a-grocery-store example:

Mommy has to do some last-minute shopping late one afternoon, and takes Toddler with her. Toddler did not have her regular nap that day, and is more tired and cranky than usual. Mommy did not get enough sleep the night before, and is *also* more tired and cranky than usual. (Never a good combination). Toddler walks along with Mommy, but is quickly bored and wants to go home and play. Although the shopping only takes fifteen minutes, in Toddler's world it takes forever. Suddenly, Toddler sees a small display with Skittles. She loves Skittles, and runs over to grab some. What joy! The first exciting moment of the entire trip! Just as she grabs a bright red package of sugary delicious treats, Mommy yanks it out of her hands and says something about *No candy before dinner.* A full-on meltdown ensues: crying, screaming, stomping feet, hitting Mommy's hand away, the whole nine yards. Mommy's face flushes with frustration and embarrassment. Mommy grabs Toddler by the wrist to go back to the shopping cart, but Toddler goes completely limp and continues to scream and cry.

Pause. Many parents have experienced this, or similar situations with their toddlers. The little one is reacting loudly and publicly to something she does not like. Toddler feels angry and powerless, and acting out in this way is the only control she has over the situation. How Mommy handles it will teach Toddler a very important lesson. Will throwing a meltdown temper tantrum get Toddler what she wants? Is that a viable strategy? Will Mommy cave in to try and get her daughter to stop making a big scene, or will she withstand the outburst calmly and leave the store without giving undue attention to the unwanted behavior?

Toddlers are testing all sorts of strategies to see what control they have, and what they can do to get what they want. This is not malicious or planned ahead: if something has worked in the past to get them what they want, they will try it again. Even if throwing a tantrum has *not* worked in the past, it might happen anyway just because Toddler is overly tired, angry, and does not know what else to do with the intense emotions she is experiencing.

ESSENTIAL

Because toddlers are constantly testing boundaries and trying to assert their will, it is helpful to give them choices. This empowers your child to make a decision that you have control over framing. For example: "Do you want to wear the dinosaur t-shirt or the polar bear t-shirt?" (In your mind: "Either way, you're getting dressed!")

Although this is a dramatic example, it shows how toddlers experiment with different social situations to see what will happen. They also enjoy experimenting with the laws of physics (e.g., gravity, sliding things across ice) and experimenting with what they are physically capable of (e.g., running, jumping, climbing). This is how they learn about cause and effect; this is how they develop an understanding of the dynamic relationships between themselves, other people, and their environment.

Although toddlers develop a basic understanding of the words "yesterday" and "tomorrow," their definitions basically amount to "it already happened" and "it hasn't happened yet." A toddler's sense of time is still anchored entirely in the present moment.

Physical Milestones

A toddler's body grows fast, and he works hard to keep up with the new things his size and strength will allow him to do. Both his large and small muscle groups develop quickly, particularly when stimulated by different activities that build his strength and refine his physical capabilities.

ALERT

Toddlers need to move. They need physical engagement, sensory stimulation, and as much interaction with you as possible. It can sometimes be difficult to muster the energy to play with your child; however, it's important to do your best. The benefits of play *far* outweigh the consequences of normalizing a sedentary lifestyle with your child.

Throwing and Kicking a Ball

Throwing and kicking a ball with your child develops important gross-motor skills. An interest in throwing things will likely arise before your child begins walking; however, during the toddler phase it can develop into a more intentional and interactive game.

Here are some ways to support these skills:

- Roll a soft ball back and forth on the ground. Increase the distance between you and Toddler as he is able to roll farther.
- Let Toddler throw a soft ball to you that you can then roll back to him.
- While standing and holding hands, take steps with Toddler by swinging your legs out in front of you. As he is able, do the same thing together without holding hands.
- Show Toddler how to kick a soft ball with his feet, and roll it back to him.
- Standing close together and using a large beach ball, ask Toddler to grab the ball from you. Once he is accustomed to grabbing and holding the large ball, try gently tossing the ball back and forth from a close distance.

Pushing and Pulling

As Toddler begins walking more confidently, he will enjoy being able to push or pull different toys or objects. This develops balance, strength, and coordination, and gives Toddler a chance to imitate adult actions.

Here are some ways to support these skills:

- Buy or make toys with wheels that Toddler can push or pull. This can include a baby doll stroller, a mini grocery cart, or a small wagon.
- Attach a string to a little car or a leash to a stuffed animal. This is particularly fun for toddlers who want to take a stuffed animal for a walk around the house. (Make sure there is supervision so the string does not create a risk of strangulation).
- Give Toddler a large cardboard box he can push and slide across the floor. You can even decorate it with Toddler to turn it into something he likes, such as an airplane, train, boat, or car.

Squatting

Toddlers typically bend over to pick things up; however, you can show them how to bend their knees instead. This will help to develop their balance as well as strengthen the muscles in their legs.

Here are some ways to support these skills:

- First, show Toddler how to bend his knees and squat. When you are both in the squatting position, you can pretend to be a rocket taking off. Count down with Toddler (5, 4, 3, 2, 1), and when you say "Blast off!" both of you jump up.
- Pretend to be frogs, and hop around the floor in a squatting position.
- You and Toddler stretch as high up as you can and pretend to pick an apple. While standing normally, pretend to eat the apple; then squat down, and pretend to plant the apple seeds.
- Line up a few small toys on the floor. Have Toddler squat down to pick them up, then stand and toss each toy into a bag or bucket you are holding. This is a particularly useful trick during cleanup time: as often as possible, turn cleanup into an interactive game!

Climbing

In the never-ending push for risk and challenge, toddlers will begin climbing and hanging off of anything that seems suitable. Why? Because it is fun! Don't be too quick to discourage this behavior. Instead, help your toddler understand what is safe to climb and what is not, and make your expectations brief and clear. He will need your help to understand what is safe to climb and what isn't.

Teach your toddler to come and ask you when he wants to climb, so you can stand behind him and make sure he stays safe. As a safety precaution, make sure to anchor furniture like bookshelves to the wall, and remove objects that could easily fall. Put gates up around staircases, and notice places in the house that might invite unwanted climbing (such as kitchen chairs that can reach the stove).

Here are some ways to support these skills:

- Give Toddler plenty of safe opportunities to climb. This can happen at a toddler-friendly playground, in a backyard tree, or on a couch cushion mountain you create yourself.
- With your support, lift Toddler to monkey bars at playgrounds so he can practice hanging and swinging from bar to bar.
- Practice climbing up and down stairs together, and climbing onto and out of beds.

Running

Running requires a fair amount of strength and coordination. Toddlers need access to wide-open spaces to practice this skill safely, and places like parks or the backyard (anywhere with grass or sand) are among the best places to do so. Running on concrete is inevitable, as are the scrapes and bruises that come with learning this invaluable skill. Let Toddler know he's all right, clean the cut, put on a Band-Aid, and let him get back to it. Toddlers take their cues from you; that's how they learn resilience.

Here are some ways to support these skills:

- Play tag, and get creative! Try using a predator-and-prey theme: a shark chasing a fish, a dog chasing a cat, an owl chasing a mouse, etc.
- Create backyard obstacle courses.
- Kick a beach ball and encourage Toddler to go get it. Then switch, and let Toddler kick or throw the ball while you go get it.
- Make a "base" where Toddler is safe, such as a tree or picnic table, then chase him around. When he needs a breather, he can stay on base. (Then switch if he wants to chase you!)
- Run for fun! Choose a "finish line" and run alongside Toddler. Dramatically collapse and cheer when you both reach your target, then repeat.

Jumping

Jumping is another way to develop strength, balance and muscle control. Providing safe and fun ways to practice this skill is easy, because opportunities to jump off of things are everywhere! As your toddler learns to assess risk, make sure to ask him what he thinks looks safe and what doesn't. Guide him in making healthy decisions, and hold his hand if he wants to jump off of something high up.

Here are some ways to support these skills:

- When doing regular daily errands with your toddler, take any opportunity available to jump onto or off of a curb. Hold hands, and say "1, 2, 3, jump!" together.
- When going for a walk in the woods, help Toddler climb, balance, and jump off of things like logs and small boulders.
- Hop like kangaroos, and measure how far Toddler can hop.
- Pretend that you and Toddler must cross a river. Tape paper plates to the floor or put down baseball bases, and hop from one "stone" to the next until you both make it to the other side!

Other Physical Milestones

Toddlers acquire many new skills as they grow. The following is a general list of things you might notice and encourage.

- Stacking and balancing two blocks on top of each other
- Scribbling with crayons and markers, eventually creating pictures
- Drinking from a straw
- Feeding himself with a spoon
- Walking backward
- Putting on his own clothes and shoes (with varying levels of success)
- Opening and closing cabinets and doors
- Washing and drying his own hands
- Walking up steps with alternate feet

Mindful Potty Training

Children are ready for potty training at different ages, and it is a difficult thing to rush. In fact, trying to rush something like potty training will often backfire on parents. Applying mindfulness to the timing, planning, and following through of potty training can help you keep your cool, plan ahead, and understand your child's needs.

Your Toddler's Experience

Be patient. Bowel movements are an intense physical experience for children at this age, and they might run out of the room or go to a place where they have relative privacy to poop. It is helpful to remember that toddlers have little control over what happens in their day-to-day lives, because their schedule must conform to the adults who care for them. Even though they cannot choose *when* it will happen, *how* toddlers go potty is one of the few things that are entirely up to them. To know when a toddler is ready for potty training, look for signs that indicate her interest.

Tips for Parents

When your child is ready to potty train it helps to plan ahead and keep extra sets of clothes, shoes, wipes, and paper towels on you at all times. It takes a while for toddlers to recognize the physical signs telling them they have to go, and by the time they realize it, it may already be too late.

Praise her for noticing when she has to go, even if she gets to a toilet and nothing happens. When she has an accident let her know that it's okay, reinforce that she is doing her best, and tell her that she can try again next time, it just takes practice. Toddlers are usually more comfortable trying to go in a smaller toilet, so having a potty-training toilet that you keep next to a regular-sized toilet is worth the investment. No matter what, when your child is ready to start using a toilet instead of diapers, there will be signs. Signs that your toddler is ready for potty training include:

- She tries to take off her diaper when it is soiled.
- She is excited by the chance to wear "big kid" underwear.
- She does not like having a dirty diaper.
- She has the vocabulary and self-awareness to communicate when she thinks she has to go.
- She squats or crosses her legs when she has to go, which shows that she recognizes the physical signs.
- She asks lots of questions about toilets, is curious about how they work, and will potentially ask outright to sit on one

Cognitive and Social-Emotional Development

Much of the cognitive development happening at this age revolves around learning language and communication skills, understanding emotions, and learning how to interact with others.

Attention

It is important to note that toddlers thrive on attention, and it does not actually make a difference if the attention they receive is positive or negative. When a toddler receives more attention from Mom or Dad through mistaken behavior than through acceptable behavior, he will continue with the mistaken behavior because it puts him in the spotlight. This calls for parents to reinforce the behaviors they want to see, and to give as little attention as possible to behaviors they do *not* want to see.

Toddlers also spend a lot of time observing adults and mimicking what they see and hear. This makes it all the more important for parents to set a good example. Act and speak in ways you would like your toddler to imitate, because for better or worse, you are the role model they will imitate most!

Milestones

Toddlers reach a number of cognitive and social-emotional milestones that influence their behavior, their personality, how they process information, and how they are able to interact with other people and their environment.

Major achievements include:

- Parallel play: Toddlers tend to play alongside one another and have limited interactions.
- Individuation: As your child explores how he is separate from you, he will push boundaries and exert control by saying "No!" and challenging your authority.
- Blossoming language skills: At this stage, toddlers understand more than they are able to communicate. Your child's vocabulary is growing steadily; he is able to speak in simple sentences, and he is by and large able to verbalize what he wants and how he feels.
- Grouping: Toddlers can begin grouping objects by color, size, texture and other basic categories.
- Showing excitement when simple tasks are completed.
- Beginning to solve simple problems through trial and error.

- Beginning to engage in basic self-care: Toddlers start learning to wash their own hands, put on some of their own clothes, feed themselves with a spoon, etc.
- Realizing things still exist even when out of sight: Your child will come to understand that even when he cannot see people or toys, those things will still continue to exist.

Ways to Support These Skills

There is much you can do to help your toddler develop his cognitive and social-emotional skills, including different ways to interact, stimuli you can expose him to, and helpful games you can play. Some ideas include:

- Sing songs and make up rhymes as much as possible.
- Cultivate prereading skills by reading with your child every day and talking about the stories and characters.
- Nurture your child's independence and let him practice the things he is capable of, such as zipping zippers, putting on shoes, and fastening his own seat belt. This takes patience and the self-control not to do simple tasks for him if you know he can do it himself.
- Play basic sorting games like dropping red pictures in a red pail, blue pictures in a blue pail, etc.
- Engage in dramatic play with your child, which often imitates adult situations (such as cooking pretend food, building a pretend house, or talking to each other on pretend phones).
- Play match-the-shape games.
- Put large four- to six-piece puzzles together.
- Play hide-and-seek with toys.
- Show pride in your child's efforts, and share their joy in accomplishing small tasks.
- Set up play dates so your child can spend more time with other children.

A major element of a toddler's mental and physical development is nutrition. The food children eat in the first years of life has a significant impact on things like memory, neural-processing, concentration, behavior, and more. All children should be encouraged to eat five portions (roughly 500g) of fruits and vegetables each day.

Raising a Toddler

Toddlers are very exciting because they have developed enough motor control to engage with the world in much more substantive ways than infants. Whereas infants are largely helpless and immobile, toddlers seem to be constantly in motion.

Children between the ages of one and three need between ten and thirteen hours of sleep each night, plus a one- to two-hour nap during the day. Having a consistent sleep routine is the best way to ensure your child can sleep through the night; it can actually be more difficult for children to fall asleep if they are overtired.

The Joys

The intrepid curiosity of toddlers can easily be contagious (when it isn't infuriating), as they touch and play with anything and everything they can get their hands on. For you as a parent of a toddler, this can renew your own enjoyment of the world as you tap into some of your toddler's curiosity and excitement.

Toddlers are constantly experimenting and pushing the boundaries of their own capabilities as they try to master new skills. There are near-daily triumphs along the way, and your toddler will relish each and every one as she expands her agency in the world. You can get in on the sense of accomplishment by supporting her achievement and sharing in her enthusiasm. You are also perfectly correct to feel pride in your child as she grows and develops.

One of the biggest changes between infancy and toddlerhood is the development of language. Toddlers gain language skills rapidly, and are capable of ever-increasing communication. This opens up powerful new ways of engaging your child as she learns about herself and the world.

The Challenges

There are many challenges that come during the toddler years. The most obvious is that toddlers can take many more risks than infants because they are independently mobile. This means that your child can get into trouble in ways that were previously impossible, and it is your job to try to keep up with her and keep her safe. It is very easy for parents of toddlers to end up feeling like human safety harnesses.

FACT

Because toddlers are not yet able to distinguish between fantasy and reality, nightmares can be particularly distressful. Your child may wake up and call out for you, even multiple times in one night. The best thing you can do is stay calm, reassure your child verbally, listen if he needs to talk about the dream, and soothe him by rubbing his back.

The energy of toddlers is also famously challenging. Toddlers seem to have only two speeds: full-tilt and asleep. Keeping up with your little one can be exhausting. Toddlers' emotions also tend to parallel their energy level, and are completely unmodulated by any self-awareness. A tired toddler will not declare his exhaustion; he is much more likely to continue trying to play, resist going to bed and become hyper-emotional. He can seem to fight you at every turn.

Toddlers also tend to develop strong preferences about many things in the world, be they clothes, activities, or food, and are rarely shy about communicating these preferences. All of this can leave you feeling fed up, as if it doesn't matter what you do, because your toddler will do whatever he wants to do. This is not true, of course, but it is helpful to notice and acknowledge the feelings of anger or frustration that sometimes come up. This simple act of noticing and acknowledging will help you to respond more constructively to difficult circumstances, instead of reacting from intense emotions.

Mindfulness and Toddlers

Toddlers will push your buttons. It is not a question of if, but when. Because they have so much energy and curiosity and so little sense of safety or propriety, toddlers are constantly pushing limits, both their own and yours. It is inevitable that you will find yourself having negative reactions to your toddler's behavior, but this need not ruin your day.

How Mindfulness Can Help You Manage Intense Emotions

Mindful self-awareness will help you to respond to your toddler as opposed to react, and help you to be more the parent you want to be and less at the mercy of your own emotions. This isn't to say that you will have fewer emotional reactions to your toddler; that's simply not possible. Through this practice of noticing and acknowledging (without judgment) whatever emotions arise, however, you can experience more choice in the midst of these intense emotions. This helps you create a space where you can respond constructively more often than reacting emotionally.

The first step is recognizing when you are having an emotional reaction. The more familiar you become with yourself and your habits of thought, the more readily you will be able to recognize when you are reacting.

When you feel a strong emotion taking hold of you, try to pause for a moment: What do you notice? Was there a progression of thoughts or feelings that worked you up? Are there particular stories playing out in your mind? Do you notice any physical sensations in your body, particularly tension? It may be difficult to do this in the heat of the moment, because the world is not likely to stop and allow you time to reflect. This is why it is so helpful to practice this form of emotional mindfulness during the calm times; when you develop the habit of self-awareness during calm periods, you are more likely to access this skill when life (and emotions) hits the fan.

As you notice what is happening in your mind and body, try to take a brief moment before you act. Of course, if your toddler is doing something dangerous, a quick reaction is totally appropriate. That being said, the reaction need only last long enough to take her out of harm's way. After you have accomplished this, the challenge is to stop your reaction from going any further and turn it into a conscious response. This is where you should take a moment, just long enough for a single breath. Try to reconnect to the moment as it is now: here you are. You are safe. Your toddler is safe. Okay. What next? By taking the time for just a single breath, you can open up new options about what to do next instead of automatically launching into a lecture based on anger, frustration, or fear.

ESSENTIAL

The great Japanese Zen master Hakuin once said that a single instant of practice in the midst of activity is worth infinitely more than an eternity of practice in peace and quiet. Don't lose heart; this is exactly as it should be!

How Mindfulness Can Help You Explore with Your Toddler

Toddlers play almost constantly. This is how they meet the world: by touching it, tasting it, trying it out, and seeing what happens. While it can be exhausting, it is also quite beautiful and potentially a lot of fun. One of the best things you can do to connect with and guide your toddler is to follow her as she plays and engage with whatever she is curious about. In this exercise, you should consciously give your toddler control of what to pursue or play with. Obviously you still need to keep her safe, but for the most part you can just follow your little girl and respond to whatever catches her interest.

You may want to stand beside your toddler or you may want to follow her from behind. Whichever you choose, do as she does: run when she runs; sit down when she sits; pay attention to what she is paying attention to, and talk to her about what you are doing. If your toddler picks up an object such as a toy dump truck, let her play with it and pay attention. She may try to show you something or hand it to you to play with as well. Don't worry if she isn't using it properly. As long as she is playing safely, exploring is at least half the fun! If she invites you to play too by handing you something, feel free to show her how it works by pushing a button or putting the cylinder through the round hole in the box, but don't consciously try to teach her. This activity is all about creatively exploring the environment; there is no other goal or objective.

How Mindfulness Can Help You with Guided Communication

One of the most exciting milestones in a toddler's life is the development of language skills. Finally, you actually begin two-way verbal communication with your child! It is important to bear in mind that a critical part of communication derives from awareness, and that self-awareness is only just beginning to emerge for your toddler. This is a particularly ripe time to help her develop her communicative skills, because toddlers very quickly acclimate to patterns of behavior that become the foundations for their future selves. If you help your toddler develop her self-awareness and the language skills to communicate effectively, she is much more likely to be able to access these skills throughout her later stages of development.

Try to keep in mind that a toddler is only just beginning to discover what can be done with language. As an infant, she got what she wanted largely through crying, so you need to be aware that you are teaching her completely new ways of doing things. This process will take time and there will inevitably be many bumps in the road, but if your toddler learns that she can get what she wants through positive communication, she will learn not to resort to other, less savory means.

To engage your toddler in guided communication, you must first recognize when she wants or needs something. Particularly in the early stages of toddlerhood, the cue will likely be some form of noise or physical behavior. You are probably quite familiar with your toddler's patterns of behavior by this point, and are fairly certain when she is hungry, is sleepy, or needs attention. This is extremely helpful, and is the first step in practicing guided communication: recognizing that your toddler has a need. It is important to realize that you don't necessarily have to know *what* she needs, just that she needs *something*.

When your toddler indicates a need through a negative behavior (such as throwing a toy), you should calmly act to stop that behavior by removing the toy or removing him from the situation. When intervening in a toddler's unwanted behavior, you usually don't want to say anything more than "No" as you remove or redirect him. If he is calm and not crying or throwing a fit, then you can engage your child directly and ask, "What do you need?" He may or may not have an answer. If he does, listen to him and respond accordingly. If he does not have an answer, it is your job to redirect him so his attention is focused on something else.

ESSENTIAL

Toddlers will often communicate that they have a need of some kind by acting out in one form or another. Try to understand whatever your toddler does as an attempt to get your attention, nothing more. If the behavior is inappropriate (such as pulling someone's hair, hitting, or yelling), once you have removed him from the conflict and identified that he has a need you can engage him appropriately.

To redirect your toddler (assuming he is calm and receptive), you can ask him a couple of questions one at a time or outright suggest a new activity for both of you: "Are you hungry?" "Do you want some attention?" "Here, help me build this train!" These simple questions prompt your toddler to look inward, think about what he wants, and articulate his need. It is not always successful; however, there is value in helping him begin to develop these basic building blocks of self-awareness and verbal communication. Sometimes the best thing to do is to avoid prompting questions entirely, and redirect his attention by starting a new activity with him. Remember, your attention is sunshine and he will most likely go along with whatever activity brings interaction with you.

If you are able to identify what your toddler wants, you then have an opportunity to help him learn how to ask for it appropriately. If he is an older toddler, encourage him to think of possible options by asking him "What do we say when we are hungry?" or "What do you say when you want something?" If he is a younger toddler and lacks the vocabulary and practice, model an appropriate way for him to express his desire. You can say, "Mommy, can I please have a snack?" or "Daddy, will you please play with me?" With younger toddlers it helps to model the pattern of speech you want him to use, and that means saying his desire for him. The benefit of this practice is twofold: first, you help your toddler develop self-awareness of what he wants; second, you help him learn appropriate behavior and communication skills to get what he wants.

CHAPTER 10

Children
(Three to Nine Years)

Children are incredibly social creatures who enjoy playing, exploring, and testing their physical and mental abilities. Growth happens at a slower pace than during infancy and toddlerhood, which gives the body more time to adjust and integrate the neural connections that continue to form. They also begin to engage with peers in parallel play and then later in cooperative play.

Children develop a more solidified sense of self during these years, and are increasingly aware that other people have their own needs and interests. This age range is a ripe window for children to learn empathy, or the ability to vicariously experience another being's thoughts and feelings. Empathy helps children connect with and relate to others, which informs their maturing value system.

ESSENTIAL

Competence is a key word for children. As children develop more motor control, they are better able to tend to their own needs and enjoy the independence that comes from doing so. Going to the bathroom alone, dressing themselves, and feeding themselves all help to build a child's sense of competence.

Through the Eyes of a Child

A child's experience of the world is very me-centric, with a gradually increasing awareness of the needs and interests of others. Through trial and error, they discover new ways to find a balance between what *they* want versus what their friends or family members want. This is an important period of socialization; as children move away from parallel play (playing next to or alongside other kids) to cooperative play (interactive collaboration with other kids toward a common goal), new social-emotional skills emerge.

Overview

Physically speaking, children develop much more control over their bodies during this stage and learn to start, turn, and stop effectively when playing movement games. As their balance improves, children also learn how to hop on one foot, skip, jump, and walk on their tiptoes. Children's bones and muscles become stronger, their lung capacity increases, and their energy levels are extremely high. You'll notice that your child's fine motor skills and coordination get markedly better, and she will demonstrate greater dexterity in drawing, writing, tying shoes, buttoning buttons, and more.

ALERT

It is very easy for adults to trivialize the small, repetitive tasks that children can enjoy. To grownups, tracing, buttoning shirts, zipping zippers, and lacing yarn can seem pointless and insignificant, but for children they are hugely important. Through all of these tasks, children continue to develop and refine their fine motor skills, and develop a sense of mastery over their environments that forms the foundation for their confidence in meeting the challenges of the world later in life.

One of the most developmentally significant cognitive advances to occur during this stage is signification, the ability to attach meanings to symbols (i.e., associating sounds with written letters, quantities with written numbers, etc.), which changes how the brain processes information. This improves communication, memory, and learning, and helps children think about and remember things that are not physically present. It also alters the way a child can engage her imagination, as she can now give attributes to objects or people that don't actually have them (such as imagining that a cardboard box is a train, or that a peg board is an electric guitar).

The primary interests of children revolve around learning about themselves, others, and the world through play. Play is at the heart of how children learn and process their experiences; at this age there is literally no separation between living, playing, and learning. Those arbitrary divisions are typically introduced in school.

What Are Children Learning about Themselves?

As they begin playing cooperatively with their peers as opposed to alongside one another, children enter a new phase of self-understanding that is shaped by these interactions. When a child is introduced to the art of compromise with friends, new social-emotional skills are forced to develop.

It is during this stage that children fully realize that they cannot always have their way. This is a challenging fact to accept; it's hard when you cannot get or do what you want, and this is just as true for adults as it is for children. The primary difference is that the adult brain is fully developed and has had years of practice regulating emotions and exercising impulse control. Between the ages of three and nine, however, a child's ability to delay gratification or to respond constructively to frustrating situations instead of reacting emotionally is just starting to develop. These are major elements of what children begin to learn at this stage.

ESSENTIAL

A parent's role in helping his or her child learn this lesson is absolutely critical. It can be very tempting to try to placate your child when he is upset by helping him to get his way or giving him something else to distract him from his feelings of upset. This is a huge mistake and denies your child the opportunity to develop the psychological coping mechanisms for dealing with disappointment. Instead of trying to turn his feelings around, help him learn to live with disappointment. It is inevitable in life.

When faced with the reality that they cannot always have their way, children try out different coping methods (such as tantrums, pleading, bartering, and more). One of the most effective strategies for balancing personal desires with the desires of others is compromise. In their naturally me-centric universe, children refine the art of getting as close to what they want as possible.

Take six-year-old Joey, for example, who wants to borrow the race car his younger brother David is playing with. David says no, so Joey sweetens the deal by offering to let David play with his new Lego Spinjitzu toys. David agrees, and both children get something they want. Though it does not always go this smoothly, children quickly learn to negotiate what they want by offering incentives as part of their strategy to compromise.

Through trial and error, children begin learning how to compromise, how to manage their emotions, how to navigate the conflicting desires that come up in relationships, and how to listen to and communicate with others. This work continues throughout their entire lives; most adults are still learning how to do the same thing. It can be helpful to remember that children this age are at the most nascent stages of learning about relationships and self-control. They need patience, guidance, and time to learn from their victories and mistakes.

Children learn a lot about their bodies as they get stronger, gain more muscle control, and test their physical capabilities in new ways. Add in their high energy levels, and it's no wonder kids are constantly on the move and seeing what they can do. They experience pride and a real sense of accomplishment as they are able to master new skills, which gives them motivation to push themselves a little further. For example, six-year-old Morgan was able to climb up to the fourth branch of his backyard pine tree last week; now he's strong and confident enough to climb up to the sixth branch. Four-year-old Marie was able to hang from the monkey bars the other day; today she's able to swing from bar to bar, and shows off to her mom. Discovering what their bodies can do is exciting for children, and is a driving element of how they play.

Children are also discovering and deciding who they are and who they want to be. Their identities become more defined during this stage and take shape based on their likes, dislikes, interests, and social relationships. This is when they develop a true sense of self that is separate from parents, family, and friends.

What Are Children Learning about Others and Their Environment?

By the age of nine, children are much more aware of the inner emotional lives of others and are realizing that other people (peers in particular) also have opinions and make judgments. Children begin feeling their way around social groups and hierarchies, and come to care more intensely about what other kids think of them. And so comes the early dawn of social scrutiny.

The ability to empathize with other people and living beings also manifests during this stage. Through explorations of the natural world, meaningful encounters with plants and animals, and relationships with other people, children can begin to experience connections with other living beings in visceral ways. For some children empathy comes very naturally; however, *all* children benefit from the guidance of adults who take time to nurture this skill. Empathy not only connects children to their immediate environment and local community; it also helps them cultivate an identity in the context of their particular web of relationships. It helps children understand that they are part of a greater whole.

Empathy is not just a nice moral or psychological idea, it is a neurological reality. Empathy occurs in the brain in two ways: When you see somebody else stub her toe, for example, the same intuitive sensory circuits in your brain experience an echo of that sensation. There is also an "empathy center" in part of the cerebral cortex that lies between the temporal and frontal lobes and processes empathetic emotions in a much more sophisticated and nuanced way.

Social boundaries are a new frontier for children, and much of what they are learning revolves around understanding and experimenting with relationships. There are many types and categories of relationship to be explored: child-parent, child-sibling, child-teacher, child-friend, child-stranger, and so on. The dynamics of these different relationships and the skills required to navigate them are all brand new to children: verbal and nonverbal communication skills, the vocabulary to express thoughts and emotions, the art of compromise, how to interpret the words and actions of others.

The other major concept children learn about is cause and effect, and how this translates into both social relationships and the laws of physics. Children quickly learn that all events have causes: in the physical realm, if a ball rolls past four-year-old Sarah she will look in the direction from which it came to determine what caused the ball to roll in the first place. ("Did Daddy roll it to get my attention? Did it just fall off the couch?")

Children are naturally self-centered to a great extent. This is developmentally appropriate, but also affects their calculations of cause and effect. Children will often deduce that they are personally involved in causing something, particularly something that affects people they care about, even if there is no logical basis for that. This means that it is critically important for parents to explain the causes for their own strong emotions to their children.

This same search for causes occurs in the social realm as well. If eight-year-old Jessica is crying, her friend Brian will ask her what happened and try to cheer her up. If Daddy starts yelling at someone on the phone, seven-year-old Chase will try to figure out what might have gotten his father so angry (and may wonder if he himself is somehow to blame).

Peeling back and exploring the different layers of cause and effect will improve children's problem-solving skills, and give them new insight into how they affect the people and environment around them.

Physical Milestones

Strength and control is the name of the game. Through a combination of free-play and structured activities, children's gross and fine motor skills steadily improve; the same happens with balance and coordination. Endurance also goes up as children's lung capacity increases. (This is all dependent upon healthy nutrition, of course).

The following abilities are categorized under strength, dexterity, balance, and coordination, as these are the areas in which children can physically progress the most by the age of nine.

Strength

This category refers to your child's gross motor skills, meaning his body's large muscle groups. As children become taller, leaner, and more physically active, large muscle groups (such as the quadriceps and calves in the legs, the biceps and triceps in the arms, or the pectoral muscles in the chest) become capable of handling more demanding activities. To take advantage of this, children need oodles of physical activity and play. Your child's increasing strength will allow him to run faster and for longer periods of time, to climb higher than before, to push and pull objects of greater mass, and much more.

Here are some ways to support your child's strength:

- *Climbing.* Children naturally want to climb just about everything in sight. This requires you to set clear expectations with your child about what he can and cannot climb. He will be better able to meet those expectations if you give him plenty of supervised opportunities to climb, and show him how to do so safely. This might mean climbing stairs, trees, rocks, playground structures, and more.

- *Running.* Give your child as many opportunities to run as possible. It helps when you participate! Play running games like tag or kick-the-can; introduce him to sports such as soccer or basketball; set up relay races with other neighborhood kids; or just chase him for fun. Visit places with wide-open spaces such as parks, beaches, or high school soccer/football fields.

- *Pushing and pulling.* If you watch closely, you will notice that pushing and pulling are seamlessly woven into children's play. You can encourage your child to make snowmen, pull a friend or sibling in a wagon, slide something heavy across the floor, play games like tug-o-war, pull himself up and on top of things.

- *Hopping and jumping.* Activities that involve hopping or jumping go a long way toward building your child's leg muscles. Encourage creative variations of activities like hopscotch and leap frog; measure how far he and his friends can jump; help him create obstacle courses that require jumping over things, or for fun jump up each step of a flight of stairs together.

FACT

There are evolutionary reasons for children's high energy levels. While adults have to convince themselves to go to the gym or exercise to stay in shape, children are still developing their muscles and the brains systems that allow them to control their bodies. The primary way they do this is through physical play. Their naturally high energy levels are one way in which nature ensures they are active enough to fully develop their bodies and minds.

Dexterity

This category refers to your child's fine motor skills, specifically the coordination of small muscle groups in her hands. During this stage your child will learn to do things that require more finesse and control, such as buttoning buttons, using tweezers to pick up small objects, or drawing pictures in great detail.

Here are some ways to support your child's dexterity:

- *Lacing.* As a project, you can ask your child to draw a shape or picture on a piece of cardboard. (Something like a cereal box is useful because it is fairly thin). Cut it out, and use a hole-puncher to punch holes all around the perimeter of the picture. Show your child how to lace shoe strings or yarn through the different holes. Other options include making Cheerio necklaces or popcorn strings. Older children may show interest in knitting, crocheting, or stitching something together.
- *Legos.* Having Legos of various colors and sizes is a fun way to encourage creativity, spatial thinking, and dexterity. The act of pushing small Lego pieces together and pulling them apart is a wonderful way to strengthen the small muscle groups in your child's hands.
- *Drawing and writing.* Learning how to hold and control writing utensils like crayons, markers, and pencils requires a certain amount of strength and concentration. Jump on any opportunity to write, draw, color, or paint with your child.
- *Cutting with scissors.* Learning how to cut with scissors takes time, and you will have to teach your child how to use this tool safely. Begin by showing him how to properly hold a pair of child scissors, then let him get accustomed to opening and closing them. Give him different colors of scrap paper, and you can make confetti together. Try cutting along a line; when he is ready, move on to cutting out shapes or pictures. Although this sounds too simple, just giving your child opportunities to cut paper into smithereens will help his hands develop small muscle strength and control.
- *Sculpting.* Whether with clay, Play-Doh, or mud, your child's fine motor skills get plenty of practice when shaping 3-D objects. The squishing, squeezing, pinching, and smoothing are fun and important ways to exercise the hands.

Balance

To balance properly, the large and small muscle groups must work together to make sure the body does not fall over. Finding creative ways to engage your child in the following activities will cultivate her sense of balance.

Here are some ways to support your child's balance:

- *Balance beams.* Almost anything can be used as a balance beam. Hold your child's hand if need be, and show her how to bend her knees to drop her center of gravity.
- *Hopping on one foot.* Any reason to encourage your child to hop on one foot is helpful. Some ideas include a hopping race, hopping up stairs, a potato bag race, or playing games like hopscotch.
- *Skipping.* By alternating between doing a double hop on one foot then a double hop on the next, children figure out how keep their balance in the midst of movement. Encourage skipping in games, during family walks and just for fun. This also develops whole-body coordination.
- *Walking backward.* This can be done in conjunction with some of the balance beam ideas, or just by asking your child if she can walk backward from point A to point B.
- *Simple yoga poses.* Doing one to three yoga poses with your child is a great way to support her balance, among other things.

Coordination

This category refers to the brain's ability to connect what the eyes see with an intentional physical reaction. Coordination involves a combination and synthesis of strength, balance, and fine and gross motor skills. This can mean catching a ball, doing a cartwheel, or riding a bicycle. Any opportunity to engage your child in the following activities will help her improve her coordination.

Here are some ways to support your child's coordination:

- *Catch, throw, and bounce balls.* Whereas the ability to throw objects develops earlier, learning how to catch tends to develop between the ages of four and seven. Bouncing requires variations of both throwing and catching, and can even incorporate running at the same time. Playing old or invented games that involve any combination of catching, throwing, and bouncing will help your child improve her coordination.
- *Jump rope.* When teaching the basics, have your child jump over a stationary rope on the ground. Once that is mastered, wiggle the rope like a snake on the ground while she jumps over. Regular jump rope games require your child to hop in synch with a rope that she or two other people are swinging over her head. To keep the rhythm going, it helps to say rhymes as she jumps.
- *Soccer.* Learning to control and kick a ball while running develops great coordination skills. If joining a soccer team is not possible, do not worry. The only thing you need to nurture these skills is a soccer ball and some space. You can play games like kick, keep-away, or obstacle ball (maneuvering the soccer ball through a line of cones), or have dribbling races with your child and her friends.
- *Swimming.* When your child learns different ways of moving her body to keep her head above water, many neural connections are made that connect her mind with orchestrated physical movements. Learning how to do strokes like freestyle, breaststroke, backstroke, butterfly, and even dog paddle will build your child's strength and coordination. Any games done in the water can help build these skills.
- *Riding a bike.* By the time your child is six or seven, she will most likely be riding a two-wheeler bike with no training wheels. Between steering with the arms, pedaling with the feet, and maintaining her balance, learning to master the art of riding bikes will build your child's physical skills and confidence. To build up the necessary strength for this more advanced activity, start out by giving younger children tricycles and standing scooters first before graduating to bicycles with training wheels.

- *Gymnastics and martial arts.* Although it may not be possible to sign your child up for gymnastics or martial arts classes, they deserve to be mentioned because of the many benefits they offer to children's physical development, coordination, and self-discipline.

QUESTION

Why are so many of the things my kid does so endlessly repetitive?
Because your child is learning mastery. To us as grown adults things like throwing a ball or hopping on one leg are easy and become boring quickly. This is in large part because the muscles and nerve circuits necessary for these activities are well developed. For children, these activities are not easy. These muscles and nerve circuits are not yet well developed in children. Because of this, children get more enjoyment out of the stimulation they receive from doing things over and over again. It is all part of the learning process.

Other Physical Milestones

The following is a general list of things you will notice and can encourage before your child is nine.

- Feeding herself without making a mess
- Walking or running up steps using alternate feet
- Building large, complex towers out of Legos or blocks
- Writing and drawing with crayons, markers, pens, and pencils in controlled and intentional ways
- Catching, throwing (overhand and underhand), kicking, and bouncing balls of different sizes
- Going to the bathroom and washing her hands by herself
- Riding a bicycle
- Moving forward and backward with balance and agility
- Pouring liquid from pitchers or containers
- Brushing her teeth by herself
- "Pumping" on the swings to keep himself going
- Doing somersaults, cartwheels, and handstands
- Tying shoes, zipping up coats, and dressing himself

Cognitive Milestones

Significant changes in how a child's brain processes new information and experiences will occur over the course of early and late childhood. The cognitive shifts that take place revolve around using written and verbal language, differentiating between fantasy and reality, using symbols, grasping the nature and identity of things, understanding cause and effect, and developing a firm grasp of time.

Language

Your child's ability to understand and use language will improve by leaps and bounds during this stage. He will go from using short, simple sentences to using complex, multiclause sentences; he will gain a solid grasp of grammatical rules; he will learn to associate sounds with written letters and develop his reading and writing skills; he will learn how to use the past, present, and future tenses properly; his pronunciation and articulation will improve; he will go from asking more concrete who/what/when/where/why questions to asking higher-level hypothetical questions ("What would happen if . . . "); his vocabulary will grow exponentially, thereby giving his descriptions of feelings and events more nuance and depth, and more.

FACT

Words have meaning in much more complex ways than just their definitions. There are the denotative, or dictionary, definitions of words, but to be able to use a word, you have to understand much more about its context, nuance, and associations. Children learn this through experimentation and word play. Although you may sometimes be startled at the things that come out of your child's mouth, even when they are totally inappropriate try to treat them as learning opportunities.

There are many ways that parents can support language development in children. Teaching your child through stories, games, and engaging activities will add a lot to his development.

Here are some ways to support your child's language development:

- Read together every day.
- Ask questions and discuss situations happening in stories.
- Ask your child questions that engage his memory and chronological thinking (e.g., retelling a story or something that happened yesterday).
- Sing, rhyme, and play with sounds and words together.
- Word of the Day: You and your child take turns finding a new word, writing its definition, and drawing a picture (if possible) to put up on the fridge. See how often you and your child can correctly use the word of the day during a snack or meal.
- Put pictures from a family trip (or pictures of a family member at different ages) in chronological order.
- Make up stories together (both verbal and written); draw pictures to turn them into books, or make audio recordings.
- Give your child pictures of different facial expressions (could be of animals as well as people), and have him write little word bubbles describing what the person or animal is thinking or feeling at that moment.
- Encourage your child to make his own cartoon strip or mini-magazine.

Understanding Identities

One of the changes that takes place in a young child's brain during this stage is the ability to understand that superficially altering something does not change its true nature. Similar to how as a toddler he learned that objects and people do not disappear when they are out of sight, he will come to understand that changing how somebody looks (for example) does not change who that person is.

Here are some ways to support your child's understanding of identities:

- *Encourage dramatic play.* As children are forming their own sense of identity, they enjoy experimenting with different roles. Having a large Tupperware bin full of costumes, styles of clothes, shoes, and accessories to play with helps your child experience changes in appearance without changing who they (or you, or friends) really are. Face painting is another fun way to do this.

- *Play classification games.* Grouping toys or pictures by similar features is helpful to developing your child's observation and categorization skills. It shifts how he identifies things and understands the associations between them. For example, he could group toys by their size, color, or function, or he could group animals by where they live or what they eat. In so doing, he will realize that a single toy (or person, or profession, etc.) can be identified in multiple different categories.
- *Disguise objects or toys, and play hide-and-seek with them.* This could be a sock hidden by stuffed animals, or a superhero figurine wearing a doll's clothes.
- *Play "opposite" games.* This can be done either verbally or with pictures. You say one thing and your child says the opposite, then switch. For example, you say "big," and your child says "small."
- *Play comparison games.* You can find pictures in books and even online that look *almost* exactly the same, but have a couple of small differences. Give them to your child to examine, and ask if he can spot X number of differences.

FACT

Symbols are largely processed in the left hemisphere of the parietal lobe of the brain.

Using Symbols

The ability to use one thing to symbolize or represent something else is a major cognitive milestone. Signification helps children think about people or objects that are not physically present (such as seeing the number 7 and understanding that it represents a quantity of something), and enhances their imaginations by letting them pretend that people or objects have properties they do not have in real life (such as imagining that a stuffed animal is a baby brother). Such thinking also helps your child understand the relationship between a picture of something (such as a treasure map), and the physical space it represents.

Here are some ways to support your child's understanding of symbols:

- Pretend play is magical for your child, and involves a mental flexibility that you will find refreshing. Accept your child's invitation to imagine with him, and immerse yourself in the impromptu world of pretend play.
- Any and all language activities are helpful to your child as he learns that letters symbolize sounds and that words symbolize people, places, things, actions, and more. Games that reinforce these associations will help him understand how to use and interpret various written symbols.
- Counting and number games will help your child make the association between a word, a physical quantity, and its written symbol. Count everything, point out numbers in the environment, play board games that require pieces to move along a path.
- Maps are incredible tools for developing your child's symbolic understanding. Beginning at about four years old, your child will be increasingly able to connect images from a map to physical space. Especially early on, it will be easier for him to associate symbols on a map to places he knows well, like his bedroom or the backyard.
- Code breakers: Write a word, joke, or tongue twister in some kind of code and help your child decipher what it says. You can use numbers to represent letters, or your child can even create shapes or little designs to represent letters (e.g., A = 1 or A = ^).

Distinguishing Fantasy from Reality

Children are increasingly able to tell the difference between things that are made-up, and things that exist and happen in real life. Although her imagination will remain rich, playful, and flexible, as your child gets older she will become much better at distinguishing fantasy and imagination from reality.

This process does not need to be rushed. This milestone occurs naturally and does not require much effort on your part; however, if you want to gently probe your child's understanding, you can occasionally sprinkle questions like "Does this sort of thing happen in real life? Can that cow *really* fly over the moon?" into your conversations while reading stories or watching cartoons together.

ALERT

The magic of this developmental stage does not last, and to some extent should be protected. Avoid slamming your child's pretend play with questions or comments about "real life," as an overly realistic approach to imaginative play will crush her freedom and flexibility of mind. On the contrary, use this opportunity to quiet your own heavily realistic mind and rediscover your expansive imagination, where *anything* is possible.

Keep in mind that too much realism at this age can backfire. In a child's mind, discovering that the tooth fairy isn't real can quickly snowball into serious doubts about other legendary figures. This can be very tricky ground for parents. Whatever beliefs you want to encourage in your child, prepare yourself for the inevitable conversations about what is real, what isn't, and why you encouraged those beliefs in the first place.

Understanding Cause and Effect

Children are constantly learning how things work, and how they can influence the things, people, and course of events in their lives. "If X happened, what might have caused it? If I do X, what will happen?" This is the foundation for more complex problem-solving as your child gets older.

Here are some ways to support your child's understanding of cause and effect:

- Play detective with your child. Set up a mystery and point her toward clues she can use to reason out and solve it.
- Make up short "What happened?" stories with your child. Give her a statement, and come up with different possible scenarios. For example, if the statement is "A dog ran across the yard," possible causes might be that a snake spooked the dog, or the dog was chasing a squirrel, or (on the more imaginary side) the dog was playing tag with a ghost.

- Draw or create Rube Goldberg machines with your child. Rube Goldberg machines are contraptions or devices that perform a series of physical causes and effects to complete a simple task. For example, a marble rolls down a tube and knocks into a car, which rolls down a ramp and hits a line of dominoes, which fall in an elaborate spiral and end by setting off a mousetrap, which sends a small carrot flying into your gerbil's open cage for lunch. Start simple, be creative, and build from there.
- Teach your child games like checkers and chess. This will help her learn to think ahead, consider possibilities, and develop problem-solving strategies.

Social-Emotional Milestones

The most significant social-emotional developments at this stage involve empathy, animism, and anthropomorphism; playing cooperatively with others; having greater independence; and cultivating a more defined sense of self.

Empathy

Vicariously feeling how other beings feel (both physically and emotionally) is an important skill to have. It helps children put themselves in the shoes of others, and helps them develop a sense of compassion for others. When your child can relate to someone or something else in this way, he will begin taking the needs and well-being of others into consideration as he acts.

Here are some ways to support your child's empathy skills:

- Have your child choose a small plant to take care of in the house, and/or plant a small tree with him in the yard. Have him name the plant, and teach him what he needs to do each day to keep the plant healthy and strong.
- If your family owns a pet, begin giving your child more responsibility in caring for the pet. Depending on the animal, this might mean going for short walks with you and the animal, making sure a water bowl is

full, feeding the animal with your help, or setting aside special play time for the animal.

- As you read, watch, or listen to stories together, ask questions that prompt your child to think from someone else's point of view. For example, "How do you think she feels right now?"

Anthropomorphism

Anthropomorphism means to attribute human characteristics (such as emotions) to animals, nonliving things, or natural phenomena like wind or clouds. This ability goes hand in hand with empathy, and helps children relate to other beings and events. It plays a major role in children's pretend play and imaginations, and is often encountered in stories. Books regularly explore human social roles and relationships through anthropomorphized animals, and can teach your child about values and appropriate behavior in meaningful and indirect ways.

Here are some ways to support your child's anthropomorphic skills:

- Read and discuss stories about animals, inanimate objects, and/or natural phenomena that give these nonhumans human characteristics.
- Ask your child questions about the animals or plants he encounters in stories or in real life—for example, "How does the Giving Tree feel when the boy cuts down her branches? Why?" or "How do you think that ant feels when you shine a magnifying glass on her?"
- When participating in pretend play with your child, you can project different human emotions, reactions, and situations onto baby dolls, action figures, or stuffed animals. Put toys or puppets in circumstances your child might encounter in real life, and through the toys you and your child can explore various social roles, interests, behaviors, emotional reactions, and more.

Cooperative Play

Socialization is a key component of this age range. Where your child previously played alongside other children, during this developmental stage, she will come to interact and play cooperatively with others to achieve mutual goals.

Here are some ways to support your child's cooperative play skills:

- Demonstrate the appropriate language to children who are learning to communicate and resolve potential disputes. On the younger side of this stage, children lack the necessary vocabulary to work out disagreements with words and might react physically instead. Anticipating these struggles and modeling ways to talk are invaluable to young children. For example, if three-year-old Jessica rips a toy out of four-year-old Aidan's hands, immediately return the toy to Aidan and say "Jessica, you have to ask. Say: Aidan, can I please have that toy when you're done?" (Jessica will repeat you). It's important to emphasize *when you're done*, so Aidan understands that he doesn't have to give away the toy at that moment. When he agrees, reinforce it by asking him, "So Aidan, who are you giving that toy to when you're finished?" and do some combination of looking at, pointing to, and saying Jessica's name. Then promptly redirect Jessica to another toy or activity so she doesn't fixate.
- Do group games or activities that require teamwork and cooperation. By facilitating activities that ask your child to work with others (like building a fort or working as a team to build a giant block castle), she will learn to communicate, listen, and compromise effectively.
- Create a team atmosphere at home, and invite your child to participate and pitch in however she can. This could mean helping you cook dinner, putting dishes into the dishwasher, helping you fold clothes while you talk or watch a show together, and much more.

Greater Independence

It is a big deal for children to be able to do things for themselves. When a child learns how to pour her own milk, tie her own shoes, or master any number of new skills, it is very exciting. It teaches your child that she is intelligent and capable, and encourages her to take new risks. The more you can nurture her independence, the more self-sufficient and confident she will become.

Sometimes nurturing your child's independence requires patience. The more often you can step back, be patient, and encourage him to do things for himself, even when you might be in a rush, the more rewarding his achievements will be. Even minor accomplishments such as learning to open the door can mean a great deal to a child.

The best ways to support your child's independence are to give her new responsibilities that show you trust her and count on her as part of the family team; show respect for what she can already do; give praise for specific actions and behaviors (e.g., "Nice job controlling that marker!" or "I'm proud of how you used your words"); and provide encouragement in the face of difficult tasks (e.g., "I know you can do this," or "Let's figure this out together").

Avoid giving generalized praise like "Good job!" To reinforce particular actions, skills, and behaviors, your praise must be specific. Instead of making a bland comment about liking something ("I like the picture you drew"), point out exactly what caught your attention ("Look at all the bright colors you chose." This gives your child actual feedback, and focuses her attention on a specific skill or behavior instead of on whether or not you "liked" it.

CHAPTER 11

Practicing Mindfulness with Children (Three to Nine Years)

As your kids progress through childhood, you begin to catch glimpses of who they may be as adults. Childhood is an exciting time in which possibilities seem to expand nearly every day. By late childhood, your child will have developed considerable dexterity and motor control, and will be able to do many things for himself. His growing independence can feel like a mixed blessing. While it is a tremendous source of pride to many parents, your child's ability to meet his own needs also fundamentally changes your relationship.

Your child's ever-growing ability to communicate with you is also very exciting. Kids possess an innate curiosity about the world, which instigates many questions and conversations. You, as the parent, will usually be your child's go-to person for information about anything and everything. Children are also exposed to a wealth of new ideas through school, and discussing what your child learns each day can be a great source of joy for you both.

As your child begins providing for some of his own needs, it is natural to mourn the change in your relationship and it can sometimes be challenging to find new ways to connect. Rest assured that your child still needs you and will continue to need you throughout his life; it is just that what he needs from you will change over time.

The Challenges

Childhood carries many challenges for you as well as your child. Children are very high-energy creatures who need to move regularly. As their strength increases during this stage, children are able to take many more physical risks, but their judgment and sense of safety do not develop at the same rate as their bodies. This can lead to lots of bruises and scabs, and hopefully not too many trips to the emergency room!

Children are also very opinionated and tend not to be shy about sharing those opinions. At this stage they have a growing sense of self, but still struggle with the idea that other people are just like them and deserve the same amount of respect. This can manifest as selfishness and a lack of consideration for the feelings of others. One of the great challenges of parenting children is helping them learn to consider how their behavior impacts others.

Finally, children are very inconsistent. Their abilities can vary on a daily basis and it can be infuriating for a parent when a child cannot do something today that he did perfectly well yesterday. Knowing that this is a natural part of their development can help to some extent, but you may still struggle to keep your patience.

Failure

Another aspect of this inconsistency is failure. Children are great experimentalists and are constantly pushing limits, testing boundaries, and trying new (and occasionally foolish) things. It can be very tempting for parents to attempt to intervene at every turn, trying to protect their child from failure, but it is a mistake to do so. Every person must learn some lessons through experience, and being overprotective does not teach your child how to make competent decisions.

QUESTION

How do I know when to intervene and when to let my child fail?
The most important guideline is physical safety. If your child is in harm's way or her actions pose a significant risk to herself or to another, then of course you should intervene. However, short of that, it is really a judgment call on your part. Try to remember that you need to equip your child to make decisions for herself.

Although it can be excruciating, it is sometimes necessary to stand back and watch your child fail in ways both large and small. Harder still is watching your child deal with disappointment. It can be helpful to try to remember that disappointment is an inevitable part of life, and that your job as a parent is to help your child to be prepared to deal with the world as it actually is. No matter what, remember that you will be there to support your child as she learns some of the difficult and outright painful lessons every person must learn at some point.

How Mindfulness Can Help Through Fantasy Play

Earlier childhood is marked by fantastic play that gradually gives way to more concrete forms of play. Regardless of whether the fantasy is of slaying dragons or winning the World Series, it can be a powerful practice to participate in your child's fantasy life. Doing so benefits you both by strengthening the relationship between you; however, it is particularly beneficial to the child, as it allows you to dialogue with him through the fantasy play and help him learn safety, social-emotional skills, and appropriate limits to his behavior.

To participate in your child's fantasy play, you first need to surrender your control over what happens in the fantasy. Of course you should continue to use your adult mind to set appropriate limits and ensure your child's safety, but you must also relinquish the leadership role that you usually play as parent. Instead, practice a radical form of acceptance in which your child is the one who gets to set the stage and define the action.

Getting Into the Game

Begin by approaching your child and inviting him to play (or by accepting as often as possible when your child invites you). If he is already suited up for an adventure, ask him if you can join. Sometimes he might say no. Try not to take it personally; he is establishing his own separate identity, after all.

ALERT

When your child invites you to play, it is a very special thing. It is also an inherently vulnerable place for your child. Your life as a parent is very stressful and you have to juggle many demands, so it can be tempting to use the time you get from your child playing independently for other things, whether they are jobs that need doing or just to relax. Try to recognize the opportunity your child is giving you. If you turn her down often, it won't be long before she stops asking.

When he says yes, ask him to describe what is going on. "Who are they? Who are you? What are you trying to do?" Sometimes your child's responses may be illogical or nonsensical, but try to accept them anyway. Resist any adultlike urge to impose rational order to what's happening. Notice the reactions of your adult mind to what your child says and the games you play together. Be honest with yourself about the thoughts that come up for you as you play together, but keep them to yourself. Children can be very prone to embarassment, so don't be negative about the fantasy you are sharing. Remember, it isn't really about the fantasy itself, but rather the different roles a child can try on through fantasy. It is just another form of experimentation.

Learning Through Questions

Fantasy play is ripe with opportunities to teach your child, and this is done most effectively through questions. Try to stay "in character" when asking your child questions, maintaining the illusion of the fantasy. You will find that there is very little you can't do from within the game if you are playful enough. If your child is about to steal some treasure from another child (who may or may not be participating in the fantasy), you can get him to pause and reconsider his actions by asking "How do you think so-and-so will feel if you steal their treasure?" If your child is about to jump from a place that is too high to do so safely, caution and redirect him by saying "Wait, Captain Blackbeard, that cliff is too high! There must be another way down, what can you see from up there?" or perhaps "I see guards down below. We need to find another way to sneak past them." Be creative and have fun!

How Mindfulness Can Help You Nurture Your Child's Independence

It is quite common to mourn the loss of these forms of connection as your child grows more and more independent, and it can be very helpful to have a way of working with those emotions directly.

Bear in mind that it is a parent's job to prepare his or her child for adulthood. This means cultivating independence and autonomy. Next, it is critical to own your multitude of feelings about your child growing up. While you may mourn the fact that she can now dress herself, your girl is rightly proud of her accomplishment and wants you to be proud as well. Recognize that any feelings of loss you experience are not your child's responsibility, but your own.

The first step in working with these feelings is to acknowledge them. You may not immediately recognize them, but there are signs that can clue you in that you may be being "overly helpful" to your child. Generally speaking, the rule of thumb is this: are you doing something for your child, or are you helping her learn to do it for herself (even if she struggles)? Whenever you are doing things *for* your child, check in with yourself. Why are you doing it instead of your child? If it is something she cannot do for physical or safety reasons, then there is nothing to worry about. However, if it is something within your child's scope of ability, really ask yourself why you feel the need to do it for her. Is it in your child's best interest that you do it for her, or would she learn more from doing it for herself?

ALERT

Try to be clear about whose feelings belong to whom. It is only natural that your feelings about and for your child are very strong. It is very important for you to be clear that this is your experience and the feelings that come up are your responsibility, not your child's. Take responsibility for your feelings about your child growing up and don't make them issues for your kids.

Working with Your Feelings

It is important to take time to attend to yourself when you find yourself getting stuck like this. You must give yourself the time and emotional space to experience these feelings; otherwise they will continue to have power over you and may interfere with you being the parent you want to be.

Try sitting comfortably and breathing evenly and deeply. Let your body find a natural rhythm. Scan your body for tension and try to draw your breath into the tight places, one at a time. Now, turn your thoughts toward your child and the specific activity that has you stuck. Visualize what you did together (such as you zipping her coat for her, perhaps against her will), and open yourself up to whatever feelings come up. Give each feeling space to express itself regardless of whether it is positive or negative. As new feelings arise, let them come in too. What thoughts and feelings passed through you when you decided to zip up your child's coat instead of letting her do it for herself? How did your child respond when you did it? What did it mean to you? Do not judge the thoughts and feelings that come up, just let them arise and fall at their own pace. All you need to do is notice.

Now, when you are ready, imagine your child doing this particular activity for herself. Imagine yourself as a fly on the wall, just watching. Notice the feelings that come up as you watch her struggle, unable to successfully zip her own coat. Give each thought and feeling some space as they arise, witnessing your child's frustration. What do you notice?

Now imagine your child successfully accomplishing the task at hand, and finally zipping her coat all by herself. How does your child feel when she does this? What expression is on her face? What does she say? Imagine she comes running up to you to share her triumph. How do you respond? Can you share in her feelings of pride? Can you feel your own sense of pride in having raised a child who can do this for herself?

QUESTION

It is impossible for me to find quiet time to do this. Is there something I can do without having to put everything else down to do it?
Yes, of course. You can use the same basic process for this or any other exercise while you continue through the activity of your day. In fact, this is ultimately the goal: To be able to practice mindfulness in the midst of activity. Taking some quiet time helps to get the practice down, especially in the beginning, but you can do it anytime.

How Mindfulness Can Help You Support Problem-Solving Skills

When you realize that you will not always be there to supervise your child, it can be easier to focus on helping him develop his own good judgment and problem-solving skills. One of the most powerful ways to do this is through guided problem solving.

In guided problem solving, you take the time to talk through a situation with your child and engage his native intelligence in coming to a resolution (instead of just telling him what to do). This is an incredibly important method of teaching mindfulness to your child as well, as he will literally learn what to be mindful of by having you draw things to his attention. This is one of the best ways to show him what to take into consideration when resolving a particular issue. Moreover, your child will also learn mindful consideration itself as a process by gradually internalizing the conversations that you guide him through over time.

Making Contact

You have two choices when it comes to correcting your child's behavior: prevention or intervention. In intervention, your child has already begun to act out or do something inappropriate and you are engaging them to stop the behavior. In prevention, you have anticipated your child's negative behavior and move to take action that will redirect your child and prevent the negative behavior.

Regardless of which situation you find yourself in, you will need to make contact with your child. Do so by calling their attention to you, but be careful of your tone of voice, particularly if you are acting to prevent a behavior. Children are very emotionally sensitive and will react to the emotion you communicate in your voice very quickly. This will set the tone for whatever happens next, so you want to try to engage your child as an ally as this will make your child more receptive to whatever you have to say. In this interaction, try not to assume the worst about your child's behavior and the motivations behind it. Rather, try to tap into his or her own good judgment. Whenever possible, make it a positive learning experience or a teachable moment.

Stopping the Behavior

For example, if five-year-old Billy looks like he is about to knock over his older sister's block castle, distract him by asking, "Hey Billy, what are you doing?" (Physical proximity helps; yelling this across the room is not ideal, but work with whatever the situation calls for.) Help Billy identify what he wanted or was trying to do; if he avoids your gaze and does not answer, kneel down and say, "I noticed you staring at your sister's block castle. Would you like to build one of your own?" This is one way to redirect Billy's focus. Perhaps he feels jealous, needs attention, or maybe he just impulsively wants to destroy something. Either way, this question forces him to think about what he is doing.

If Billy says no to building a block castle of his own, you might ask him, "Were you thinking about knocking your sister's castle down?" It is okay to smile as you say this, because Billy has not done anything wrong yet and this will likely help him to feel safe in telling you the truth. When he replies, "Yes," you can simultaneously normalize his impulse to knock something down while helping him to consider the consequences of doing so. "Billy, I totally understand wanting to knock down a castle. Sometimes I like to knock stuff down too—it can be really fun! There's only one problem here. Can you guess what that problem is?"

ALERT

Tone of voice is absolutely critical whenever you speak to your child, regardless of their age. Tone is one of the easiest things to let slip when you are tired or dealing with stress. Children attune to their parent's emotions very early on in life and remain sensitive to them throughout. Your tone can dramatically impact how your child understands what you say, what you mean, and how he responds to you. Sometimes children's perception is even clearer than your own, so notice how your child reacts when you first start to speak; it may show you something about what you're putting out there.

This gives Billy the chance to think about and articulate why knocking down his older sister's castle may not be the best idea. Chances are, he will know what the problem is right away and say so. (If not, you can always ask, "Whose castle is that?").

Redirecting

"Exactly, you nailed it. How do you think your sister will feel if you destroy the castle she worked so hard to build?" Here, Billy may say something like "Bad" or "Angry." Feel free to expand this, which reinforces more vocabulary and nuance. "Yes, you're right. I think she'd be pretty angry and hurt if her brother destroyed something she cares about. Would you like it if she kicked down something that *you* built?" (Of course he'll answer no). "Yes Billy, I wouldn't like it either. I have an idea, though. If you want to knock something down, what can we do about that?"

Not only does this help Billy consider his sister's feelings, it helps him put himself in her shoes. Then you reinforce the lesson and empathize with Billy by adding that you wouldn't like it either. By ending with an open-ended question about what else Billy can do if he wants to knock something down, he now has a chance to come up with other ideas while receiving positive attention from you for doing so. You might even suggest building a bunch of small buildings together, and pretending that he is Godzilla—a good distance away from his sister's castle.

ESSENTIAL

One of the biggest challenges when guiding your child to consider another person's feelings is leaving guilt and blame out of the conversation. The way you talk to her has as much to do with this as what you actually say. Try not to sound accusative or angry; instead, try to engage her natural curiosity and consideration. Do your best to keep it light, despite how frustrated or angry you may feel.

Guiding the conversation in this way takes practice, and will help your child think through his actions in new ways. Feel free to ask questions like, "Did you think about this?" to help him consider other possibilities or perspectives. By gently guiding your child in such a way, you will help him come to learn how to empathize with others, how to better manage his impulses, and how to think through the likely consequences of his actions. Try to facilitate these types of preventative discussions so that your child discovers for himself what the best course of action is.

If it is a matter of intervening in an unwanted behavior (such as Billy destroying his older sister's castle before you could stop him), part of the conversation's resolution should include asking him, "What can you do the next time you start feeling angry/jealous/like you want to knock something down?" If Billy doesn't say it himself, make sure to mention that he can always ask an adult for help or attention.

The skillfulness in guided problem solving comes from teaching your child to consider things for himself instead of just telling him what and what not to do. When a child responds only to the demands of an adult (instead of practicing how to think and choose for himself), he is engaging an external locus of control. This means he is only doing things in a particular way because he was told to; this happens when a child just seeks approval or is afraid of reprisal. By guiding your child through the problem-solving process, you are helping him establish an internal locus of control guided by an internalized value system. That is the ultimate goal.

When not closely supervised, children with a strongly externalized locus of control often behave unpredictably, are more prone to inappropriate behavior, and may take unnecessary and dangerous risks. This is usually a form of rebellion against adults always telling them what to do instead of empowering and guiding them to make healthy decisions for themselves. By guiding your child through the problem-solving process and helping him use his own faculties to evaluate a problem and decide how to act, you promote an internalized locus of control. Children who internalize this way of considering situations before they act are much more likely to do the right thing when they are by themselves or with friends.

CHAPTER 12

Preadolescence, Adolescence, and Beyond

Adolescence is a time of transformation as children begin to make the transition from childhood to adulthood. The decade from age ten to age twenty is characterized by rapid changes in both the body and the brain, making for famously volatile personalities and difficult interactions, both at home and out in the world.

Children at this stage of development require a great deal of support, but are often much more loath to accept that support, making a parent's job all the harder. By better understanding the adolescent experience as well as the many major developmental changes of this time, parents can become much better equipped to support their adolescent's emerging independence and weather the many storms that come with these changes.

Through the Eyes of Adolescents

In early adolescence, the preteen or "tween" years, children still have much of the exuberant energy of the earlier stages of childhood but have a vastly expanded social consciousness. Fully aware of themselves as distinct individuals, early adolescents' attention moves toward social groups and group-based identities. Children at this stage become famously cliquish, forming close groups of friends and distinguishing themselves from other groups. This is an important part of their identity formation.

Overview

Puberty marks the beginning of the second most rapid stage of growth in human life and typically begins between the ages of twelve and thirteen, although it can arrive earlier or later for some kids. At the onset of puberty, there is a massive neurological bloom in which millions of new connections are formed in the brain. These connections begin to get pared down almost immediately after flowering. Those that are used regularly persist, strengthen, and accelerate while those that are not used fade. Much of the adolescent experience is defined by this neurological bloom and the subsequent challenge of learning how to coordinate all of these new faculties of the mind.

ALERT

Adolescents of almost any age are inconsistent in their behavior and performance. It often seems that they cannot do today what was quite easy for them yesterday. This is a natural part of the process as they learn to coordinate activities across their brain.

With puberty comes the emergence of stronger sexual awareness and urges. Adolescent children begin to take an interest in romantic partners and begin to explore their sexual identities. Puberty also brings with it the final stage of physical maturation. Children's bodies rapidly grow into their adult forms and develop adult sexual characteristics.

With the physical growth of the body comes the capacity for independence: Whereas earlier in childhood they could not physically provide for many of their own personal needs, adolescents become capable of doing so, at least in theory. With this often come attempts at actualizing their independence. It is quite normal for teenagers to begin branching out, putting greater emphasis on social relationships as opposed to familial ones. Whereas a child might previously have been glad to receive a parent's help or support, teens are often hostile to their caregivers.

What Are Teens Learning about Themselves?

As the teen years progress, individuals become more aware of others as selves and often become hypersensitive to the judgments of others. Teens also develop a more sophisticated sense of identity and begin to grapple with the question of who they want to be in the world. With this inevitably comes a certain degree of confusion and experimentation, particularly in outward appearances. Teenagers' fashion choices often change dramatically and quickly, sometimes in ways that can be quite startling to parents.

As identity is one of the primary issues with which teenagers struggle, they are inevitably narcissistic to a certain degree. This can manifest itself in apparent selfishness or self-centeredness, a disregard for the feelings of others, particularly parents or other family members, and a considerable degree of hyperemotionalism.

Teens are ultimately on a cusp: they are almost adults, but not quite. They have all of the necessary pieces, but struggle to get them working together successfully. They look forward to an autonomy and independence in the future that they cannot yet have. For many teens, this often leads to strong experiences of frustration and of being overwhelmed.

Part of the challenge of raising adolescents is that they are developing their own independence and are so often much less engaged with or responsive to their parents. The stress on parents is only exacerbated by the fact that adolescents increasingly live their lives outside of their parent's field of view and the risks that they are capable of taking can carry much more serious consequences.

FACT

Slang is a subset of language that becomes part of adolescents' identity formation as they identify with particular groups. Slang sets various groups apart, and is used as a form of expression. This is true for differentiating social cliques within a generation, as well as being a generational marker.

Physical Milestones

Adolescence begins at puberty when the child's body begins its final leap forward into physical adulthood. While the brain may lag somewhat, adolescents' bodies rapidly acquire their adult characteristics and, with this, the ability to provide for themselves. Adolescents no longer need help tying their shoes or pouring milk into their cereal bowls. Their gross and fine motor skills are fully developed and they gradually take on more adult responsibilities, such as food preparation, self-care, shopping, and, eventually, driving.

With puberty comes sexual maturity. Girls will experience their first menstrual cycle sometimes as early as age nine, and both genders will develop mature sexual characteristics. With this sexual development comes a natural degree of sexual curiosity and interest in romantic partners. This is also the time in life when many individuals come to recognize their sexual preferences, be they heterosexual or homosexual.

Parental Control

For parents, adolescence can be a particularly scary time, as your child is physically fully capable, but she has yet to reach her full maturity. It is only natural to be concerned about her safety and the choices she makes, particularly as pertains to sexuality. Enforcing rules, limits, and boundaries often becomes substantially more difficult, as teenage children are capable of defiance in ways that younger children are not.

When parenting adolescents, you must recognize that whether you like it or not, you have completely lost your ability to control your child. This is not to say that you don't still have substantial leverage; however, parents of teens must make a mental shift and increasingly rely on dialogue with their young adults. Your goal is no longer to control them, but rather to maintain an ongoing conversation with them. This also means that you will have to occasionally accept that they will make decisions you disagree with. It helps to maintain focus on absolute limits, such as personal safety.

Sexual Development

Particularly as it pertains to your child's sexual development, this may put you in an uncomfortable position. It is difficult to know how to respond when your adolescent wants to discuss sexuality, which may bring up uncomfortable and unresolved feelings for you.

On the other hand, it is difficult when you know the "sex talk" needs to happen and your teen is not interested in discussing it with you. Regardless, it is totally appropriate and indeed well-advised for you to open this dialogue with your young adult when she appears ready for you to do so. She may begin to approach you with questions, or you may notice that she has passed a particular milestone, such as beginning menstruation. (The voice change or growth of facial hair is an equivalent marker in boys).

This first conversation should cover the basics and leave an open door for future discussion. Most parents agree that as uncomfortable as discussing sex with your teen can be, you would rather have your kids coming to you than seeking information from who knows who else.

When you do discuss these topics, recognize that they are at least as raw and sensitive for your child as they are for you, and try to be respectful. Your teen will cue you about what she needs and how far to go. Particularly if she comes to you with a question about sexuality, it is important to notice not only her intense vulnerability in doing so, but also the enormous amount of trust she is putting in you. Try to take it as an honor, and leave her feeling glad that she came to you and that she can do so again in the future.

Supporting Adolescent Physical Development

Often the biggest challenge for parents as their child matures into adolescence is to step back and let him figure things out for himself. You have developed a close relationship with your child over many years, and much of this closeness has come from doing things together or from your doing things *for* him.

As children grow into adulthood, their capabilities expand and they become able to provide more and more for themselves. This is totally natural and appropriate, but can be challenging for parents, as you are understandably reluctant to change the established patterns of behavior and control that have become comfortable.

Shifting Responsibilities

When parenting adolescent children, try to notice the things you do for them and identify tasks that they may be able to take on for themselves. Perhaps this is waking up with an alarm clock, preparing their own breakfast, or folding their own laundry. Look for things that are within your child's grasp and are appropriate for him to take responsibility for.

This change in your relationship can be challenging for your child, too. He has also become comfortable with certain patterns of behavior with you, and is accustomed to the closeness and other benefits that this brings. A sudden change can be as jarring for him. Therefore, it is critical that you have a discussion about whatever changes you want to make. Let your child know what will change, what you expect of him, and why. Be particularly careful to emphasize that this is part of the process of growing up, and does not mean you love him any less. It is just a natural part of becoming an adult.

The Importance of Dialogue

Recognize that having a conversation about shifting appropriate responsibilities to your teen is an important part of that shifting process. When your child was younger, he was not capable of participating in conversations like these and so you made decisions for him independently. That was part of your role as a parent, but a parent's role changes as his or her child grows and changes. Engaging your child collaboratively is a key skill to parenting older children.

Cognitive Milestones

At the onset of puberty in pre- or early adolescence, there is a massive neurological bloom of new connections across the brain. These connections bring with them the capacity for new kinds of thought, particularly in the areas of abstract reasoning and the ability to understand more complex nuances of cause and effect. These new abilities are a result of being able to draw on information from across the brain, but doing so remains a challenge throughout adolescence and well into young adulthood. Much of the adolescent experience is defined by the ongoing development of the brain, and the many challenges in learning how to use the powerful new tools it provides.

How the Brain Connects

After the initial neurological bloom of new connections across the brain, things begin to change. The connections that appear early in adolescence almost immediately begin to pare down as the brain seeks efficiency. Neural connections that are not used will wither and die away, while those that are used regularly persist.

The connections that are used regularly survive and will continue to strengthen and accelerate throughout adolescence and the twenties. Myelin sheaths, or the layers of fat along nerve axons that can accelerate nerve signals up to one hundred times, develop in direct response to their regularity of use. The pathways in the brain that are used consistently will develop more myelin, and the unused connections from that initial bloom will die out.

The development of myelin generally follows a pattern in the brain, going from the bottom of the brain up and from the back to the front. This is the final stage in the physical development of the brain, a process that continues well into the twenties and is not fully complete until about age thirty.

Brain Development and Teen Behavior

Some of the last parts of the brain to fully develop are those most responsible for the kinds of reasoning that adolescents are most famously bad at, such as risk assessment and impulse control. The part of the brain most involved in these kinds of calculations, the prefrontal cortex, is one of the very last to develop.

FACT

Adolescents need about nine hours of sleep each night for their brains and bodies to function at their best. Lack of sleep is a chronic problem for teenagers, with one study finding that only 15 percent of teens polled got eight and a half hours of sleep each night. Lack of sleep limits an adolescent's memory and ability to listen, concentrate, and problem-solve.

Also slow to develop in the adolescent brain is the corpus callosum, a veritable information superhighway in the brain that carries connections between almost every brain region. The lag in the development of these two areas goes a long way toward explaining the noted inconsistency in adolescent behavior and performance. As a parent, it is helpful to recognize that there are very real biological reasons behind the inconsistencies in your teen's behavior.

Supporting Adolescent Cognitive Development

The flowering of neurological connections in early adolescence provides a ripe opportunity for every child to cultivate her skills and talents. This is a time when it is totally appropriate to encourage your child's exploration of her various interests. This may mean taking on new hobbies, picking up an instrument or two, or engaging in the arts.

What You Can Do

Parents can support this development by encouraging their child's interests and providing opportunities to discover new things. Outings to museums, historical sites, or performances are great ways to encourage your adolescent in her growth and development.

The challenge to you as a parent is to help make these outings interesting and enjoyable to your child by engaging with her, not just expecting your teen to find things interesting because you believe them to be inherently so.

The Most Important Thing

As a parent, the single most important thing you can do to support your adolescent's cognitive development is to encourage your teen to be active and get involved in the world. It is very easy for teens to isolate themselves in certain ways. Video games, TV, cellphones, and the Internet offer ample distractions that can be all the more tempting for teenagers because of the high levels of stimulation these media provide. Many of these activities also invite adolescents into fantasy worlds of ever-increasing depth where teens may be able to exercise choices that they do not have in the real world.

Encourage your teen to get involved in extracurricular activities of any type. It is practically certain that your teenager will have her own ideas about what she wants to do, be it academics, athletics, performance, or service work of some kind. All of these activities bring tremendous benefits for teenagers. As a parent, you should bear in mind that it matters less what your teen does than that she get involved and be somehow active in the world at large.

Social-Emotional Milestones

Adolescence is ripe with many changes in how young people see themselves and the world around them. Continued development of the adolescent brain allows for enhanced understanding of complex social relationships, social roles, and social groups. Teens are newly aware of the opinions of others about them and are often very sensitive to these perceived judgments.

Identity

One of the key issues for teens is identity: "Who am I?" and "Who do I want to be?" Teens spend much time grappling with these questions both inwardly and outwardly as they try on different roles and identities, change fashions, identify with different social groups or cliques, and fantasize about their future as independent adults. It is common to see sometimes dramatic changes in identity signifiers (such as fashion or media preferences) as teens experiment with their identity.

Because identity is so central to adolescent psychological development, a certain degree of narcissism on the part of all adolescents is both normal and developmentally appropriate. Teens' first psychological priority is figuring out who they are in the world, a question that lends itself naturally to a self-focused attitude.

Teen Sensitivity

Teens are notably emotionally sensitive. This is a natural part of their development and a result of the complexity of their emotional experiences. Your teen's emotional life remains subject to the influence of the complex hormonal changes that are occurring within his body, even long after the outward changes of puberty have completed.

ESSENTIAL

Having a support network makes a big difference. When parents have a community in which they can ask questions, vent frustrations, share stories, and spend time with other parents who are experiencing similar joys and challenges, the joys and difficulties of parenthood become normalized and parents realize they don't have to do it all alone.

Adolescents are still in the process of developing their own emotional self-awareness and often struggle to find the vocabulary to communicate about their experience of the world. This on top of crazy hormonal changes, a forming identity, and a social vulnerability and turbulence unlike any they have previously experienced can understandably lead to emotional reactivity and sensitivity.

The emotional intensity and volatility of teenagers can be particularly challenging for parents. It is often hard to know what to do when you see your adolescent in the throes of emotional struggle. Often, the most appropriate thing to do is to wait for your adolescent to approach you. While observation and direct intervention is appropriate for younger children, as your child grows it is appropriate to let him take more responsibility for reaching out to you.

ESSENTIAL

If you make a mistake, the best thing you can do is admit it and apologize to your teen. This shows respect and acknowledges that you are not perfect either. Atoning for a mistake models the kind of responsibility you want your teen to take for her actions, and can serve to bring you closer together.

When you do reach out to your teen, do so as gently and warmly as possible. Should you have a concern, it is often appropriate to share an observation that has aroused that concern as a way of opening the door to a larger conversation.

Supporting Adolescent Social-Emotional Development

As your child progresses through her development, you have less and less direct control over her as a parent. This becomes particularly clear in adolescence when your child begins to develop fully functional independence. At this point your influence over her is directly proportional to the strength of your relationship, so it is well advised for parents to put the relationship first.

ALERT

Whatever boundaries or rules you have set in place with your young adult, it is imperative to follow through on the agreed-upon consequences. Not following through on consequences to mistaken behavior undermines your position as parent and teaches your teen that he can do whatever he wants.

Setting Boundaries

Putting the relationship first does not mean letting your adolescent get away with anything she wants, or backing away from confrontations or disputes. On the contrary, it is all the more important that you share your voice, but you must learn to do so differently than you did when your child was younger. You are no longer in a position to dictate to your child, and instead must become comfortable and adept at engaging her in conversation and consideration.

The Shift Away from Family

A particularly difficult aspect of parenting adolescents is seeing their focus shift away from you and the family and toward their social lives. Adolescents are notably involved in their social relationships and are often embroiled in social dramas, be it as a participant or as a support to a friend. Try to bear in mind that this shift in their relationship priorities (social over familial) is actually natural and appropriate.

There is, in fact, an evolutionary origin to this shift in relationship priorities. The longevity of modern humans is a very recent development, and throughout most of human history life expectancy only ran into the late twenties or early thirties. Therefore, historically speaking, adolescents could not rely on their parental relationships to support them in adulthood. They needed to seek out their own social networks and supports, completely independent of their parents.

Although parents today often live well into their seventies and beyond, it remains appropriate for teens to seek out and develop their own social networks.

Mindfulness Exercises for Adolescence

One of the greatest challenges of parenting adolescents is backing off and letting them take more responsibility for their own lives and solving their own problems. This can be stressful for parents, as it often puts you in the position of having to watch your child suffer.

Self-Care Mindfulness

It is very easy for parents of teens to worry about the future. Based on a combination of your own experiences and your concern for your child, you may often find yourself telling anxiety-based stories about what might happen. If you try to engage your teen from this place, he is likely to be less than grateful, and perhaps even hostile. It can be very helpful to have a way of attending directly to your own concerns and fears about your adolescent before engaging with him. Here is a technique that can help:

1. Begin by identifying a worry or concern you have about your teenager.
2. Think about what you have seen that gave rise to this worry. What was it that got your attention? Why do you take this as cause for concern? Be particularly sensitive to any associations you may make between what is happening for your teen and things that happened in your own life. It is very easy for parents to relive challenges they faced in their own lives when similar things come up for their children.
3. Try to identify specifically what you think will happen to your child. What are you afraid of? Let yourself tell this story for a while. As you play it out in your mind, notice what other thoughts arise. Are there any sensations in your body that come up? Where do you feel them?
4. Now sit with these thoughts and sensations for a while, breathing deliberately with them. Try to recognize them as just stories. You are not trying to dismiss them, just to put them in the proper context. When you are ready, take three deep breaths and move on.

The purpose of this practice is not to let go of any thoughts or fears you may have, but rather to contextualize them more appropriately so that you can be there for your child as he needs you. When you are gripped by your own fears for your child and the stories you tell based on those fears, any attempt to engage your teen will be colored by that emotional cloud. What you say to your teenager will be driven by these fears, and you will act in a way that focuses on your own concerns instead of attending to what he is dealing with. This practice can help you to be more available to your teen through almost any circumstance.

ESSENTIAL

Rites of passage are common across cultures. They are ceremonies of one sort or another that acknowledge a particular transition in a person's life, marking a new societal role. A common rite of passage occurs when children reach adolescence, and helps to facilitate a change in personal behavior and public status.

Active Listening

It can be very difficult for parents to really listen to their adolescent children. Often, when you engage your adolescent, you can be completely overwhelmed. Adolescents regularly talk very fast and with great intensity. It can be hard to keep up with all the people involved and their relationships, let alone the slang and other language your teen may use. Throughout, it can be very tempting to offer solutions to your teen's problems, and then you are left dumbfounded when his frustration boils over and he lashes out at you. To really be there for your adolescent you need to practice active listening with him, and then deal separately with anything that may come up in your own mind as you do so.

Whenever you are listening to your teen, give him your full attention. Stop doing anything else and use your body language to help create a warm and safe space for him to share. As he begins to talk, anchor yourself with your core practice. Breathe deeply and deliberately. Listen intently to what he says as he speaks, and notice the way that he expresses himself. You may not be able to follow the cast of characters involved, and may also have trouble keeping up with exactly what happened, but these are just details. Remember that the most important piece of this interaction is your presence.

By listening intently, whether or not you fully understand what is going on and why, you give your teen an opportunity to vent some of his emotions and process events for himself. Do not interrupt him; just try to let him talk. Resist the temptation to offer advice unless he explicitly asks for it. The purpose of this exercise is to be a sounding board for him, letting him express his feelings about a situation and explore it in his own mind. He will figure out for himself what he needs to do about it, and this may include asking for your help—but it very well may not. Either way, you can support him with your presence as he sorts things out.

CHAPTER 13

Teaching Your Child Mindfulness

Parents should not teach mindfulness in the same way that a subject is taught in school. Your child will learn mindfulness primarily through the way you model mindfulness in your own life, and secondly through conversations with you about circumstances as they arise, and different ways to navigate them. This chapter presents a basic framework for engaging your child in these conversations, and then will explore specific aspects of mindfulness and how to apply the framework in those situations.

The Framework for Teaching Emotional Mindfulness

The following four-step framework is helpful to parents who want to nurture emotional mindfulness in children.

Step One: Seize Opportune Moments

As with most instruction you want to give your children, mindfulness is most effectively taught in context. Sitting your child down and "trying to teach her mindfulness" is not likely to be successful. You must wait for opportune teaching moments.

Begin by mindfully noticing the qualities and habits of your child. You already know her quite well, and can probably tell when she is feeling exuberant, self-important, or perhaps sensitive for some reason. Look for signs that your child either is experiencing or is about to experience an emotional reaction to a situation. Depending on the nature of your child's emotional reaction (e.g., angry, sad, embarrassed), common signs might include:

- Has withdrawn into herself
- Is suddenly quiet or loud
- Avoids eye contact
- Frowns
- Glares
- Clenches fists
- Face flushes
- Eyes tear
- Arms are crossed in front of body
- Turns away from others

FACT

Body language is another way that all people communicate. When paying attention to what someone is saying, being mindful of his body language (e.g., how he is holding himself, where his arms are, what he is doing with his hands, what subtle facial expressions you notice) will give you a subtext for what he is saying.

Step Two: Make Contact

After you have identified that your child is having an emotional reaction to another child, your next job is to intervene and establish contact. The first priority is to ensure the safety of everyone involved. Particularly if your child has just acted out by redirecting frustration at a playmate, it may actually be more appropriate to remove her from the spotlight and attend to the other child first. This is absolutely fine. Reconnect with your child afterward, perhaps by taking her aside or to someplace more private.

ALERT

Remember that one of the most important things in your child's life is your attention. Whatever behaviors you give your attention to will be reinforced, so choose carefully when and how you give it and never be afraid to attend first to the child who got hurt (be it physically or emotionally).

Step Three: Start a Conversation

Once you have engaged your child and created a safe space for her, you want to begin a conversation about what just happened. If she has just acted out, avoid the temptation to ask why. She almost certainly will not be able to answer this question and is likely to feel overwhelmed and only retreat further into herself.

Instead, identify what just happened:

- If your child acted out, begin by asking her to tell you what happened from her point of view.
- Help your child identify with the experience of the person she acted out toward. This might require bringing in the other child and hearing his point of view.
- If you saw what took place, share what you observed from your point of view.

Step Four: Wrap Up and Move On

Regardless of how responsive your child is to the conversation or how much or little she participates, be confident that she is learning immensely from the way in which you respond. Give her plenty of space to reflect during the conversation. You are responsible for maintaining an atmosphere of calm and safety by remaining steady and helping the children to remain emotionally steady as well.

Once you all have had an opportunity to share what happened from your own points of view, begin moving the conversation toward a resolution by asking, "What can you do differently the next time you feel X?" or ". . . the next time your friend does/says X?"

This facilitates a conversation about how your child (and the other child) can handle these emotions and situations more constructively in the future, and helps the kids brainstorm better ways of managing their emotions under frustrating circumstances.

Internal Awareness

One of the most important aspects of mindfulness is raising self-awareness. When you are aware of how you feel, you can take action to address these feelings directly rather than letting your behavior be driven blindly by them. The ultimate goal is conscious choice; that is, intentionally acting and being the kind of person you want to be in the world. This kind of self-awareness is even difficult for adults, and is particularly difficult for children. There are a number of reasons for this.

1. Children are overwhelmed by the constant stream of data pouring into their brains through their senses. The things they see, hear, taste, touch, and smell demand their attention, making it difficult to listen to and identify their inner experiences and emotions (let alone articulate them).
2. Children often lack the vocabulary they need to communicate their feelings. They often do not have the words necessary to describe their emotional experiences, or the necessary faculties to communicate these experiences to others. Further, they may not fully understand what different emotions "feel like" and be unable to identify specific feelings.

3. Children struggle with impulse control. Emotional experiences bring with them very real chemical reactions in the brain that are designed to drive behavior. The parts of the brain that regulate these impulses are some of the slowest to develop, making it much harder for children to assert self-control and to not lash out when emotionally provoked.

Overcoming these challenges is the work of a lifetime, and indeed many adults continue to struggle with the same issues. Nonetheless, mindfulness practice—particularly as it relates to emotional mindfulness—is a powerful tool that is accessible to children and adults alike. Through the guided support of an adult it is possible for children to make significant progress in all of these areas, not only raising their self-awareness but also learning to communicate about their inner states.

ALERT

Parents should keep in mind that learning to communicate about feelings and emotions is a lifelong process and calls for patience, caring, and support. Children are inconsistent in most things because their bodies and brains are changing at such a rapid pace.

Raising Your Child's Self-Awareness

As you become more accustomed to looking for and noticing emotional cues, you will be able to prevent situations before they come to a head. Again, your own practice of mindfulness is extremely helpful in noticing potentially bad or reactive situations, and preventing them before they arise.

When the immediate situation has been defused, it is time to establish contact with your child. Do so gently, regardless of what may have just happened. If necessary, you may want to take a moment to attend to your own reaction to the situation first. This is totally appropriate and will allow you to respond more evenly when you speak with your child.

When you do turn your full attention to your child, your first job is to help him calm down and feel safe. Particularly if your child believes that he has done something wrong or has been wronged (whether or not he is correct), he may be very defensive and upset. He will likely be anticipating a particular kind of reaction from you, which may prompt his defensiveness. Make it clear to your child that things are all right, even if his behavior was not, and begin a conversation about what just happened.

ESSENTIAL

When practicing and teaching emotional mindfulness, you need not look only for signs of negative emotional reactions. Negative emotions indicate some kind of suffering, and so it is natural for them get most of the attention. That being said, mindfulness is just as powerful when it is applied to positive emotions. In fact, many practitioners report greatly enhanced experiences of joy, happiness, satisfaction, and contentment from meeting positive experiences with mindfulness practice as well.

Even if you are still upset, do your best to keep a calm and receptive voice. If you are facilitating a conversation between more than one child, make sure you indicate that everyone will have a turn to talk and a turn to listen. Under these circumstances, you are the arbitrator of fairness. "Okay, are you ready to talk? Tell me what happened from your point of view." Using clarifying and guiding questions, lead your child through a process of explaining the series of events leading up to him acting out, and how he felt when X happened. Help him draw the connections between the actions that took place, how he felt, and how he reacted.

Once all of the children have had a chance to share their points of view, begin wrapping up the conversation by asking your child (or all of the children) what they can do differently next time.

Example of the Four-Step Framework in Action

Scenario Part 1: Imagine that your seven-year-old child, Patrick, and his friend Tom were playing together outside. You see them from inside the kitchen, and can hear their voices getting louder. They are both frowning and pulling on the same Star Wars lightsaber toy, and it quickly escalates to your son wrenching it out of Tom's hands and pushing him to the ground. You immediately go outside.

Step 1: *Seize Opportune Moments*. In this example, there was no way you could have prevented the altercation from taking place. You noticed some signs that the kids were reacting emotionally to one another (the raised voices, their facial expressions, the tug-of-war), and now you are going outside to help them resolve the conflict.

Scenario Part 2: You go outside and say "Hey" loudly enough to announce your presence. Your son starts talking a mile a minute to explain why he isn't to blame, and his friend Tom is still on the ground looking angry and hurt with tears in his eyes. You walk over to your son, hold up your hand, and (as calmly as you can manage) say, "Patrick, stop talking. Give me the lightsaber and sit down." You take a deep breath to calm yourself down, too, because you're upset and disappointed that he would behave that way. Your son pouts, tears up, hands you the toy, and crosses his arms over his chest. He starts to complain that this isn't fair. You look Patrick in the eye, put your hand on his shoulder and say, "Stop. We will work this out together. Right now, I need you to sit down. Understand?" He tearfully nods his head and complies. You immediately go over to Tom, who is still on the ground. "Hey buddy," you say. "Are you all right? Let me look at those hands." Tom shows you his hands, which are red from having the lightsaber ripped out of them. Tom doesn't say anything, but lets you touch and examine his palms. You know that he's physically fine, but understand that he needs the attention and contact. You squeeze his hands, almost like you are a doctor. "Open and close your hands for me. Good. Now wiggle your fingers. Good. Give me a double high-five. Do we need to take any X-rays?" Tom smiles a little bit and says no. "Okay, little man, I think you'll be all right. You ready to talk about this?" Tom nods his head yes. You look at your child, and invite him to come join you and Tom.

Step 2: *Make Contact*. You have successfully intervened, defused the situation, removed the child who acted out most aggressively from the spotlight, ensured everyone's safety, and given attention to the child who needed it. It is now time to start a conversation.

Scenario Part 3: You are feeling much calmer than you were initially, and the boys are both ready and emotionally steady enough to talk. Your son is still a bit teary and worked up, and that's all right. You sit in a three-person circle and begin. "So you both are going to have a turn to say what happened from your point of view. When it is not your turn, your job is just to listen. Understand?" Both boys nod. "Tom, why don't you start?" Tom goes on to explain that the two were playing Star Wars together, and that both of them wanted to be Mace Windu with the purple lightsaber. Patrick got to be Mace Windu last time, and Tom wanted a turn so he grabbed the purple lightsaber. (At this point Patrick begins to interrupt to argue and explain. You put your hand on his knee and calmly say that it will be his turn to talk in a minute, and right now he needs to listen to his friend.) Tom goes on to say that Patrick got angry, started yelling at him, and then pushed him down. "Okay Tom, thanks for sharing your side of what happened." Turn to Patrick and say, "Patrick, what happened from your perspective?" Patrick gushes his side of the story, that it isn't fair because Tom *always* gets to be Mace Windu and that it's *his* lightsaber, and that he wanted a turn and Tom wouldn't let him. "So you got angry and pushed your friend to the ground?" Patrick looks down and says yes, clearly feeling a little ashamed. "Thanks for telling us your side of the story, Patrick. What I saw from the window was both of you trying to pull the lightsaber away from each other. I could hear you yelling, and then I saw you (Patrick) push your friend to the ground. It looked like both of you were feeling pretty angry. Is that how you felt?" Both boys nod yes. "Well, I definitely know what it feels like to get angry with a friend. Was pushing Tom the best way to handle all that anger?" Both boys say no. "I agree. There's nothing wrong with feeling angry; the question is, what do you do when it comes up. Do you lash out, or can you find a better way?" Both boys agree they can find a better way.

Step 3: *Start A Conversation*. Everyone needs a chance to calmly say their piece and be heard. You've helped both boys calm down and successfully facilitated a conversation that explored everyone's perspectives. You helped the boys identify what emotions they experienced, notice and articulate how they each reacted, and agree that they can find better ways to deal with anger. Now it's time to wrap this up and move on.

Scenario Part 4: "So the next time you feel yourself getting angry, what else could you do instead of lashing out?" The boys think for a minute and come up with some good ideas, like walking away to cool off, just taking turns, coming to get an adult to help solve the problem, and more. "I think these are really good ideas. I'm proud of how you both have been listening to each other and talking about this. You ready to get back to playing?" Both boys smile and say yes. "All right, so who gets to be Mace Windu first this time?" you ask, looking first at Patrick. Patrick says that Tom can have a turn, then they can switch. "That sounds great. High-fives all around!"

Step 4: *Wrap Up and Move On.* Keeping things brief and to the point, you encouraged the boys to brainstorm alternative strategies for handling their anger the next time they notice it arising. You reinforced how the boys listened to one another and worked out their disagreement, and immediately segued back into collaborative play between them. With this four-step process you have modeled and taught them about social and emotional awareness, self-regulation, strategies to self-soothe and conflict resolution skills.

Body Awareness

Children are constantly learning about the mechanics of their bodies through play. This is part of the reason they are so active. However, most children are not particularly aware of how they use their bodies. This may manifest itself as inappropriate body language, risky play, or recklessness.

ESSENTIAL

It can be helpful to draw your child's attention to her body when she identifies that she is feeling a particular emotion. "So you said that you're angry right now. How does 'angry' feel in your body? What do you notice?" The areas of the body most commonly associated with negative emotions include the jaw, stomach, hands, chest, and face. If your child can identify how her body changes depending on how she feels, you can guide her to intentionally relax that part of her body.

Handling High Energy

Children often act out physically in response to both their emotions and their latent energy levels. It is perfectly natural for children to be energetic and active, but it can be quite a handful to positively direct this energy, and it is all too common for children to be overactive in places and at times where it is not appropriate. By drawing your child's attention to her body, you not only reduce the stress of these instances, but you give her the tools she needs to be more intentional as she moves through the world.

Raising Your Child's Body Awareness

The easiest way to raise your child's body awareness is to ask questions about how it feels in her body when she is excited, hyper, anxious, etc. When your child identifies how she feels when she's got too much energy, for example, she may say her body feels jumpy or bouncy. Once she has connected the emotional feeling to how it feels in her body, you can brainstorm ideas for what she can do when she has that much energy but can't run around as she wants to (e.g., getting a toy, saying something to Mom or Dad so they can help, dancing in place).

Opinions and Personal Preferences

The model introduced previously provides a powerful four-step framework for engaging with your child to examine any aspect of her inner experience. It can be particularly useful in relation to you child's opinions about practically anything, and everyone knows how opinionated children can be.

Handling Reactive Opinions

In the case of opinions, you may notice your child's emotional reactivity getting triggered while she is expressing an opinion (such as "I hate salad!") or disagreeing with the opinions or desires of someone else. This is your cue to intervene and engage. Ask her why she feels that way, or what's wrong with someone else feeling a particular way. Your child is fairly likely to have an answer to this question, but it may not be much more than "Because!"

Once your child has responded (or even if she won't), your challenge is to help her examine her point of view through probing questions. Ask her if there is a specific quality about the thing she suddenly feels so strongly about. Your goal is to help her discern her experiential basis for her preference. You are guiding your child to explore her reaction. Use your own good judgment throughout this process, and try to imagine why she might feel a particular way and ask about that. Throughout the conversation, be aware of your own feelings as they arise and try not to hold on to any judgments about what your child says (even if she doesn't like what you cooked for dinner).

For each reason your child gives for her opinion, gently challenge her to examine those reasons. The object here is to determine what about her experience gave rise to that opinion. Try to help her connect with the experience itself without judging it. One way to do this is by sharing other interpretations of that experience. For example, if your child doesn't like petting dogs but you do, share your own memories and experiences of petting a dog, what you like about it and why. This may help your child connect to a new experience that she initially doesn't like or is scared of.

The Goal

Remember that the goal is not to change your child's mind, but to help her learn how to notice her preferences about things and question why she might feel that way. The lesson here is about accepting an experience as opposed to outright rejecting it. This is a profound lesson to teach children, because regardless of their personal preferences there are many things in life that they will have to deal with despite how they feel.

By helping your child learn to examine her various opinions at an early age and explore how she might come to appreciate aspects of an experience she initially finds distasteful, you equip her with the tools of mental flexibility, self-awareness, and reflection.

Awareness of Others

Empathy, or consideration of others' feelings and experiences, is one of the highest virtues a person can develop. Children of all ages are prone to being self-centered, and even narcissistic. While this is developmentally appropriate, it can be a huge source of stress both at home and at school. By helping your child develop sensitivity to how his actions affect others through mindfulness, it is possible to raise children who are kind, considerate, and polite.

Other as Self

The beginning of empathy is simply recognizing that others are selves just like you, and that like you, they have feelings not particularly different from your own. Teaching this basic idea to children can be very difficult because they are so involved in discovering their own selves.

When you find an opportune moment to engage your child on this topic, do so gently. The opportune moment may occur as you watch your child and see that he is about to do something harmful, or when your child declares an intended course of action, or even after he has done something and seen its affect on another person.

ALERT

Remember that it is actually appropriate for children to be self-centered. Much of childhood and adolescence is about discovering who you are, so it is totally healthy and correct for children to be self-involved to a certain extent. That being said, there will be many opportunities to help them develop empathy.

It is also very appropriate for you to create opportunities to discuss the feelings of others with your child. Perhaps there is a birthday coming up for a friend or family member; you could discuss what to do for the occasion to help make that person feel loved and special. Maybe someone your child knows is ill or in need of help or support. Any of these opportunities is ripe for a discussion about the feelings of others. Although initially you will be guiding him through this process and reminding him to think about other people's feelings, over time he will take up the practice on his own.

Empathy

A particularly great opportunity for teaching your child about the feelings of others occurs whenever he bears witness to another person's feelings. This may come up in many different contexts: seeing somebody at home, on the playground, or while on an outing; or through a story, movie, or TV show. Whatever the opportunity, invite your child to think about how another person might feel, then ask him to imagine himself in the same circumstances. "How would you feel if X happened?"

Empathizing is a powerful way to teach consideration of others, and this simple practice can have profound, lifelong impacts on your child. When your child shares what he thinks of another person might feel in a given situation, you can help him develop his reasoning by asking him why he thinks so. Remember that the point is not to come to any definite conclusion about how other people feel; you are just imagining how they *might* feel. It is important to hold these ideas loosely and remain responsive to the situation. You and your child will only ever go with your best guess; there are no "right" answers. You can teach this by telling your child "That's a good idea" and asking "How else could they feel?" This invites your child to engage with the complexity and subjectivity of human experience, and helps him see that different people often have different reactions to the same circumstances.

ESSENTIAL

Teaching empathy need not be confined to connecting to other human beings. Animals, fictional creatures, and even plants or trees can all be used to teach empathy. If it is a living thing, there is an opportunity to connect with the experience of that thing and your child will benefit from that connection.

Empathy is generally associated with negative emotional experiences and helps you and your child connect to the inner emotional lives of others. The positive side of empathy is called sympathetic joy, and it is simply sharing in and experiencing happiness when others around you are happy. This is a particularly important quality to cultivate in children, because it is very easy for kids to get jealous when others have cause for joy.

Speech

Speech is a particularly rich area to practice mindfulness, and presents a minefield of challenges for adults and children alike. Think about how many times in your own life you have said something innocuously to another person, only to have it blow up in your face.

Talking to other people can be particularly difficult because you can control at best only half of the situation. Your speech is colored by your own inner feelings and directed by your intentions, but it is then interpreted by a listener whose interpretation is colored by her own emotional state. This is all particularly difficult for children, because children are often less consciously aware of their feelings and are prone to more immediate reactivity.

In Buddhism, speaking skillfully is an important part of practice. The original Buddha gave three questions to reflect on when considering whether it is skillful or not to speak: Is it true? Is it helpful? Is it the right time? You might find these questions helpful when considering whatever it is you might have to say.

What You Say

The most overt aspect of speech is what you say, or the actual words you choose to express yourself. There are ways of speaking that are kind and polite, while there are at least as many ways to say things that are rude, inconsiderate, and unkind.

As an adult, you have a lifetime of experience about how people react to different words and sentence constructions. Children are at a huge disadvantage here, not only because they lack the same volume of experience, but also because their vocabularies are much smaller, which gives them far fewer options when trying to express themselves verbally.

In teaching mindful speech to a child, the opportune moment will usually occur after the child has said something (although it is possible to examine the speech of someone else, either real or fictional, as a means of teaching mindful speech). Particularly if your child has said something rude, you are likely to have your own emotional reaction to what she has said. Your first challenge is to practice with your own reaction before engaging with your child. It is very important that you do not react to her speech, no matter how unskillful it is. A sharp rebuke from you will put your child into a state where it will be much harder for her to engage with you and learn a lesson from what has just transpired.

When a child speaks unskillfully, it is usually for one of two reasons: either the child has not considered how her words will affect the listener, or it is because the child's words are being colored by her own emotional state (or a combination of the two). When your child speaks rudely, examine her demeanor for signs of emotional distress. If you see indications that your child is speaking from an emotional place, you should respond in a way that draws her attention to what she is feeling as a means of raising her self-awareness.

If, however, you do not see evidence of emotional reactivity beneath your child's speech, it is an appropriate opportunity to invite her to reflect on how she expressed herself and how someone is likely to feel when hearing her words. Invite your child to reflect on the words she used, how they might make someone feel, then help her come up with better ways of expressing the same idea.

ALERT

As with most of these techniques, your child will learn more effectively if *he* is the one who comes up with the solutions. Resist the temptation to tell him how he should have done it, and instead engage him in a creative problem-solving process where you try to guide him toward finding more appropriate answers or solutions.

How You Say It

The "how you say it" aspect of speech is particularly difficult for children to master. How something is said is most often interpreted based on tone of voice. The tone of someone's voice is often a subconscious expression of their emotional state.

When your child expresses herself in an inappropriate tone of voice, it is best to draw her attention to it. Help her notice and identify any feelings that may be affecting how she is speaking, and help her practice other, more appropriate tones of voice.

CHAPTER 14

Mindfully Teaching Children Through Stories

A good story will grab your attention, hold your interest, and bring you on a journey with characters that are going through some kind of learning process and/or transformation. A good story can transport you into a realm where social roles, cultural norms, the laws of physics, and reality itself may be tested or questioned. When you read a good book you can learn to see things from different points of view, and often learn something about yourself in the process. This is why stories are the perfect avenue to teach your children mindfulness.

Stories and Children

For children, stories are a great way to learn about the world. They become an extension of pretend play, and help children learn about new experiences.

Addressing Serious Topics

Serious topics concerning family, values, relationships, growing pains, and more can be explored in less threatening ways when they are addressed in the context of a story. Children can easily relate to a young turtle who gets in trouble for telling a lie, or a little boy who is scared of going to school for the first time; this gives parents opportunities to teach in meaningful ways that do not focus directly on their child.

ESSENTIAL

Stories are a powerful way to explore different values with your child and to support social-emotional development. Children have a monkey-see monkey-do mentality, and learn vicariously from what other people (or characters) do.

Just as you model behaviors for your children, so do the fictional characters in books and on television. Knowing this gives you a chance to bring more attention to the books you choose to read with your child, the media you allow them to be exposed to, and the subjects that they address.

How Stories Can Teach

Books present you with countless topics, characters, and circumstances to choose from. Reading is a fantastic way to connect with your child while cultivating his literacy skills, imagination, and critical-thinking abilities. Reading every day with your child does incredible things for his cognitive development, and yet there are ways to take it further and have a more significant impact.

Active participation versus passive participation when reading makes a world of difference in terms of your child's ability to comprehend and connect with what is happening in a story. In other words, the more your child understands the story's characters and the world those characters inhabit, the more likely he is to empathize with and learn from those characters' experiences. This opportunity to empathize with and learn from a story is enhanced by multiple readings.

FACT

Research has shown that reading is one of the most important things your child can do. Reading is closely correlated with success in school, in college, and throughout almost every area of life. Most readers develop their love for books at an early age, so it is important to start young!

Interactive Reading

The following section describes a unique form of interactive reading that has been used in classrooms and home settings to great effect. This particular take on dialogic reading uses a combination of probing questions, interactive reading techniques, and related games or activities as a means of teaching particular social-emotional skills and values.

When used regularly, this way of reading with your child can increase your child's vocabulary, nurture his love of reading, support his literacy skills, and improve his social-emotional learning. This is all on top of how it creates fun opportunities for you both to spend quality time together!

The Arc

The overall arc of interactive reading is a three-step process. Each step is valuable and builds upon the previous one:

1. Preview books before reading them.
2. Read books with your child in dynamic, interactive ways.
3. Do related games or activities.

Whether it happens through books or while running errands, every positive interaction you have with your child has a positive impact on his development, and any amount of time spent reading together is a great thing.

QUESTION

I don't always have time to do each of these steps. Can I still use this method?
Sometimes the best you can do is to grab a random book from the shelf and read it with your child before bedtime. That's just fine. You can still use some of the ideas from interactive reading to make things more fun. It doesn't always have to be a process; you can improvise and you and your child will both still benefit.

Preview Books Before Reading Them

Scanning through books before bringing them home to read with your child is necessary when choosing a "teaching story." Teaching stories refer to fictional stories that you intentionally want to use to explore particular values, behaviors, or social circumstances. This vetting process allows you to select particular books that relate to your child's interests, or that touch on a timely social-emotional subject (such as honesty or self-control when those topics have come up recently in your child's life).

ALERT

This is not to imply that you should choose all of your child's books. It is important for him to be able to explore libraries and choose books for himself. Doing so respects your child's interests and agency, and helps him develop criteria for choosing good stories. (You of course maintain the power of veto!)

Things to Consider

The following is a list of things to consider as you preview different stories and determine whether or not they are helpful and/or appropriate teaching tools:

1. What types of characters does the story have?

    When choosing a teaching story it can be useful to think about what kinds of characters your child relates to the most. Does your child prefer books about animals? Is he particularly interested in firemen, train conductors, or superheroes? Whatever story you select, you want the characters to be interesting and easy for your child to connect to.

2. Are there good illustrations?

    Particularly when reading with preliterate children, it helps to have interesting and attention-grabbing visuals that support the plot. Good illustrations will spark your child's imagination while also giving him something concrete to focus on as he listens to the story. Illustrations help younger children concentrate for longer periods of time, and allow them to look through the book on their own and "retell" the story using the pictures as prompts.

3. What kind of plot does the story have?

    When selecting a teaching story, this is the most important question to consider. Part of what makes reading through books ahead of time so effective for parents is that you can choose plots that reflect the most relevant topics for your child. There are two sides to think about when it comes to a story's plot:

    - Are there particular genres that your child loves?
    - Does the plot appropriately address the social-emotional situation you want to explore with your child and create opportunities for interesting dialogue?

    When you find books that have interesting characters your child can relate to, strong illustrations that grab his attention, and a plot that is relevant to his life, you have struck gold.

What to Look for in a Plot

Stories and pretend play offer a safe setting for your child to investigate various social and emotional situations. This enables him to explore social interactions and emotional landscapes through someone else's lens, and to learn about healthy values and behaviors.

To engage with a story is to learn about somebody else's actions and the consequences of those actions, whether the story is real or fictional. This is a form of vicarious reinforcement. According to Dr. Sherry Thompson (2008), vicarious reinforcement occurs when a learner observes another's actions and the consequences of those actions.

Knowing the potential of vicarious reinforcement, what kind of social-emotional topics does it make sense to address with your child? What values do you want to explore with him through the lens of a story and its characters? The point here is not to lecture or get onto a moral soapbox; it is to help your child hold a value (such as cooperation) in his mind and turn it to see it from different angles. The beauty of helping him do this through a story is that the focus is not directly on *him*, but on the characters. This gives him some distance from the topic, and gives you both an opportunity to discuss it without it becoming too personal.

When previewing books to find a teaching story, some of the major social-emotional topics you might look for include:

- Honesty
- Empathy
- Generosity
- Follow-through
- Respect
- Self-control
- Cooperation
- Self-help
- Helping others
- Trustworthiness
- Active listening
- Reliability

Taking your child's interests, proclivities, and recent experiences into account makes this method of teaching all the more effective. For example, perhaps your child needs help understanding what follow-through means.

Maybe he's angry because one of his friends lied to him. Or perhaps your five-year-old daughter just got caught taking something without asking. Another way to address this latter situation might be to use the Intentional and Interactive Reading Curriculum (IIRC) instead of just lecturing or punishing her. The ultimate goal is for your child to learn from her mistakes and establish an internal value system, after all; the IIRC is a helpful tool in making that happen.

Read Books in Dynamic and Interactive Ways

There is overwhelmingly positive research supporting the value of reading aloud with children. Regularly reading with your child:

- Develops vocabulary, memory, listening, and language skills
- Encourages imagination and creativity
- Connects children and adults
- Teaches information about people, social relationships, and the world

This is all well and good, but all too often reading is a passive experience for children. They sit back, look at pictures, and an adult reads something to them. In this scenario, the child's involvement is rather limited. Reading this way involves little interplay between reader and listener; it does not require children to fully think about, process, and connect with what is happening in the story.

Luckily, there are techniques like dialogic reading available to parents who want to turn reading into a more dynamic and interactive experience.

Dialogic Reading

In addition to providing an interactive format through which you and your child can engage in storytelling together, dialogic reading shifts the role of storyteller toward the child. This involves more than one reading of a story over time; the repetition helps to reinforce vocabulary (among other things), and the added familiarity with a book empowers your child to have a larger role in telling the story.

Based on six different studies that involved over 481 preschool students, the *What Works Clearinghouse Intervention Report* (2006) found that dialogic reading had positive effects on oral language development, and potentially positive effects for print knowledge and early reading and writing (U.S. Department of Education). It is frequently used in early childhood classrooms across the country.

The fundamental technique underlying dialogic reading is the PEER sequence:

Prompt: Invite your child to say something about the story.

Evaluate: After asking your child a question, what about his response was correct? Where might he need guidance?

Expand: Give your child's response more depth by rephrasing it and/or adding information.

Repeat: Say an important word or piece of information again to reinforce the expansion, perhaps by asking your child if he can say it.

This is particularly effective with toddlers, who at that age still have relatively limited vocabularies. Here is an example of how you might use the PEER sequence with a toddler:

If you and your three-year-old are reading a picture book about a happy family of insects, you might point at one of the pictures and ask:

"What's that?" (prompt).

"*Bug*," your toddler answers.

"That's right!" (evaluation), "It's a red and black ladybug!" (expansion). "Can you say ladybug?" (repetition).

Interactive reading uses the dialogic process as a foundation, and builds it into a system for teaching social-emotional skills through stories (and beyond).

Use CROWD Questions as You Read

When using dialogic reading for the first time, it is helpful to briefly cue your child to what is about to happen. Tell him that you are going to try a fun new way to read, and ask him if he would like to help you tell the story. If for any reason he says no (highly unlikely), don't worry about it. Sprinkle in a few CROWD questions here and there, and see how he takes to it.

There are five basic types of questions or prompts that you can use to help your child become actively involved with a story. These prompts are easily remembered through the acronym CROWD: Completion, Recall, Open-ended, Wh-, and Distancing.

In a completion prompt, you leave the end of a sentence blank for your child to fill in. This is easiest to do with rhymes, or if your child is already familiar with the story. If your child is not sure what word he should say, you can give him a hint (such as pointing to a picture, or articulating the first sound of the word). For example, you might say:

- "The cat in the . . . " (and pause for him to say) "Hat!"
- "Three blind mice, three blind mice, see how they . . . " (pause) "Run!"
- "Eenie, meenie, miney . . . " (pause) "Mo!"

Recall prompts are questions about a book your child has already read. These kinds of questions hone your child's memory about a story, and can be used to help him reconstruct the chronology of events. For example, if you just finished reading Shel Silverstein's *The Giving Tree*, you might ask:

- "How did the boy and the giving tree like to play together when he was little?"
- "When the boy needed wood to build a house, what did the giving tree do?"
- "What did the boy and the giving tree do together at the very end of the book?"

Open-ended questions tend to focus on a book's illustrations, and can sometimes leave things open to your child's interpretation. For example, you might point to a picture and ask:

- "What do you think is happening in this picture?"
- "How do you think this character is feeling right now?"

Wh- prompts refer to questions that begin with Who, What, When, Where, Why, and How. There is often overlap between Wh- questions and the other types of CROWD questions. For example, you might ask:

- "Where did the baby raccoon go?"
- "Why is the wolf cuddling up to the boy?"
- "Who stole the cookie from the cookie jar?"

Distancing questions ask children to relate some aspect of the book to their own lives. These are important questions to ask, because they help your child make direct connections between what is happening in the story and what is happening in his own life. This guides your child to put himself into a character's shoes, or to imagine what he might do differently in a similar situation. For example, you might ask:

- "Have you ever broken something by accident? How did it make you feel?"
- "If you were hungry like Aladdin and saw other kids who were even hungrier than you, what would you do?"
- "If you were home alone and The Cat in the Hat showed up without permission, what would you say to him?"

It is easiest to think of some of these questions before reading with your child, although with some practice you will become good at thinking up questions on the fly. Initially, however, it may help you to brainstorm a few different CROWD questions you can ask ahead of time.

ESSENTIAL

The key to all of this is to make your child an active participant in the reading, not just a passive listener. At every opportunity, turn to him for a response. Be creative! If you get your child participating, you are doing it right!

Read with Voices

How you read with your child changes the experience and what he can learn from it. One of the techniques you can use to make story time more dynamic is to give characters different voices, accents, or affectations.

ESSENTIAL

Not everyone feels comfortable using silly voices. Some adults get shy about looking or feeling silly or about not accurately imitating accents, or simply don't want to put in the effort. When it comes to being silly with your kids, however, you will never have a more enthusiastic and accepting audience.

Using different voices will make the characters in a story stand out, particularly if you use the same character voices in the same story more than once. It is a wonderful way to spice up your child's auditory stimulation and memory, and makes it easier to use your regular voice for narration and CROWD questions.

FACT

The auditory memory can be a powerful way for your child to remember characters, circumstances, or lessons they have learned from a story. Giving story characters unique voices is just another associative link your child's memory can draw upon.

Don't go thinking that any of this requires great vocal impressions or imitations. No one expects you to do professional cartoon voices, or to win any voiceover awards! Besides, the differences in characters' voices do not have to be drastic. One small change in speed, tone, or volume is all it takes. All this requires is for you to loosen up and play around with different ways of saying things.

Here are some exercises to loosen you up.

- Make nonsensical noises. This will relax your tongue, your mouth, and, hopefully, the judgmental part of your mind.
- Play with octaves. Say "Hello" (or any word you want) as low as you can, and work your way up to saying it in as high a voice as you can.
- Play with dynamics, meaning how softly and loudly you speak.
- Combine the octaves and the dynamics. For example, say "Hello" really loudly in a high-pitched voice, and then softly in a medium-pitched voice.

- Play with the speed at which you speak. For example, how might a turtle say "Good morning"? What about a rabbit or a caterpillar?
- Try speaking with an English accent. It does not matter if it sounds anything like a real English accent.
- Combine different accents with various octaves, dynamics, and speeds. Get wild and have fun.

Once you are comfortable using different voices, it may be helpful to plan the major voices you want to use with a particular teaching story ahead of time. If you are super-motivated, you might even practice reading the story (with funny voices) by yourself first to practice.

Bring Stories to Life

Beyond using CROWD questions and giving voices to different characters, there is another great way you can really breathe life into a story: incorporate movement.

Children have lots of energy, and it can sometimes be a struggle to sit still during a story. One of the great tools available to you when reading with your child is finding opportunities to let him move and engage his senses in relation to the story. This is a wonderful technique that activates his imagination, and helps the story pop off of the page in ways your child can physically interact with. There are many creative ways of doing this.

For example, when characters in the book are eating food, pretend to grab some of the food off the page and eat it. This is a fun way to engage some of your child's other senses through his imagination.

When pictures show the characters doing something like knocking on a door, you and your child can knock on the page and say, "Knock, knock!" If characters in the book are doing simple movements like clapping, jumping, stretching, or tiptoeing, do those movements along with your child. It often helps when you do the action too, because then it is something you and your child are doing together; kids love shared experiences with their parents.

When there are pictures of flowers or yummy-looking soup, pretend to smell them together; if there is a picture of something like a skunk, pretend you caught a whiff and it stinks. If characters in the book are climbing a tree or riding a bike, pretend to do the same thing from where you and your child are sitting. Move your arms and legs as appropriate, and it becomes a mini-game. This is great when you come across more complex movements that cannot actually be replicated while reading, only imagined.

FACT

When you recall a vivid memory (such as what it tastes like eating hot apple pie or what it smells like at the beach), 91 percent of the same brain circuits are activated. This means that recalling vivid memories is strikingly similar to experiencing the event again. So when you and your child pretend to eat something familiar out of a book, you both can literally taste what you pretend to eat.

By enhancing dialogic reading with CROWD questions, character voices, and movement opportunities that bring stories to life, you and your child will have plenty of dynamic and interactive storytime experiences.

Do Related Games or Activities

You've vetted the possibilities, chosen a teaching story, and now have the tools to turn storytime into an interactive event. Ready to take it one step further? Teaching social-emotional skills and values takes time. Your child will learn and relearn the same lesson again and again in different contexts; by reinforcing elements of a teaching story through related games or activities, you will build more associations between the stories you read and your child's actual life.

Incorporating Multisensory Approaches to Games and Activities

Kids are bundles of sensory experiences. Engaging your child's physical senses is the ultimate way to help her explore, experience, and understand the world around her. When a child has more than one of her senses engaged, neural connections across the brain are strengthened. Such engagement makes every activity more interesting, and increases the likelihood that your child will retain any knowledge gleaned from such an experience.

Game and Activity Ideas That Build on a Teaching Story

For people who are new to the idea of reinforcing elements of a book through games or activities, it will be helpful to have some ideas of what you can do. First off, timing is important. The ideal time to do a game or activity that relates to a teaching story you and your child have read is within a day or so of reading it. Often there is an even greater impact if a meaningful game or activity happens after the *second* reading, because then your child is more familiar with the plot and any lessons it vicariously reinforces. Children have short attention spans, so it helps to build upon a story while it is fresh in your child's mind.

Secondly, when planning a game or activity, it helps to consider which intelligences your child is most inclined toward and how you might incorporate multisensory components into what you and your child will do. When these two factors are taken into consideration, the activity you do with your child will be all the more meaningful and effective.

The primary purpose of doing games or activities is not necessarily to reiterate a social-emotional skill (though that can certainly be part of it). What you are really doing is helping your child connect with teaching stories in a real-life dimension. Doing so furthers her interest in the characters and the plot in one way or another, and creates more mental connections between the teaching story, the experience of reading it with you, and the related activities that happen after the fact. A web of experiential memory associations is established, and the story (and the lessons your child takes from it) stays in her realm of awareness for more substantial periods of time. Keep in mind that these games or activities can be done with larger groups of children, including reading the teaching story itself.

ESSENTIAL

There are always creative opportunities to include basic writing and math skills in various games or activities. For example, if you and the kids are acting out a story, everyone should write his or her name on a piece of paper (or whiteboard) next to the character they will be. To incorporate math using the same example, ask the kids to count how many characters there are in the story and how many children there are in the "play."

Examples of Possible Activities

- *Act the story out.* Several children can play the same role, or one child can play multiple roles. Making costumes and backgrounds is an option, but is not at all necessary. It is easiest if you are the narrator; jump alongside whichever character is speaking, say their part, and the kid(s) can repeat what you say. The only real setup required is to assign character roles and to decide which parts of the room or yard will represent which locations in the book. Make sure that at the end everyone comes together, takes a bow, and cheers (even if there is no audience).

- *Act out the story using puppets.* Although this takes more time, for children who enjoy art projects, it can be a lot of fun to make puppets and maybe even background scenery. A large cardboard box can easily be transformed into a puppet theater. There are a couple of options in terms of the "show": either you can continue to be the narrator and feed the kids their lines, or they can look at pictures from the book and just improvise their lines.

- *A kinesthetic game using character names/themes from the story.* This is as simple as adapting games like tag, hide-and-seek, or Simon Says to fit with the theme and/or characters of a book. For example, if you just read a Winnie the Pooh book where Pooh Bear and Piglet get lost and Christopher Robin has to find them, two children can be Pooh Bear and Piglet and go hide together, while the other child or children can be Christopher Robin.

- *Do something similar to what the characters did in the book.* If you read a story like *The Very Hungry Caterpillar* by Eric Carle, you might consider getting a caterpillar "kit" with your child. This will allow her to see natural science in action, and give her the chance to care for another living thing until it "grows up" and becomes a butterfly, which she can then release in a park or garden (social-emotional skills: empathy and helping others).

- *Science experiments.* After reading about Humpty Dumpty, perhaps you can make "egg parachutes"; there are also baking soda volcanoes, testing out different kinds of paper airplanes, experimenting with colors. . . . There are many kinds of science experiments that can fit with all sorts of stories; it's just a matter of finding what works best with the book you want to read.

- *Make homemade instruments.* If there is music in the story, one fun and easy activity is to make instruments like maracas, bongos, rubber band guitars, etc. Don't forget to use kitchen items like pot lids as cymbals or buckets as drums. You can have a musical parade once the instruments are ready!

- *Go on a related outing.* This is an easy way to expand and nurture your child's interests. For example, if you read a story involving dinosaurs, you can go to a nearby natural history museum. If you read about different kinds of animals, you can go to the zoo. If you read about camping, you could pop a tent in the backyard and create a similar experience with the kids.

Getting the Most Out of Reading

Strong foundations in literacy are built upon a love of books and stories. A lifelong love of learning begins with reading and storytelling, which provide opportunities for children to discover the world while having meaningful interactions with adults. These factors give kids important reasons to *want* to learn the letters and sounds of the alphabet, and create a sense of excitement and self-satisfaction in doing so. All forms of educational achievement hinge on each student's ability (and motivation) to read and write. Literacy is the bedrock of academic success; it is essential that we help children form positive attitudes toward reading.

For children to get the most out of reading, the experience must be more than just passive listening. Children have a natural desire to learn and develop new skills. When you turn reading into an interactive process that involves thought, imagination, and discussion, you play into these innate desires and increase your child's hunger to learn.

CHAPTER 15

Mindful Parenting Pointers

Parenting is a tricky and rewarding experience. While paying attention to the present moment might sound simple, learning how to integrate the tool of mindfulness into your spectrum of parenting strategies is a challenge. It is important to remember that raising mindful children requires mindful parents. Just as you can't teach algebra to a friend without first knowing how to do it yourself, it's impossible to teach mindfulness to children without practicing mindfulness in the context of your own life. To get you started, here are some helpful pointers to consider.

Positive Language

It's important to be mindful of the language you use when interacting with your children. Children are concrete, imaginative thinkers who often visualize or picture things as they are said. (Adults do this too!) Knowing this will help you choose your words more carefully, so your child hears and pictures what you *want* him to do instead of directing his attention to what you *don't* want.

Testing This Out

When you hear someone say, "Don't think of a pink bunny," what do you think of? Go on, admit it. You thought of a pink bunny. It's completely normal. Unless you put your full concentration into thinking of something else, a pink bunny will be the first image to pop into your mind. That's how the mind processes sentences: the subject and/or verb stands out first. The "don't" part of the sentence is an afterthought.

Here's another example: Imagine being out to dinner with a friend who says, "Don't look at the man behind you." What comes to mind when you hear that sentence? Most adults might be able to control their impulse to turn around and look at the man, and instead inquire why their friend does not want them to look. Even so, most of these adults would also be quite tempted to sneak a glance. What stands out in the previous sentence is ". . . look at the man behind you." If anything, the word *don't* just ups the ante by tapping into your innate curiosity and coaxing you to see for yourself.

Applying This to Children

What do you suppose your child thinks of first when he hears you say, "Don't run"? When you frame expectations using negative language, you are subtly and unintentionally reinforcing the behaviors you do not want to see. This type of language does not set you or your child up for success, because it emphasizes the word "run," exactly what you want your child to *stop* doing.

Let's say you and the family are all driving in the car together. Both of your kids are sitting in back, and for some reason one child starts hitting the other. Frustrated, you react by frowning at them and yelling, "Don't hit each other!" You turn back around, and lo and behold a few moments later the kids are hitting each other again. The scene repeats itself, and your frustration escalates. Depending on your children's personalities, they might even do it again, not because they want to be disobedient, but because they both want to have the last punch. As you can imagine, it's all downhill from there.

FACT

Make it easier for your child to do what you ask by emphasizing the behavior(s) you want to see. This makes your expectations unequivocally clear, and plants the seed of what you want from your child directly into his mind. When used consistently, you'll notice that this subtle difference in language has a real impact on your child's behavior and how you communicate with him.

Behavior like this can be infuriating to parents who don't understand why their kids just won't *listen*. Perhaps part of the problem is that they *are* listening, and conveniently (or defiantly) ignore the "don't." These types of reactive episodes produce disharmony between parents and children, and can unnecessarily strain family relationships. If you consistently use positive language to frame your expectations, however, your kids are more likely to do what you ask.

Here is a list of common things parents say to their children that distinguishes between the subtleties of positive and negative word choice:

▼ **COMMON PHRASES PARENTS USE WITH THEIR KIDS**

Negative	Positive
Don't hit/kick	Keep your hands/feet to yourself
Stop running	Use walking feet
Not so rough	Be gentle
Stop playing with your food	Eat like a grown-up, please
Don't yell	Use your inside voice
Don't be mean	Be nice/kind
Don't chew with your mouth open	Chew with your mouth closed
Stop making a mess	Put your toys where they belong
Don't talk back	Be respectful or be quiet
Don't touch that	Hands-off, leave that alone

Being mindful of the language you use is a powerful way to improve communication and support the relationship with your child. When you say exactly what you *want* your child to do, his success rate will go up and you will both be happier.

Teach By Example

Children learn perhaps 10 percent from what parents *say*, and 90 percent from what parents *do*. The old saying that actions speak louder than words is completely true, and children are constantly watching and learning.

Modeling Behaviors

Teaching by example is also known as modeling appropriate behaviors. Because children are such "monkey-see monkey-do" creatures, it is important for you as a parent to model the behaviors you want to see in your kids. This is easier said than done, but is a wonderful invitation for you to practice being exactly the kind of parent you want to be.

Living Your Values

Whether you intentionally live your values or not, your child will absorb and internalize what you do. This is similar to the point that you can't teach what you don't know. If a parent is not mindful of her own actions, how can she teach a child (who has vastly less impulse control and self-awareness) to be mindful of his? When you teach by example, your child learns through experience.

For instance, there was once a little girl whose family went to her grandparents' house every year for Thanksgiving. The whole family was there, including aunts, uncles, and cousins. They spent the entire day cooking and playing games together before enjoying a massive Thanksgiving feast. Once dinner was over, the little girl immediately wanted to get up and play with her cousins; however, her mother always asked her to help clear the table and clean the dishes. This happened year after year: Mom was always the first person to help clear the table and clean up the kitchen, and the little girl would sulk as she helped.

For the first couple of years, the little girl asked her mom why *they* were always the ones who had to clean everything up after the Thanksgiving feast while everyone else got to rest or play. Every time, her mother replied, "We are guests here. Your grandmother bought all the food, and your aunts and uncles spent all day cooking it for us. This is a team effort, and we all have to do our part. The least we can do is help clean up. It's how we show them our love and gratitude." The little girl continued to absorb this lesson until one year her mother didn't even have to ask for help, because the little girl was the first person clearing the table and cleaning up after the meal.

ESSENTIAL

Modeling the behaviors and values you want to see in your child means taking a longer view of successful parenting. Teaching by example may not change your children's behavior overnight; however, as they grow into adults, you will see the values they have absorbed from the childhood environment you created.

Another story that illustrates the power of modeling behaviors comes from a kindergarten classroom. There was once a feisty six-year-old boy named Felix who was having a rough day. All morning Felix said mean things to upset the other students, and his teacher, Ms. Joanna, was increasingly frustrated by his poor behavior. At one point Felix mouthed off directly to Ms. Joanna and said something hurtful and rude. The entire room went silent, and all eyes fell on the teacher to see how she would react. Her cheeks were flushed in anger, and to the students' surprise she simply closed her eyes and breathed deeply. Felix tried to say something, but Ms. Joanna raised her hand to stop him. "Felix, I'm very upset with your behavior right now. I need time to cool down before we can talk."

Felix sat down and colored for a few minutes, glancing at his teacher to see what would happen. Ms. Joanna opened her eyes and kept breathing slowly to calm herself down. When she was ready, she invited Felix to sit with her and they discussed what happened and came to a constructive resolution.

The most interesting part of the story happened a couple of weeks after this incident. Felix's kindergarten class was outside for recess when Ms. Joanna noticed that Felix and another boy were arguing in the sandbox. As she watched to see how the boys would handle the dispute, Felix stood up and walked away. He sat under a tree for about five minutes, then returned to the sandbox and continued playing with his friend. They seemed to have worked it out by themselves.

As the class went inside for lunch, Ms. Joanna pulled Felix aside and asked what had happened. Felix told her that the other child had taken his shovel, and that he was so angry he wanted to hit him. "Wow, what did you do when you felt all that anger come up?" Ms. Joanna asked. "Well, I didn't want to get mad and hurt my friend, so I walked away and cooled down under the tree. Once I felt okay, I went back to the sandbox and he gave the shovel back to me."

This story illustrates another aspect of teaching by example. When things go wrong and parents get angry, how they manage this intense emotion is one of the greatest lessons they teach their children. When a parent yells, swears, or spanks out of frustration, those behaviors become normalized and their children learn to do the same. Luckily in Felix's case, he absorbed a different lesson about how to deal with anger. Because Ms. Joanna was mindful of her emotions, she was able to notice her rising anger and take steps to calm down before engaging with Felix. To her amazement, he was able to learn from that experience and use the same technique on his own a few weeks later.

Teaching by example is not about being perfect; it's about making your best effort. Just remember that no one "gets it right" all the time. It may not always feel this way, but it is a real gift to know that everything you do teaches something to your child. Being mindful of this knowledge can guide you and act as a north star in your decision making. When you act like the kind of person you want your child to become, this is mindfulness in action.

It Isn't Personal

Children are wrapped up in their own worlds. They are discovering who they are and who they want to be, learning the ins and outs of different types of relationships, learning about empathy and compassion (it comes more naturally to some than to others), and for very developmentally appropriate reasons everything is some way or another about *them*.

When Your Child Is Rude

Intense emotions often cause kids to react intensely, but even when your child is calm or happy she might say or do something rude, selfish, or short-sighted that just hits you wrong. It may even be hurtful, which is more often the case as children grow to be teenagers and power struggles with parents become more of an issue.

The truth is, nothing your child does is about you. People speak and act in ways that reflect their own emotional state, their own needs, their own interests, their own agendas, and their own desires. Even children can spout emotional venom from time to time, and it is particularly easy for your child to push your buttons (and vice versa). Such is the nature of your very close, intimate relationship. You do not have to take the bait, however. You have a choice, and you do not have to take someone else's bad attitude or hurtful actions personally.

Taking things personally automatically makes you defensive, and defensiveness is simply the launching platform for anger and aggression. (The best defense is a good offense, right?) If you take it personally, your child's snarky under-the-breath remark will offend you and trigger all sorts of reactions.

When you react from this emotional stance, something that was relatively small is now a big deal and snowballs into a fight.

As the Adult . . .

You are light-years ahead in terms of being neurologically equipped to keep your cool in the face of frustration. You can expect your child to be selfish sometimes, and to say or do rude things. You know this will happen from time to time, and you should absolutely correct the unwanted behavior. The point behind not taking things personally, and realizing that your child is simply acting out because she has not learned to control herself and respond instead of react, is that you suddenly have more space to decide upon your course of action. Do you take it personally and get into a fight? Or can you recognize the venom for what it is, refuse to be bitten, and choose another way of addressing your child's behavior without mirroring her emotional immaturity and opting into an argument?

FACT

Not taking it personally and not accepting someone else's venom does not mean that you won't feel angry or hurt. The difference is that through practice, you will see your child's reactivity for what it is—a developmentally appropriate reaction to emotions and circumstances he is still learning how to deal with—and choose not to act from a place of anger as you correct his mistaken behavior.

It's easier to say this, think about this, and discuss this than to live it in the heat of the moment. When your anger or hurt is triggered, it is *really hard* not to act on those emotions. It's not always possible to see the venom for what it is, and even when you see it for what it is, sometimes it's just not possible to respond constructively. Children know how to push your buttons, and sometimes it's hard not to let them. This is where your mindfulness will help. Keeping in mind that your child's rude words or hurtful actions (anyone's, really) are not personal, that it's not about you but *them*, is a helpful reminder that you do not have to react in kind.

"Say It Out Loud"

Assumptions are a part of life. You assume that drivers will stop at stop signs, that your spouse will take out the trash, that your child understands what you have asked him to do, and so on. Assumptions are made countless times a day, and it is illuminating to notice what you presume and with whom. It is easy enough to make assumptions when you are with other adults, but all the more so when you are around children.

How Assumptions Happen

Assumptions often arise from predictable experiences, such as expecting that your computer will start or that your neighbor will wave to you. Most of these assumptions are so common that you don't even notice that you are assuming anything. Besides, many assumptions are automatically in the background and actually simplify how your mind processes life (such as expecting that the sun will rise each day, that objects will fall if dropped, that children become cranky when overly tired, etc.) On the other hand, some assumptions can cause a lot of problems.

The most problematic assumptions tend to revolve around communication. It is surprisingly easy to misinterpret somebody's words, facial expressions, and body language. For example, when you ask your twelve-year-old to take out the trash and she says, "Okay," you might assume she understands that you want her to do it *right now*. In her mind, she might interpret your request to mean take the trash out sometime tonight, perhaps after dinner and certainly not now while she's on the phone with a friend. Another example might be asking your teenager if he has any homework that night, and he replies, "No," assuming you mean does he have any homework due *tomorrow*. It is very easy for children to misinterpret the nuance of your words, or the direct cause of your emotions. For example, if you are extremely busy and your child tries to show you something she made at school that day, she might interpret your unenthused response as disapproval.

Don't Assume

Why are adults more prone to making problematic assumptions with children than with other adults? The assumptions you make are based on repeated life experiences. You have the benefit of a fully developed brain that can process and integrate large amounts of information, and has had much more experience interpreting the social cues of others. The problem is, your child hasn't had those experiences yet and so he will not always make the same assumptions. Your child doesn't know what you know, and you cannot assume that he does. So what is a concerned parent to do? All you have to do is say it out loud.

When you take up the "Say It Out Loud" principle, you make a pact with your family to avoid assumptions by talking things through. It is simply a matter of checking in and making sure that the person you are talking to is on the same page, even if your meaning seems perfectly obvious to you.

Parallel Processing

One of the most effective tools in your parenting toolbox is parallel processing. People tend to go about their days with an "us and them" mentality: Here you are, looking out from behind your own eyes and everyone else is "out there." It is natural to engage people from this perspective: you on your side, everyone else on their side. It can feel like two armies facing off across a battlefield engaged in a struggle for power, especially when there is frustration and conflict.

Power Struggles

Power struggles happen all the time between parents and children. Maybe your son has done something wrong, or maybe you just need to get him to finish a particular chore; either way, it is easy to walk into those sorts of conversations with an underlying battle mentality. This creates an atmosphere of automatic opposition, and the conversation can feel like two armies facing off across the battlefield.

You see yourself as the authority, the force of good, trying to maintain peace and order in the universe, and your kid is over there being self-centered and messing everything up. If only he would do what you say, there wouldn't be a problem! Unfortunately this combative approach causes more harm than good, because when you approach a power struggle with a battle mentality, you take away the common ground between you and your child. The underlying assumption of this view is that children should be blindly obedient because they are your children. This does not respect their individuality, interests, or priorities, which automatically discounts their personal agency as the living, learning human beings they are.

Opportunities for Growth

Whenever you "get into it" with your kids, you are probably focused on the immediate issue at hand and just want to get it fixed quickly so that you can get on to the next thing on your checklist or busy schedule. What you are missing out on is a growth opportunity with your child. Instead of facing off across the battlefield, when you put yourself beside your child as a partner and ally who wants to collaboratively figure things out as adults usually do, you are putting the relationship first. This approach will help your child learn and grow through a dynamic conversation that helps him see things from other people's point of view, rather than just demanding that he obey.

Instead of the tyrannical do-what-I-say-because-I-told-you-to approach, what if you visualize the two of you as commanders on the same team, standing side by side, surveying the terrain and working things out together? This is the essence of parallel processing. It is the practice of standing beside your child and guiding him through the process of negotiating a solution that takes everyone's needs and responsibilities into account.

ALERT

Parallel processing can be used with children of any age. It is particularly important to use as your child gets older. This way of approaching issues is collaborative, and demonstrates your respect for your child's (or teen's) interests, priorities, and growing independence. It reinforces healthy problem-solving skills and an internal locus of control.

Engaged Listening

Listening is one of the most important skills in your parenting toolbox. It is an important way to support your child and demonstrate that you care, not to mention that it can help you strengthen your relationship at any age. Listening is a tricky concept because it is not immediately obvious what you actually do when you listen. Engaged listening, otherwise known as active listening, is a process by which you give someone else your complete attention.

Setting Distractions Aside

All too often people multitask their way through the day. This is a coping mechanism you have probably developed as a means of juggling the many projects, tasks, errands, and obligations that you are responsible for. Although it is a common approach to managing the multiple things you have to do, it splits your attention in ways that distract your mind and actually lessen the quality of your attention. In reality, heavy multitasking causes your work and social interactions to suffer because of how it divides your focus.

To avoid this becoming an issue between you and your child (and to make sure you're modeling the kind of focus and engagement you want your child to manifest in her own life), make sure to practice engaged listening when you are at home with your family. This means setting aside other distractions, making eye contact, and giving the speaker (in this case, your child) your full attention. Ironically there are many people who believe that they are strong and active listeners, when in reality this is not necessarily true. In fact, research suggests that people remember between 25–50 percent of what they hear. This is not a good sign.

Where Is Your Mind?

Even if you set down what you are doing and are looking at the person who is talking, check in with yourself. Is your mind focused on what the person is saying, or is it still planning, scheduling, remembering, projecting, or worrying? It is very easy to only half-listen, and this can be especially true when it comes to listening to children.

The stories your child tells are not always relevant or very interesting to your adult life. The idea behind active listening is not that you suddenly care about little Joey in first grade who lost his favorite pencil and started crying, but then found it again at the bottom of his backpack; it's that you care about your daughter, and she wants to tell you the funny, strange, or interesting things that she experienced that day.

It's true that you probably don't care two wits about the insanely detailed description of the Diego, Mickey Mouse, or Scooby-Doo cartoon your son is telling you about. You do not have to care about the cartoon at all (although you may have a soft spot for Bugs Bunny); the important part of this interaction is that your boy wants to share his joy, curiosity, and interests with you. He wants to interact with you, he wants to share parts of himself and his life with you, and this is one of the ways he can do that. Please don't miss out on this gift, even if the subject itself bores you. You'll be surprised by the interest you may develop in these things as you listen to your child talk about whatever; when a person you love cares about something, it becomes easier to see that "something" through his eyes and come to appreciate it all the more.

Looking Ahead

Engaged listening is particularly important when conversing with teenagers, who are much moodier and prone to withdrawal from parents. If your teen is telling you something, *anything*, it will go a long way to actively listen to whatever it is she is talking about. Not giving advice, not talking about yourself (unless asked), but simply listening. Sometimes that is the best form of support you can possibly offer.

ESSENTIAL

There are times when your child wants to talk and tell you about something, and you have something else that needs to get done first. If you know you cannot give your child the attention he needs, communicate your own needs! "Hey, my friend, I can't wait to talk to you and listen to your story. Before I can do that though, I need to finish XYZ. How about you give me a hug, go play, and as soon as I'm finished you can tell me all about it. Sound good?"

How to Practice Engaged Listening

Here is a list of ways to practice this and hone your active listening skills during conversations:

1. *Remove distractions and tune in.* It's impossible to really listen to what someone is saying when there are distractions in the background. Turn off the television or radio, stop what you are doing, and make it clear to the other person that the conversation is your top priority.

2. *Pay attention to the person speaking.* Engaged listeners provide many clues that they are paying attention. Eye contact is important, and demonstrates to the person speaking that you are right there with them. Body language (such as leaning slightly toward the speaker) does the same thing. Verbal and nonverbal cues (such as nodding your head and saying "yes" or "Mm-hmm") encourage the speaker to continue.

3. *Connect with the speaker.* Even if the content of the conversation is not initially interesting, remind yourself that you care about the person talking. Use that as your gateway to caring about the content. Think to yourself, "I care about you. What you're talking about is important to you, and I like that you are inviting me into your world."

4. *Asking clarifying and reflecting questions.* These are great ways to show that you are engaged with the subject matter. Repeat/reflect different points to make sure you understand (e.g., "So wait, if I'm hearing you right . . ."), or when appropriate ask questions that expand the topic or invite different perspectives (e.g., "What do you think about . . .")

5. *Listen, don't plan.* Often times in conversations, people are simply waiting for their turn to talk. This is the opposite of listening. Although it is tempting to formulate responses in your mind, hold that impulse at bay until the other person is finished talking.

6. *Be aware of your mind.* Thoughts have a tendency to wander, and are often sparked by the topic of conversation at hand. When you notice your mind wandering, gently turn your attention back to the speaker. Just like in meditation when you notice thoughts arising and refocus on your breath, you can notice your mind beginning to wander during a conversation and bring your focus back to the speaker. Your core practice is a helpful tool!

Engaged listening is another way to show how much you love and support your child by intentionally making her a priority, and how you model this skill will heavily influence how your child learns to communicate with family, friends, and teachers. When you practice engaged listening with your child, it demonstrates that you care about her, her opinions, her experiences, and her ideas. It indicates that you value her, because what she has to say is an extension of who she is and you recognize that she is trying to share that with you. In turn, you model for your child what it means to give someone your full attention. It's a powerful gift to you both that will keep you connected by putting your relationship first.

Manners and New Technology

New technology brings with it many opportunities and possibilities, but many questions as well. Questions about manners and etiquette regarding new technologies are particularly difficult. It is difficult to figure out how to handle things like text messages, e-mails, and social networks when most people now carry devices that keep them plugged in all the time.

QUESTION

How do manners relate to mindfulness?
Manners are nothing more than the practice of mindfulness in interaction with others. All manners are based on paying attention to those around you and being mindful of how they may be affected by what you do and how you do it. You practice showing them due respect with your words, actions, and body language.

As a rule of thumb, it makes sense to show respect to those who are actually in your presence. This should receive priority over those you are interacting with remotely, by whatever means. This means giving the people around you your attention and using body language that demonstrates you are engaged with them and attentive.

Teach Communication

One easy way to show respect to those around you in almost any circumstance is to communicate about what you are doing. This is an important rule to instill in your children and practice on your own. Most people know that it is only polite to excuse one's self when leaving the table to use the restroom. The same rule should be applied to use of technology: If you get a call or text, excuse yourself before you check your phone. If the call or message is not critically important, put your phone away. It can wait until later. If for some reason you have to respond, again, communicate to those around you that it is important and you will need a moment to respond. In the case of a text or e-mail, it is fine to remain where you are.

Get Face to Face

One of the key ways to demonstrate politeness is through eye contact. Human beings' primary sense is vision. For human beings, things we see grab our attention in ways that most other senses do not. Historically, this is because one of the main reasons for sight was to detect threats. When you speak to someone, it is polite to turn toward them, stop whatever else you are doing, and look them in the eye when you speak to them. When you do this, they will feel more connected to you and you both will be able to get your points across more readily.

ALERT

Looking someone in the eye is not possible for everyone. In fact, in some cultures, it is considered confrontational to do so. It is also inherently intense, in part because of the wealth of information the brain gleans from someone's face. Looking at someone's face activates systems all over the brain to collect and interpret information and then make inferences about the person from that information.

CHAPTER 16

Living a Mindful Life

Living mindfully includes recognizing the complex web of relationships that make your life possible. The saying, "No man is an island" is very true. Every person depends on other beings for love, support, company, food, and care. Your ability to survive and flourish depends on others, much as others depend on you.

Interdependence

Interdependence is a reality of life, and every person lives and grows within the grace of this truth. Food is a wonderful example of this. The vast majority of people in the United States do not hunt and forage for sustenance, but instead buy their food at grocery stores. Have you ever stopped to think about all of the people and beings who make this possible, or how you are connected with them? It's pretty incredible, when you think about it.

Interdependence Through Space

Vegetables are grown, processed, and shipped without you having to do a thing. Animals are raised, killed, and butchered by other people (or are caught in the wild). The meat you find in the store is either precooked or prepackaged, or at the very least cleaned, wrapped in plastic, and ready to take home.

All of this food comes from a mishmash of local and international farms that depend on a healthy environment, the right climate, fertile land (or lots of pesticides), animal feed, and other aids to produce what they do before shipping their goods to your grocery store. The shipping itself requires resources to pack the food safely (such as plastic made from crude oil), semi trucks that can act as massive refrigerators, drivers, pilots, or ship captains who transport the food, gasoline to make this happen, store employees to unload the food and organize it on the shelves, butchers who slice the meat for you, and so on.

Even in this brief example, the fact that you are intimately connected to and depend on countless others around the world is crystal clear.

Interdependence Through Time

The example with food not only crosses space, but also time. Humans stand on the shoulders of those who came before them; the life you now lead is in part the way it is because of the billions of lives that came before yours. Simple things like how to make bread, how to start a fire, how to build shelter, or more complex ones like your municipal water and sewage services, medical care, oil extraction and manipulation, cell phones, airplanes, cars, not to mention all of the plant and animal life that contribute to making this possible—the life you lead is what it is because of the actions of beings across space and time.

The main purpose of being aware of this is to recognize that you are a small part of a much greater whole; that each person is woven into an incredibly complex tapestry of cause-and-effect relationships. There is much to be grateful for, and part of living a mindful life is living in gratitude.

Cause and Effect

Just as a pebble thrown into a pond will never see the waves it causes or how far they might spread, it is much the same with what people say and do. It is not an overstatement to say that even a single word or action can ripple through space and time.

Every (seemingly) major or insignificant thing you do has a consequence. Every action does something to affect the surrounding world, and there are many times when you will never see, experience, or understand the consequences of something you do or have done. Each individual action affects the whole, no matter how small.

Just Imagine

You go shopping for regular coffee and a few other items, and when you get to the checkout line someone bumps into you and you drop your groceries and wallet. Glaring and cursing quietly at the inattentive person who knocked into you (who walks on in complete oblivion), you look down to see a middle-aged woman picking up your things. "Here you are," she says, handing you everything that had fallen. "People can be such nitwits, don't you think?" she says with a wink. Something about her expression and tone of voice hit your funny bone, and you both start laughing. The day's tension suddenly vanishes, and a seemingly insignificant connection with another person has made all the difference.

Intended and Unintended Consequences

In this case, the middle-aged woman's intended consequence was to do something kind and possibly cheer you up. One of the unintended consequences of this scenario is how this short exchange also compelled the mother standing in line behind you to smile and place her hand on her child's shoulder. Who is to say how this small interaction might influence the trajectory of everybody's day, and perhaps beyond?

Because you cannot know the full impact of your actions, and because there is always a series of intended and unintended consequences, to act intentionally makes a big difference. Sometimes the consequences are benign, sometimes quite positive, and sometimes quite negative. A little kindness can go a long way; a flippant remark or an angry reaction can, too. Practicing mindfulness in the light of this understanding will help you consider what you say and do ahead of time; hopefully, the ripples of your actions will lean toward the positive.

Compassion and Empathy

Being mindful of those who help make your life what it is, both human and otherwise, brings with it a sense of connection and gratitude. Cause and effect demonstrate this world's interconnectedness, and how each action ripples through time and space. When you are mindful of the link between all people and life on this planet, it becomes obvious that we are all in this together. With this knowledge, compassion arises naturally. Whether to live in a way that respects this or not is a choice each person makes.

This understanding can open your heart and compel you to consider your actions more carefully. When it is clear that harming others is the same as harming yourself (and vice versa), there is real motivation to act with compassion and intention. When you feel a connection with others and care about their well-being, you do not want to see them suffer and will take steps to alleviate their pain.

The Root of the Word "Compassion"

The word *compassion* was absorbed into written English from the French in 1340, and the French word was taken from the Latin *compati*. When you break down the roots of the word (*com* means "with," and *pati* means "to suffer"), the original meaning of compassion is "to suffer together." The Latin definition is much closer to what we now call "empathy," which means to identify with or vicariously experience the thoughts, feelings, or attitudes of others.

When you are actively aware that you care about others, you are more likely to take their needs into consideration as you act. This is compassion in action. It can happen on a massive worldwide scale, but it more commonly occurs through small acts of kindness. One is not better than the other (every person who chooses to live mindfully does what they can, when they can). By simply paying attention, you quite literally change the world one moment at a time.

Modeling Compassion

Modeling compassion is the most effective way to teach and promote it in your children. When you treat others as you want to be treated, it does not even matter if the kindness is reciprocated; you act with kindness because that is the kind of person you want to be.

Here are some examples of small acts of kindness:

- Hold the door for someone.
- Pick up something a person has dropped.
- Give away things you don't need to family, friends, or strangers who do.
- Say "Please," "Excuse me," and "Thank you."
- Ask how you can help.
- Sincerely ask someone, "How are you?"
- Give and receive hugs.
- Smile at people, even if they don't smile back.
- Help carry a neighbor's groceries.
- Tell someone that you appreciate what they have done.

Try getting your children involved in these acts as well.

Kindness and Gratitude

Another way to promote compassion, particularly with your children and family, is to casually talk about kindness and gratitude. When subjects like these are part of a regular dialogue, your child's attention (and your own) will be drawn to kindness and gratitude in new ways. Conversation starters include questions like "What's one nice thing you noticed someone do at school today?" or "What's one thing you're grateful for today?" Sometimes it helps if you go first. The point is to ask questions like this regularly, and to share what you notice and are grateful for as well. Before you know it, your child will begin sharing his answers with you before you've even asked!

Compassion Through Service

Another meaningful way to integrate compassion into your family life is through service. There are countless service opportunities available across the country; it is just a matter of looking to see how you can get involved in your local community.

Community Service Opportunities

Engaging in various types of service-oriented activities with your child teaches quite a few things, not the least of which is how each person can make a difference in the lives of others. This is most effective when the service work is oriented toward developing meaningful relationships with others and happens regularly, instead of more superficial engagements that occur once or twice every couple of years.

Superficial engagement in service work tends to make people feel better about themselves, but often does not teach any meaningful lessons about making a real difference in someone else's life. Meaningful lessons come from building relationships with others (including animals, plants, and places), seeing the positive impact of your actions, and doing so regularly as opposed to sporadically.

Possible service opportunities for you and your family include:

- Bring a trash bag on family walks.
- Volunteer at soup kitchens, food pantries, or animal shelters.
- Collect clothes and toys to donate to churches or shelters, particularly during the winter months.
- Write pen-pal letters to servicemen and women.
- Form a litter patrol with friends to keep school or park grounds clean.

- Plant trees and wildflowers.
- Hold bake sales or car washes, and give the proceeds to an important cause.
- Contribute to or participate in Meals on Wheels.
- Visit local retirement or nursing homes to read, help out, and spend time with the elderly.
- Contact your local hospital and find out what you can do to spend time with or support sick children.
- Set up your child with a younger "reading buddy" so he can mentor and spend time with another child who is learning to read.
- Set up a pen pal project with children in a local hospital, senior citizens, or children in other parts of the country or world.
- Make a book on tape and donate it to a local day care center.
- Volunteer to help out at your local library.
- Sponsor walk-a-thons or read-a-thons whose proceeds go to an important cause.
- Look for opportunities to help your neighbors.

Compassion for Yourself

Living a mindful life means being aware not only of the needs of others, but also noticing and prioritizing your own needs. Given the many demands on your time and energy, it is important that you find ways to meet your own needs and care for yourself.

Parents so often cast their own needs aside in the face of other demands, such as work and children. It is important to recognize, however, that you cannot do your best at work, as a parent, as a spouse, or as a friend when you are too physically or emotionally depleted. When you are not mindful or attentive to some of your own basic needs, it will catch up to you and get taken out on others in unhealthy or unfair ways.

It is important to have a short amount of alone time each day. Even if it is only for a few minutes, finding time for yourself is necessary to your mental sanity. Sometimes the only way to do this is to go for a short run, take a hot shower, meditate, enjoy a cup of tea or coffee outside, or simply lie in bed for a few extra minutes before getting up each morning and focus on some deep breathing. Whatever you choose to do, and however it fits into each unique day, it makes a big difference when you make this a priority.

Sleep has a significant impact on your mood and functionality. Parents are often running a sleep deficit for a million different reasons; even if all you can do is lie down for a few minutes, giving your body and mind some time to relax and recuperate is helpful. Do what you can as you are able, and notice when your exhaustion is getting in the way so you can do something about it. If your child is around, explain to her that your body is tired and that you need some quiet time so you have energy to play again. Children can be very receptive when you include them in your process, and are often eager to help you in one way or another. If there are ways for your child to help take care of you, tell her so and she will likely do her best to help.

Creating time with your significant other can sometimes feel impossible, particularly when your children are very young. This is crucial, however; although children change the dynamics of any marriage or relationship, it is important for you and your partner to make time and space to reconnect on a regular basis in ways that are unrelated to raising children. Time to be intimate with one another (and this goes far beyond just having sex) is important to how you function as a couple.

Making sure you and your partner have time together requires tapping into a necessary resource for every family: your support network. Parenting should not happen in isolation, although with the prevalence of single-family homes and the degeneration of the community mentality, this happens more often than it should.

Every family needs help and support. Learning how to ask friends, family members, and neighbors to help you makes a significant difference in how you and your partner are able to prioritize and meet your personal needs. Reaching out to others, even if it is just to vent for five minutes about how exhausted or frustrated you are, makes a massive difference. Part of this is admitting the ways that you need and depend on others. There are many people who have mistakenly internalized this as a negative thing, but the truth is that every person needs and is dependent on others. This is not a failure or a mistake, it is something to embrace, appreciate, and be humbled by.

Make time for yourself to be alone, even if for only a few minutes every day. Do what you can to get the rest you need, so you can be at the top of your game. Prioritize time with your significant other, perhaps by forging a date night every week or two. Do this with the help of your friends, family, loved ones, and neighbors. Arrange ways to help each other, so that you and the people you care about all have opportunities to care for themselves and get what they need. Notice if pride, stubbornness, or frustration is getting in the way, and take measures to let the emotion move through you instead of holding you back or bringing you down. Live a life of intention, and practice mindfulness in how you treat others, how you treat the environment, and how you treat yourself. Notice your thoughts and feelings without judgment, and respond to situations in the best way you are able to in the moment. Notice what triggers you to react, your patterns of thought and action, and reflect on what you can do to set yourself and your family up for success. Recognize that mistakes are only a problem if you fail to learn from them, and return again and again to your breath and the beauty and the grace that surround you, even when the weather is bad and your mood is foul.

Practice living a mindful life, and just notice what happens. You might be amazed by the spaciousness this practice creates.

Dangers of Multitasking

In reality, multitasking (trying to do more than one thing at a time) decreases people's quality of work because of how it divides and scatters concentration. The relative excitement you typically feel when multitasking is a result of the adrenaline rush that comes when the brain is overstimulated. Unfortunately, this strategy does not translate into greater productivity—in fact, quite the opposite.

ALERT

Multitasking is neurologically impossible. When you try to multitask, what you actually end up doing is rapidly switching between tasks. Each time you do so, you lose efficiency and concentration, so stop trying! Do one thing at a time so you can do it with your whole brain, then move on to the next.

A mind that is bouncing between the demands of trying to hold a face-to-face conversation while researching something on the Internet and checking Facebook all at the same time will inevitably fail to complete each task as efficiently and effectively as it otherwise could. This kind of scattered attention creates mediocre results and possibly hurt feelings. The best way to approach work (or conversations) of any kind is not to simultaneously juggle a bunch of tasks, but to focus on one thing at a time.

Every parent can agree that the ability to concentrate on a single task for a long amount of time is an important skill to have, both as an adult and as a child. This is especially true when it comes to having face-to-face conversations with others and knowing how to listen. It is impossible to give someone your full attention if you are also checking your e-mail or sending a text, yet these sorts of things happen all the time. Politeness and manners have been eclipsed by technology.

Though it may be tempting to idealize or romanticize "how things used to be," when cell phones or computers didn't exist, this frame of mind is counterproductive. The potential distractions we face every day aren't the problem. What matters is how we deal with them.

FACT

The mind has a natural tendency to remember the past more fondly than it may have been. This is particularly true of the distant past and even in our imagining of times before our own birth. This phenomenon arises, at least in part, because of the stress associated with the future: Because you do not know what will happen, you experience some degree of stress and anxiety about what is to come.

Now, a closer look at some of the potential distractions you and your child face each day:

The Internet

This technological feat has completely changed the world in which your child will grow up. Information has never been more widespread and easily accessible, and the public has never spent more time sitting in front of computers. The Internet is a necessary educational tool in this day and age, and using search engines to help complete projects and homework is now the norm. Entire libraries are becoming digitized, and these changes are revolutionizing the educational system.

On the other hand, the Internet is very easy for people to get lost in. Distraction is seductive, after all, especially for students procrastinating on something like a research project. If you are not careful, the Internet is a black hole of misused time and attention. One web page links into another; one question or idea leads to ten related Google searches; online games abound; and social networks such as Facebook, Twitter, Pinterest become obsessions. It is not uncommon for teenagers to spend huge amounts of time each day roaming the Internet, but the trick is teaching them to enjoy the benefits this technology brings so they do not fall into the rabbit hole of compulsive escapism.

It is tricky for people of any age to remain focused when using the Internet, because it is both an educational resource and an interest-driven playground. It is especially difficult for parents to know whether their child is using the Internet for educational purposes or as a distracting wonderland. This can understandably stress parents out.

Cell Phones

With the advent of smart phones and tablets, we can now bring the Internet anywhere we want to go. Generations are now growing up in a world connected in real time. Even before smart phones, regular cell phones brought significant change to how people communicate with one another. Now individuals can contact each other anywhere, anytime. Text messaging is commonplace, and the proliferation of cell phones among younger kids continues. This technology has caused serious issues within school systems across the country; administrators and teachers are still learning how to manage and enforce acceptable cell phone use at school.

Many families struggle as parents decide on (or fail to decide on) appropriate cell phone use at home for themselves and their kids. On the one hand, cell phones make it easier for parents to know where their children are, and give kids a way to ask for help in case of an emergency. On the other hand, when parents and their kids spend more time looking at their phones than each other at the dinner table, something is wrong. Healthy boundaries are needed.

FACT

Have you ever felt your cell phone vibrate only to check it and see that no one had called or texted? This phenomenon, called "ghost sensation," is very real. Because your mind enjoys the stimulation it receives from the many things you can do with your phone, it anticipates rings and can even subconsciously create the false sensation of an incoming call or text to give you an excuse to check your phone.

Television

TV is one of the primary sources for American entertainment. According to a May 2012 report from The Nielsen Company about television consumption, the average American over two years old watches thirty-four hours of TV a week. That is a long time! The point of bringing this up is not to bash how often people watch TV, because TV can be a fun and educational resource as well. The purpose is to help you bring awareness to your choices.

QUESTION

Why is TV so addictive?
The reason television is such a powerful draw is because of the level of stimulation you get from it. As far as your brain is concerned, a TV is a box of blinking lights that provides a wealth of stimulation to the brain. Even more than that, TV shows of all types communicate stories and offer us the opportunity to engage in fantasy relationships. This creates a perfect recipe to get the brain hooked.

Healthy parent-child relationships require conversations, interaction, physical activities, and critical thought (to name a few). It's important to keep in mind that television is passive entertainment. It requires no interaction, no communication, no critical thought, and no movement. If watching television becomes the only way your family spends "quality time" together, the relationships will inevitably suffer.

That being said, there is absolutely nothing wrong with watching TV every day. What matters is how much time you spend watching TV and what kinds of shows you watch. Each family must find its own balance and definition of healthy television use. The point here is to be intentional about what you and your child are choosing. When you choose your actions mindfully, you help your children learn to do the same.

Advertisements

Advertisements are everywhere in American culture. It is impossible to drive down a road, watch television, use the Internet, play games, read a magazine, listen to the radio, or even walk down the street without being bombarded by somebody trying to sell something. Marketers often pay lots of money to plant products in movies and TV shows to subtly promote these things *during* the entertainment instead of just *in between* entertainment. Just think—how often have you seen popular film or television characters drinking a can of Coca-Cola, smoking a cigarette, or driving a particular type of vehicle?

When you realize the extent of your exposure to marketing ploys, it can be a disturbing experience. This is amplified when you realize the extent and impact of your child's exposure to advertising.

Because young children have a less developed prefrontal cortex (the higher thinking and reasoning area of the brain) and less impulse control, they are particularly influenced by advertising. Ads typically present toys, clothes, food, and more in fun and exciting ways that appeal to children. Anything children watch on TV can quickly become "normal" to them, and what kid doesn't want to feel fun, cool, and normal?

"Pleeeaase! Everyone else has one, why can't I?!" is a common plea you might know well. Once kids are hooked on whatever an ad is selling, they work on persuading their parents to buy it. This is the linchpin behind corporate strategies that advertise directly to children: when kids are repeatedly exposed to ads and become convinced that they want or need something, parents are very likely to make the purchase.

Games

Computer and video games can be great fun. Some are mindless and silly; others are cognitively and/or physically challenging. Regardless, these kinds of games are entertaining and offer much more interaction than something like television.

Computer and video games can offer great graphics, various degrees of physical movement, compelling storylines, interesting opportunities to problem-solve, and (it is important to recognize) another venue for social interaction. People use these games as a way to have fun, decompress, and often, as a way to interact with others.

ALERT

Video games have a well-known withdrawal effect. Playing a video game creates an intense environment of overstimulation and hypervigilance in the brain. Research has shown that after as little as ten minutes of gaming, your brain becomes highly active, processing huge amounts of data very intensely. When you stop the game, your brain is exhausted and functions at a severe deficit for several hours while it recovers. The areas that suffer most are attention and executive functioning, so never let your kids play video games before homework.

According to The 2012 Essential Facts About the Computer and Video Game Industry (released by the Entertainment Software Association), 62 percent of gamers play either in-person or online with other players. In this sense, playing video games contributes to a child's ability to develop social spheres, and can have many positive social and educational benefits. But computer and video games can also be overused, and become a welcomed escape from the demands and responsibilities of real life.

Similar to the choices parents face about television, a healthy approach to playing computer and video games hinges on how often these games are played and the content of the games themselves. There are still many questions that scientists are trying to answer about the impact of video games on developing brains; however, at this point a few things are certain:

- The brain grows and develops neural connections in response to external stimuli, and computer and video games are definitely sources of stimuli for the brain. When played regularly, these games do have an impact on children's neurodevelopment.

- Those who regularly play video games with lots of action and violence are certain to have negative cognitive effects. Intensive game play such as this makes it difficult for people to appreciate slower paced and less stimulating environments (such as work or school).
- There is a connection between playing violent games and having more aggressive thoughts. This can reduce empathy, normalize anti-social behaviors, and increase confrontational or disruptive behaviors in the real world.

ESSENTIAL

Unlike video games, which make attention and executive functioning much harder for the brain after playing, physical exercise has the opposite effect. Just fifteen minutes of active play stimulates the body to release a variety of chemicals that make concentration and cognitive tasks both easier and more efficient.

Deciding on Healthy Limits

Mindfulness is an invitation to practice with every shade of experience: the good, the bad, and everything in between. The potential impediments parents face while living and teaching mindfulness are not actually problems, but opportunities for deeper and more creative practice. Every obstacle you encounter presents you with this opportunity. While there is often a temptation to rage against whatever makes life difficult or to point a finger of blame at others, the real challenge of mindfulness is to practice with the world exactly as it is.

What to Consider

Despite the many potential distractions that technology presents in this day and age, they are only distractions when they are used as such. When used with intention and moderation, things like the Internet, cell phones, television, and computer and video games have much to offer. The question facing you now is what healthy limits are appropriate for you and your children?

There is no one-size-fits-all magical formula to answer this question; however, there are many important factors to consider as you, your partner, and your children discuss what your family's healthy limits are.

ESSENTIAL

It's important to realize that when your children are old enough to communicate effectively, the process of deciding on healthy limits for your family can and should include your kids. It is possible for this to be a constructive conversation instead of a top-down decision.

- *The age and stage of your child(ren).* It has been scientifically proven that "screen time" (which includes TV, computers, hand-held games, iPhones, iPads, etc.) has negative neurological impacts on children who are two or younger. Children learn the most through active play, and should be encouraged to do as much of it as possible instead of forming habits around passive entertainment. Parents can use technology to supplement their child's education; it just requires forethought and filtering for appropriate content. Scientists have shown that prolonged screen time makes it exponentially more difficult for preadolescents and teens to concentrate on tasks such as homework. Supervision and agreements about computer/Internet use are important for these age groups.
- *Social interests and needs.* This correlates to the age of your child. Preadolescents and teens often want to participate in online social networks such as Facebook, Twitter, MySpace, or role-playing video games because "all of their friends are doing it too." This is a legitimate social sphere for youth to interact.
- *Educational interests and needs.* This mostly has to do with Internet access, as students nowadays are expected to use computers and the Internet in completing assignments.
- *Time to decompress.* Moderation is key, and that also means being clear about when it is appropriate to relax and be a couch potato. When kids first get home from school, it's important for them to have some time to decompress before beginning homework. What are healthy options for doing so that will set your child up for success?

- *Safety.* Safety is an important consideration when deciding what kind of Internet use is appropriate for your child. Chat rooms, Skype, and posting pictures and comments to Facebook present concerns over privacy.

Media Diet

It is easy to not pay attention to what kind and how much media you consume, but it is a critical part of mindfulness practice that you and your children learn to do so. Everyone knows the adage, "You are what you eat." This should be reworded to "You are what you consume."

In the case of food, it is obvious enough: What you eat gets broken down by your digestion and absorbed into your body. The same is quite literally true of the media you consume, but the path of entry is through your brain, not your stomach. You always look at your food before you eat it, right? And you are probably selective, choosing a combination of things you like and that are healthy for you (well, most of the time, anyway). Why wouldn't you apply the same rules to what you put in your mind, or more importantly, in your child's mind?

ESSENTIAL

Don't think the media you consume has an effect on you? Pay attention to how you feel after you watch a show or listen to the news. Notice the thoughts circulating in your mind. Now scan your body: What do you notice there? Now, think back to what you just watched or listened to: Could there be a connection?

It is easy to leave the TV on in the background, turn the radio on when you hop in the car, or just start watching any random show because it was on after something you really did want to watch. It is important to recognize that with these activities, there isn't any choice involved. When you consume media in these passive ways, you take it all in without any selection. This is mindlessness, the very opposite of mindfulness, and it can have surprising impacts on how you feel and behave. The same applies to your children.

Instead, try to be intentional about the media you consume. Think about the shows you watch: Why do you watch them? What about the radio stations you listen to or the websites you visit? The books, magazines, and newspapers you read? For each one, ask yourself "What do I get from this? How does this contribute to my life?" If you can't answer that question in a way that aligns with your personal values, maybe you should reconsider what you consume.

This isn't to say that every single thing you take in should have some higher purpose and it is never okay to just relax. Sometimes it is perfectly appropriate to watch something just because you enjoy it or because it helps you unwind. You don't have to be "on" all the time, but it is worthwhile to consider what you get out of what you consume. If you have a particular show you like to watch to relax, bring your mindfulness practice to that, too. Notice how you feel during and after the show: Are you really relaxed? Or does it stir you up? All humans are naturally drawn to stimulation. Giving our brains something to do and giving our emotions something to feel feels good. Even negative stimulation can feel good (hence the popularity of horror films). Just be clear about what you choose and why.

CHAPTER 17

Conversation with Mindful Parents

In this chapter you will meet two parents who actively practice mindfulness with their child, and gain a better understanding of the challenges (and rewards) associated with this practice. Melissa Blacker and David Rynick are both Zen teachers and cofounders of Boundless Way Zen. They are a married couple who have raised their daughter, Rachel, together and have practiced mindfulness in their daily lives since before she was born. Melissa formerly worked with Jon Kabat-Zinn at the Center for Mindfulness in Medicine, Health Care, and Society at University of Massachusetts Medical Center in Worcester, Massachusetts. You can learn more about Melissa, David, and their work at *www .worcesterzen.org*.

Everyday Mindfulness

One of the most difficult questions parents practicing mindfulness struggle with is how to carry their practice throughout the activities of their daily lives. It helps to see how others approach this subject, and how you can use their techniques to your own advantage.

Through the Eyes of a Mindful Mom

When asked about her daily mindfulness practice, mindful mom Melissa says:

"The main way that I've been taught mindfulness has to do with this openness to whatever is happening. Really being awake to what's going on in the body, what the sensory experiences are, what the emotional field is in any given moment . . . It's about what's going on in the mind, but not believing what's going on in the mind. There's an openness to all of the senses, to emotions, the thoughts, to whatever is coming.

"For me the breath was the original practice, both in Zen and then later in mindfulness. I can always pause and stop and remember. That's another important way of describing mindfulness: as remembering or recollecting the actuality of life. You can bring intentionality to what's going on in this moment. I'll often say to myself 'Stop,' and just take a moment in the middle of the stuff that's going on—if I'm lucky, and if I remember.

"From my point of view, it's more about this reminder to just stay open to what's going on. When that happens [when I remember to stop and pay attention], I realize that I have been missing some really crucial information about what's happening in the present moment. That's part of what mindfulness practice helps me with. It doesn't calm me down, it doesn't make me happy, it doesn't *do* anything that I might wish for—it widens the field [of my awareness]."

Through the Eyes of a Mindful Dad

When asked the same question, mindful dad David says:

"I think this issue of remembering is really at the heart of it, because there is what I call 'the mindless forward momentum of our lives.' There is this inertial quality toward faster and faster and more and more, and I think for parents it's more intense than for anyone else.

"If you have a busy life, if you don't have kids you can go home and have a meal and sit down. But if you have a busy life *and* you have kids, you go home and then there's another kind of business. There are these small beings that are specifically designed to push your buttons. Our children will push us beyond whatever wisdom or capacity or equanimity we have. I think this is pretty much guaranteed. So the question is not how do we always be open-handed and easy, because we will not be. If we set that as our goal, we will fail and feel terrible about ourselves. So how do we change what our goal is?

"To me it is about being present with what's here, and trusting that what's here might be what I'm looking for. This is the teaching of so many spiritual paths, that what we are looking for is right here. So when two children are fighting in the other room, hitting each other, screaming, and you are exhausted, how is *this it*? Unless we can stop, or slow down, or somehow bring some awareness to the present moment intentionally, we will just be swept away with the necessities of life."

Zen Practice and Mindfulness

Because David and Melissa are both parents and Zen practitioners, they have a unique understanding about the differences between the two practices, differences that may help you understand the purposes of both lifestyles more succinctly.

Mindfulness Is a Part of Zen

David: "The practice of Zen Buddhism includes the practice of mindfulness, but is not limited to that. And I think Zen has a particular take on mindfulness. Sometimes mindfulness is approached with a '. . . If I do this, then I'll get that' [mentality], and so mindfulness sometimes is confused with being calm. And we'd all love to be calm and centered, especially around this topic with our children. We would love to be 'mindfulness saints,' but I think that's missing the real point of mindfulness, which is being present with whatever is happening, including all of the things we wish *weren't* happening.

"The teaching of Zen about mindfulness is that when we really meet what is happening, there is some transformational possibility in that moment."

Melissa: "Certainly in Boundless Way [Zen], we practice mindfulness in the form of just sitting where we are, present with everything that's occurring. 'Just sitting' doesn't mean [only] sitting, it means going out and living your life with some kind of attention, on purpose, receiving whatever the world has to offer and responding to it.

"There are many different definitions of mindfulness. Jon Kabat-Zinn's definition is paying attention on purpose in the present moment without judging. I like the Zen aspect of mindfulness, which is this capacity to receive the world and respond. In concentration practice there's a focus on just one thing, almost to the exclusion of other things, but that eventually has to be complemented by an open awareness."

Embracing the Moment

With parenting comes obvious stress and struggle. How do Melissa and David practice mindfulness when they don't like what the present moment has to offer or they don't like what is coming up for them in that moment?

Handling Your Emotions

As David notes, the first thing he often does is to blame his spouse or his children.

Melissa adds: "Which works very well, because I like to blame myself, like I'm the worst mother in the world. Actually I keep thinking about an experience that I had when our daughter was five or six months old, and my older brother had had his first child a month and a half after we did.

"He called me up one day and said, 'Melissa, you're a spiritual person. I have a question for you about raising my daughter: There are moments in the day when I struggle so much that I just want to take her and throw her out the window. What can I do about that?' I said, 'I don't recommend throwing her out the window, but I know that feeling,' and the two of us suddenly had this wonderful experience of sharing how hard it is. We get angry. We get angry with these innocent little cherubs. We were both really exhausted and upset, and just sort of allowed those feelings to be so. It was very healing for both of us. It was a great moment.

"It's really important to acknowledge that we all feel like this sometimes. It is also important not to act on it. It's this pause: 'I do feel like, as much as I love you, I want to kill you right now.' It's a really useful thing to admit. It's not a problem to be upset about your child. It's not a problem to feel like a bad parent, to feel frustrated, to not know what to do. One of the things I credit my brother with in that instance is that he called somebody. You don't want to be alone in it, because then you can get fooled and start ignoring information, then you get too narrow in view, so we always want to keep the view big. One way is to have another person to talk to."

David: "And I think too, moving out of the patterns of blame. We blame ourselves, we blame our children: 'I should be better, how come I'm not more loving?' but there is the possibility of not blaming.

"I think it is powerful for all of us to meet what's arising as just what's arising, and as part of being a human. When we meet it that way, there is some possibility to be with [our thoughts and feelings] in a new way. This points to the 'not judging' aspect of Jon Kabat-Zinn's definition of mindfulness."

Melissa: "Yes. Absolutely. It is very easy, especially with those intense emotions, to start judging yourself or others because of that."

David: "My sense is that there have been other societies in human experience that have not been as isolated as ours, where everybody didn't have their own house and separate space. It is wonderful that we have the things we have today, but I think it's a structural issue. We have to parent in private now, so we don't have the support of other people unless we intentionally join a playgroup or call a friend, so I do think reaching out is something that parents have to do consciously now."

Consciously Teaching Mindfulness

Sometimes, when parents practice mindfulness in their own lives, it becomes an unconscious part of their parenting style. Did you consciously try to teach mindfulness to your daughter at any point?

Melissa: "I would say yes and no."

David: "Me, I would say no and yes. I think in the deepest sense, the only thing we've ever taught her is mindfulness. In terms of being present with her in the moment, *that's* mindfulness. Being with her as she just learned to do her buttons to put her shirt on when we had to get somewhere very quickly is still vivid in my mind. Then as she grew, really in the developmental way, to walk with her as she encountered the world, to help her be present to what was going on, and knowing when to help and fix, and when not to button the buttons for her.

Melissa: "Rachel's teacher—I think [when she was] in third grade—they were on a trip on a bus, and she taught her teacher how to meditate. Her teacher told us later, 'Rachel told me how to work with my breath,' so I think there was some kind of an absorption quality that was happening because she was around us practicing and teaching formal meditation.

"There's a great story, I don't remember how old she was, but she decided she was going to meditate. I think she was around eight. She came down from her room and she said, 'I scored four minutes!' What she meant was she'd actually timed herself, and was able to sit still and meditate for four minutes. Then she just thought it was the *lamest* thing as she got older and got to be a teenager. But she was kind of always pulled and fascinated by it. When she got older, she actually trained with Jon Kabat-Zinn. I took her out with me to a seven-day mindfulness professional training, and she has used some of what she learned. She is now a music teacher, and teaches music using some of the tools of mindfulness, and has kind of flirted with Zen practice. She definitely goes in and out of it."

David: "I'm reminded of a friend who, when our kids were younger, had a boy and we had a girl, and he was saying, 'I really want to figure out what I need to say to my son so that he won't be sexist.' And I said, 'It actually doesn't matter at all what you say to your son, it's how *you* behave.'

"I think the most important thing, if we want to encourage mindfulness in our children, is for *us* to practice. *That's* the real gift."

Transitional Mindfulness

There tend to be three different stages that children go through: initially, total helplessness and dependence on their parents; then a great closeness and affection with parents; then moving into adolescence, a rebellion from parents. Melissa and David made sure to practice mindfulness individually and with their child as she moved through those different frames.

Mindfulness Transitions

Melissa: "I agree with those three frames, and also see that they replicate themselves in smaller ways. Rachel did her adolescent piece when she was about two years old. There was the total dependence, and then there was this real closeness, and then there was rejection. It just kept cycling around, and I think that's part of how it works. There's some reactivity to the closeness in all kids, so they have to pull back to individuate. Where we see that big time is in their adolescence, and it also happens all through the early stages of life too. That's why they talk about the terrible two's, because all kids know how say at that point is 'No!'"

David: "Every child is so different. Some people talk about how adolescence is terrible—that really wasn't our experience at all. But those phases of closeness and separation are some of the hardest things as a parent.

"I vividly remember Rachel going to college, and six months before she left, Melissa was really upset about this. I didn't really get that [Rachel] would leave us. You invest so much, and you're closer to this human being than to any other human being on the planet, and then they want to leave you. Melissa was processing that before Rachel went to college, and moments of sadness would come over her, and I would say, 'Well this is what we want, and yes it is sad.' Then we dropped her off at the college and came back home, and Melissa walks in the house and says, 'Hmm. It feels pretty good here!' And I walk in the house and begin to sob helplessly, because Rachel's stuff isn't where her stuff always was, and I'm like, 'How can I survive without this young woman I love so much?'

"There is real pain and real ambivalence as our children grow up, because in some way I always want to be wonderful daddy who can make everything fine. And that's a role that's very hard to give up. I mean that's the pleasure in the dependence part, is that you can actually make it better, you know? As our children get older, we can't solve everything. And of course it's that way even as they're young, but it becomes more apparent that we cannot play the all-powerful one, and we have to play the one who cares deeply and can do nothing.

"Although I do remember when our daughter was first born, she was born cesarean, and they took her into the next room. I abandoned Melissa and went in with our daughter, and they were doing the first exam, the APGAR test. They checked things and everything looked good: they counted the fingers and toes, and then they said, 'Now we are going to take some blood to do a blood test.' I said, 'Well how are you going to get the blood?' and they said, 'We are going to prick her heel,' and I said, 'No you're not!" and they said, 'Yes, we are.'

"[Rachel] was five minutes old, and that was the first moment I got a clue that I was not going to be able to protect her from this world. So I leaned over to her and I said, 'Okay Rachel, now we begin. I can't protect you, but I will stay with you.' I think that as a parent, we want to protect and we can't [always] do it, but we can be with, and protect in some way. But as they grow older, that changing [parental] role is so important, and we're all ambivalent about that. I think kids growing up are ambivalent. It's great to have somebody else take care of you, but yet they're just desperate to grow up and be separate. So all of this developmental stuff happens within the context of great longing for the imagined past, and great longing for the imagined future."

It's Not about Good and Bad

It's so easy to conflate one's success as a parent with your ability to protect your child and give them a life of ease. As though, "If my child suffers I'm a bad parent, if my child does not suffer I'm a good parent." How did you work with that throughout your daughter's life?

Giving Up Control

Melissa: "I think we went in and out of feeling like bad parents. You know the way there are developmental steps for children, there are developmental steps for parents! But this feeling, it's sort of like the primary issue of being human, of taking responsibility for what is not our responsibility, and seeing clearly that we really are in control of almost nothing. That we are in control of this little bitty part of reality, and control in the sense that we can do actions—like if she's hungry we can go to the refrigerator and get food, and we know how to put it on the table. That's the little bit of control we have, the control to respond and the control to take action in some way. But other than that, it could be, and this happened quite a lot, that the food we put on the table is rejected. At certain ages, smeared all over the body.

"So for me, it's been this constant back-and-forth learning of carrying forward a delusion of control over outcome, and then thinking that it's true, and then discovering that it's not true. And then somehow trying again, and then thinking it's true and then discovering it's not true. That's one of the 'great' things about being a parent: it's an incredible learning about responsibility and control."

David: "And I remember one thing that was helpful for me in this regard was my experience with my father. Because when I was in college, I went through real difficulty, and was in this very dark place, and I remember talking with my father about it once and he started to get all upset and said, 'I've been such a bad parent and I'm so sorry,' and I actually interrupted him and I said, 'Dad, this is not about you, it's about me.' And I came to sympathize with his perspective later on. When our daughter is going through something, it's very hard to be with that urge to fix it and the urge, or the delusion that if we are good parents, she will not suffer.

"But I think to imagine that somehow our children will not have the family karma we do is silly. Yes, we should do what we can with what we've inherited, and hopefully we can learn and learn from our parents' pluses and minuses and be better parents, but our children will be neurotic. They will be dysfunctional in their own special way, and that's part of our gift to them. That's what they're going to learn from and grow from."

Melissa: "And stuff will happen to them too, because stuff happens, and we are not in control of that at all. It is, though, a knee-jerk reaction to feel responsible for a child's suffering. It's just really interesting, even though logically it has absolutely no ground . . . we're very creative as human beings, and we can find a way to blame ourselves."

Working with Fear

How do you work with fear as you notice it arising? (Fear of something happening to your child, etc.)

Melissa: "I have a friend who says that when you have a child, you're basically plucking your heart out of your body and putting it on the ground and it walks away from you. It's really how it feels. The connection and the love, the yearning for protection and safety—it's overwhelming. It's similar to what we've been talking about already: owning that fear. I go in and out of being terrified and then being in a happy delusional state that 'everything will be fine.'

"This is where practice is really important, that in this present moment, and also not buying into a contracted state around fear—imagining all the things that can happen—seeing that as a series of thought constructions that are habitual but not the whole story, because there is no way of really knowing what's going to happen. Really being present to it, feeling that fear when it arises, and when it's not present, when I go back into the delusion of 'everything is fine,' to really enjoy that too.

"When I was pregnant, we got an invitation from a local church in the mail that said something about, 'Congratulations on your loan from God,' and inviting us to be a member of their church. We put that in front of the refrigerator because we were both so struck by 'It's a loan,' it's a temporary thing.

"But however long you have, it's the loan of the universe. You get to have this relationship with this person, like with any relationship, but somehow more intense for a child. So fear is normal, but you don't want it to be the whole thing."

Be Present with Your Child

In those moments when you are listening to your daughter or just trying to practice being present with her, what do you do internally to work with those reactions that are really self-centered about *you*, and come back to being present with the child in a way that may serve them more directly?

Going Through the Motions

David: "I think one of the dangers of mindfulness is that we can become a kind of pathetic imitation of a gentle parent. That we can go through the motions without really fully being there. So I can go on listening, or I can go on *pretending* to listen, even after my heart closes. I can keep my eyes about the same width open, and I can keep nodding my head, and I've actually gone somewhere else. So for *me* to recognize that, first of all, is really something. Then sometimes to say, 'You know what, I can't listen to any more of this now,' or 'I have to leave,' or '. . . to take care of myself.'

"I think that the hardest thing for me was to recognize that I had limits, and *have* limits as a parent, because I didn't want to. I wanted to be able to be there all the time and be open and caring, and it's just not possible. It's a great humiliation in some way, but I think to realize as parents when we're near our limit, and then as they say, to put the oxygen mask on yourself first before your children. So how do I take care of myself so that I can restore my capacity to be present? The *first* step is actually realizing that I've gone over to the dark side."

Melissa: "This is where mindfulness really is helpful, because I can notice [my reactions] coming up. Our family style is very transparent, so we've always shared what we're feeling and thinking with Rachel, sometimes probably inappropriately, but she can sense when these things are coming up in us. If I try to pretend that I'm cool when I'm not, when I'm getting triggered by what she's saying, that's not helpful. It's somehow recognizing that these things are coming up [in me], and finding a way to be present with the other person."

Take a Step Back

How did you practice being with your daughter as she experienced or acted out on intense emotions, without getting sucked into those emotions yourselves?

Melissa: "I was a psychotherapist for a while, and now I'm a Zen teacher, and when someone comes to me who is in great distress, even my own child or a student or a client, I can get sucked into the reality of their distress in a certain way.

"My primary job as a teacher and as a parent and a therapist or spiritual director is to remember what is actually true about this person and about life. Internally it's like *come on, remember, remember, recollect the truth of the world.* That these things are temporary, that this is not who you really are. It's really great practice in not getting sucked into [someone's] constricted, delusive reality. That's a real service to another person."

David: "In coaching, we call that, 'Not getting in the boat' with the person. So the person's in the boat about to go over the waterfall: if you get in the boat with them you can't be of much use to them.

"Part of the message is 'Am I a capable person?' And part of my job as a parent is to manage my feelings and keep giving the message 'You are a capable person and you can solve problems.' Problems a three-year-old can solve are at a different level than a twelve-year-old. Another coaching thing is, if you are working harder than your client, you are doing it wrong. And I think the same way as a parent: if we are working harder than our child, then we're taking away their treasure."

Melissa: "I just want to clarify something about this, too: this is not about withdrawing into some state of equanimity, but there's also a joining, that we can sit in the bigger place and also feel the heartbreak of our child or our student. That the heart quivers in resonance with the suffering, while remembering that that's not all that's happening right now. My heart breaks when Rachel is suffering. All the time. But I don't enter [the suffering] with her, where that's the only thing that there is.

"I remember when she was around two years old, [Rachel] was really upset and I was all alone. It was just horrible. She was screaming, crying, and completely inconsolable, and I didn't know what to do. I felt terrible, and I was getting sucked into the reality of 'everything is terrible.' So I just gave myself over to it completely. She was lying down on the floor, kicking her arms and legs and screaming, so I lay down next to her and kicked and screamed. Suddenly she looked at me like, 'What are you doing?'

"It's not just about withdrawing and making space [for someone's suffering], it's also about connecting within this bigger space. And again it's trial and error, there's no way to plan it ahead of time. I didn't do this because I thought it would work, I just did it because I'd run out of options. But it immediately broke her open to, 'What's going on?' So she just stopped and I stopped, and we just looked at each other and then hugged and she cried. I don't think she had the words to say what had happened."

Advice for Other Parents

What advice might you have for parents who are interested in taking up a mindfulness practice for themselves?

Melissa: "I just say do it. I think it really is important for everybody to have a meditation practice, but that's just me. It's certainly been useful to me. But it might take different forms for different people. I would say one of the great benefits of having a meditation practice for a parent is that at least there's a little tiny part of the day where you are doing something just for yourself. Although it does benefit the child and benefits all beings. It could be that it's Yoga practice or exercise, or something that doesn't involve having to accomplish something. It could be cooking, it could be whatever, but something where that's all you are doing. Some immediacy in the day where it's not about parenting for that moment and it's just about you."

CHAPTER 18

Mindfulness Programs
in Schools

Public education is one of many sectors that can benefit enormously from learning about and practicing mindfulness. As research on the benefits of mindfulness and meditation continues to disseminate, more and more people are realizing the importance of such practices in light of the crisis that public education is currently facing.

Schools and Mindfulness Programs

Teacher burnout is a serious problem in the U.S. educational system: nearly half of all new teachers quit the profession within the first five years. On top of this, according to the National Education Association, 37 percent of the education workforce is over the age of fifty and will soon be retiring.

Between issues such as poor administrative support, difficult working conditions, and a massive amount of stress, one of our nation's most important professions is suffering a severe crisis. Sadly, this impacts students more than anyone else. Luckily, mindfulness programs are one of the tools proving to remedy teachers' stress, increase job satisfaction, and create healthier classroom environments.

Benefits

Research indicates that there are many benefits to integrating mindfulness into public schools, including staff retention. Mindfulness programs directed at professional development for teachers have been shown to reduce the rate of teacher burnout, improve their self-care and emotional regulation, aid in stress management, and make classroom atmospheres healthier and more engaging.

There are also benefits to teaching mindfulness to students themselves. Studies have shown that mindfulness courses for adolescents can improve their attention and well-being, reduce their anxiety and reactivity, and help with their self-regulation and awareness. The potential for mindful teaching and learning is massive, and in the long run could have significantly positive impacts on public education.

FACT

One research study by Robert Wall, MDiv, examined the effect of using tai chi and mindfulness-based stress reduction in a Boston public middle school. Afterward, the students participating expressed feelings of well-being, calmness, relaxation, less reactivity, improved sleep, greater self-awareness, and increased self-care.

Barriers

There are increasing opportunities for public school administrators to bring mindfulness education to their schools. Some organizations teaching mindfulness focus primarily on the professional development of teachers, and show them how to integrate mindfulness practices into their lives and the classroom; other organizations offer to come out to schools to teach mindfulness directly to students. There are also abundant opportunities for parents and other professionals who work with children and teenagers to participate in mindfulness trainings.

The two major barriers to integrating mindfulness into public education include the lack of awareness regarding the positive impacts mindfulness training can have on teachers and students, and a lack of funding available to schools to pay for such training.

Raising awareness about mindfulness education is an important step. The more that parents, teachers, and administrators in your community learn about mindfulness training and the many benefits it can bring to school environments, the more motivation there will be to seek out such opportunities.

Possible solutions to the lack of public school funding include motivating Parent-Teacher Associations (PTAs), who can fundraise to bring mindfulness training to their schools; finding individual donors who are willing to "adopt" and pay for different teachers (or potentially an entire school) to receive training; and scholarships that some mindfulness training organizations are able to offer. Grants may also be a possibility.

Although the following is far from being a comprehensive list of organizations that teach and promote mindfulness education, these are good places to begin when learning what types of programs are available to teachers, students, parents, and other professionals who work with children.

Mindfulness in Schools Project

The Mindfulness in Schools Project (MiSP) is a nonprofit organization based in the United Kingdom whose aim is to encourage, support, and research the teaching of secular mindfulness in schools. To further this mission, the

MiSP team works in collaboration with the Oxford Mindfulness Centre and the Well-Being Institute of Cambridge University.

Meet the MiSP Team

Richard Burnett and Chris Cullen are cofounders of the Mindfulness in Schools Project and coauthors of the .b curriculum; Dr. Chris O'Neil is another coauthor of the .b curriculum, and Sarah Hennelly is a researcher and teacher-training coordinator for the organization. Since 2007 they have been conducting research studies to explore the effects of teaching mindfulness in schools, and have published multiple papers.

The creators of the .b curriculum are all experienced classroom teachers and mindfulness practitioners. They have taught mindfulness in schools, experienced the tremendous benefits of doing so, and are now sharing their knowledge and experience with others. To this end, they have developed and refined a unique mindfulness curriculum called ".b" that schools can purchase.

Supported by an impressive Board of Advisors, the MiSP team is now dedicated to bringing their .b mindfulness curriculum to schools around the world as well as offering teacher trainings.

The .b Curriculum

The name of this curriculum is quite intentional: ".b" means "Stop, Breathe, and Be!" Mindfulness is at the heart of this nine-session curriculum, wherein each lesson teaches a distinct mindfulness skill to students in entertaining and engaging ways.

The weekly lessons of the .b curriculum (as written on the MiSP website) are:

1. Introduction
2. Puppy Training: First steps in focusing attention
3. Turning Toward Calm: Establishing calm and concentration
4. Recognizing Worry: Noticing how your mind plays tricks on you
5. Being Here Now: Developing present moment awareness in the every day
6. Moving Mindfully: Slowing and savoring activities, including walking

7. Stepping Back: Stepping back from thoughts that hijack you
8. Befriending the Difficult: Allowing, accepting and being with difficult emotions
9. Pulling It All Together: Looking back and making it personal

The essence of the curriculum is to raise student awareness of their inner and outer environments, and to show them how they can practice and benefit from mindfulness in their day-to-day lives. This curriculum is specifically designed for middle and high school students; however, it is flexible enough to be adapted to a wide age range.

The .b curriculum is only to be taught by educators who maintain a regular mindfulness practice of their own. Teachers interested in teaching the .b curriculum must go through a four-day teacher training program in addition to having completed a separate eight-week training program (such as Mindfulness-Based Cognitive Therapy or Mindfulness-Based Stress Reduction). This is necessary so that teachers can model the skills the .b curriculum is teaching for their students.

To learn more about the .b curriculum and how to bring it to your school system, visit the Mindfulness in Schools Project website at *www .mindfulnessinschools.org.*

FACT

The Association for Mindfulness in Education, which seeks to support mindfulness training as a component of K–12 education, is compiling a comprehensive list of schools and organizations across the United States that provide K–12 mindfulness education. People can learn more about the AME and what they do by visiting their website, *www .mindfuleducation.org.*

Inward Bound Mindfulness Education

Inward Bound Mindfulness Education (iBme) is a nonprofit organization dedicated to improving the lives of teens, parents, and professionals. This organization focuses on cultivating awareness, compassion, and kindness for all beings by offering mindfulness retreats for adults and teens, as well as in-school and after-school programs. Retreats are offered in different locations across the country.

Adult Retreats (typically five to seven days)

Adult retreats are geared toward parents and professionals who work with teenagers. iBme helps adults who work with teens restore their physical and emotional balance, while learning to recognize their personal limits. These retreats integrate approaches in mindfulness and social-emotional learning that help adults become more aware of their own physical, emotional, and spiritual needs, and also equips them with tools they can use to meet these needs.

The ultimate purpose is to learn and practice using these tools so they can be brought back home and to the workplace. The key to these retreats is mindfulness: introducing adults to the concept of present-moment, nonjudgmental awareness, and teaching them how to use mindfulness in the context of their day-to-day interactions with teenagers.

Teen Retreats (typically five to seven days)

The three core elements of iBme retreats for teens include mindfulness, authentic communication, and connecting with the natural world. Teens are taught different ways to practice awareness and concentration, and practice integrating these tools into their daily lives.

With meditation being one of many tools teens are taught, the focus of these retreats is on helping young adults learn how to settle the mind, manage their thoughts and emotions, focus and sustain their concentration, cultivate compassion for themselves and others, and learn to listen deeply and communicate with others skillfully.

One important feature of these retreats is the opportunity for teens to practice mindfulness in the midst of regular activities. To this end, there are a variety of daily workshops available including sports, yoga, art, theater, music, and poetry, as well as discussion groups on various topics for participants to choose from. This type of engaged, hands-on mindfulness practice helps teens acclimate to using mindfulness in action as well as in quiet meditation.

In-School Programs and Teaching Trainings

iBme offers to come to schools to do:

- All-school assembly presentations on mindfulness and the brain
- One-time introductory classes or twelve-week in-class instructions on mindfulness exercises, social-emotional skills, and community building
- After-school programs that focus on identity formation, interconnection, and service work
- Faculty development seminars that address issues teachers commonly face (such as burnout and stress) and how mindfulness can be used in the classroom to help both teachers and students
- Daylong service programs that include an all-school assembly, classroom visits, faculty planning period visits, and an evening session for parents

In partnership with the Mindfulness in Schools Project, iBme staff has worked to adopt their .b curriculum to high schools in the United States. This is the foundational curriculum of iBme, and is used with students during in-class instructional periods.

iBme also offers teacher trainings that certify teachers to teach mindfulness to high school students using the .b curriculum. To learn more about this and the many programs that Inward Bound Mindfulness Education offer to schools, please visit their website at *www.ibme.info*.

FACT

Ellen J. Langer, from the Department of Psychology at Harvard University in Cambridge, Massachusetts, wrote a paper entitled *Mindful Learning* in which she states that experimental research conducted over a span of twenty-five years shows that mindfulness increases health, longevity, competence, memory, and creativity while simultaneously decreasing accidents and stress.

Mindful Schools

Originally founded by Laurie Grossman, Richard Shankman, and Megan Cowan, Mindful Schools is a U.S.–based nonprofit organization whose mission is to help lead the integration of mindfulness into education. They further this mission by offering in-class instruction, professional training opportunities, and other resources that support mindfulness in education.

The History of and Need for Mindful Schools

Seeing a desperate need to help students deal with the intense levels of stress they were experiencing, Laurie Grossman (who at that time was an Outreach Coordinator) and Richard Shankman (a longtime mindfulness teacher) created a five-week pilot mindfulness program in 2007.

The results of this pilot program were so positive that mindfulness teacher Megan Cowan implemented the program in another nearby school. Since then, the organization has steadily continued to grow and spread.

To address some of the serious issues facing public schools in the United States today (including students' inability to focus, impulsiveness, high levels of stress, and lack of connection with their surrounding community), the Mindful Schools curriculum aims to develop students' "inner compass." By teaching students techniques that help them focus, resolve conflicts, and manage their stress and their emotions, it allows them to reflect and make choices more intentionally as opposed to simply reacting.

In-School Program and Adult Courses

Mindfulness Schools offers a three-step process for teaching mindfulness. The first two steps are online courses. Whether you are a teacher trying to bring mindfulness into your school or a professional who wants to learn how to integrate mindfulness into your work with children, you take the same online courses (steps one and two).

- *Step 1.* The first course (entitled Mindfulness Fundamentals) is a six-week online course that shows you how to incorporate mindfulness into your own lives. This course builds a foundation for mindful living, and teaches participants how to create their own mindfulness practice.

- *Step 2.* The second course (entitled Curriculum Training) is a sixteen-hour online course that shows you how to use the Mindful Schools K–12 curriculum with children. This curriculum focuses on teaching children how to pay attention, build empathy, cultivate self-awareness, reduce stress, and control their impulses. The course also teaches participants how to incorporate mindfulness into behavior management. Curriculum lessons are easily adapted to other contexts, such as in the home or in private therapy sessions.
- *Step 3.* Community calls are available to any and all Curriculum Training graduates. These video or teleconference calls address a number of different topics, including participants' questions.

All Mindful School courses are geared toward professionals who work with children, including educators, psychologists, social workers, parents, and others. Schools interested in the Mindful School programs pay for teachers to participate in steps one and two. (The community calls have no additional cost.) Understanding that each school has its own financial limitations, Mindful Schools suggests a few different funding options on their website, including a need-based scholarship program.

To learn more about Mindful Schools and how to bring their curriculum to your school system, visit the Mindful Schools website. (*www .mindfulschools.org*)

ESSENTIAL

Mindfulness is about paying attention and noticing things, which taps into active observational skills. What children learn may not be as important as *how* they learn it, according to Ellen J. Langer of Harvard University. When students are taught through facts instead of by exploring questions and perspectives, education becomes much less engaging.

Holistic Life Foundation, Inc.

The Holistic Life Foundation, Inc. is a nonprofit based in Baltimore, Maryland, that performs human and environmental health programs to demonstrate the interconnectedness people have with the environment in which they live.

Founded by brothers Ali and Atman Smith with their friend Andres Gonzalez, the Holistic Life Foundation offers training, classes, and workshops on various community, health, and mindfulness-related topics. In addition to offering after-school, mentoring, and environmental advocacy programs to Baltimore K–12 public schools, the HLF also offers a twenty-four-week Stress Reduction and Mindfulness curriculum.

The HLF Stress Reduction and Mindfulness Curriculum

The SRM curriculum teaches students how to resolve conflicts peacefully, improve their focus and concentration, gain greater control and awareness of their thoughts and emotions, and improve their self-regulation skills. They also teach different techniques they can use to help them relax and reduce stress.

By showing students how to effectively use tools such as yoga, meditation, tai chi, breathing, centering, and more, the SRM curriculum teaches mindfulness through two forty-five-minute classes per week. Students have assignments in between classes that reinforce the skills and techniques they are learning.

The Research

The HLF partnered with the Johns Hopkins Bloomberg School of Public Health and the Prevention Research Center at Pennsylvania State University to test out this curriculum in four Baltimore City public schools. They facilitated the first-ever randomized control study of a school-based mindfulness and yoga intervention for urban youth, from which a scientific paper was published in the October 2010 edition of the *Journal of Abnormal Psychology*.

The study's findings turned out quite positive, showing that students who participated in the curriculum were better equipped to respond to stress. Participants who encountered issues such as rumination, intrusive thoughts, and emotional reactivity learned better ways of handling their involuntary stress reactions, which led to an improvement in their social, emotional, and behavioral development.

Multiple articles have been published about HLF's Stress Reduction and Mindfulness curriculum. To learn more about this and other programs they offer, visit the Holistic Life Foundation, Inc.'s website at *www.hlfinc.org*.

QUESTION

What is Mindfulness-Based Stress Reduction, and who came up with it?
Developed by Dr. John Kabat-Zinn, Mindfulness-Based Stress Reduction uses a combination of mindfulness, meditation, and yoga to help people address health problems, anxiety, depression, and stress. Two decades' worth of published research indicates that the majority of participants who complete the MBSR Program experience a lasting decrease in their physical and psychological symptoms.

The Garrison Institute

The Garrison Institute (GI) is a nonprofit, nonsectarian organization that explores the intersection of contemplation and engaged action in the world. By applying the transformative power of contemplation to today's social and environmental concerns, the GI works to create a more compassionate and resilient future.

The Garrison Institute currently has three major program initiatives: the Contemplative Teaching and Learning (CTL) Initiative, the Transforming Trauma Initiative, and the Climate, Mind, and Behavior Initiative. The following section will focus on the CTL initiative.

The Contemplative Teaching and Learning Initiative

The sole focus of the CTL initiative is to develop the field of contemplative teaching and learning for K–12 educators and classrooms. When teachers are introduced to evidence-based contemplative methods, student academic performance improves, the teacher burnout rate is reduced, and school environments become healthier.

CTL also facilitates dialogue between educators, scientists, funders, and policy makers regarding how to develop and implement contemplative-based teacher trainings, classroom pilot programs, publications, and other resources for educators, researchers, teachers, and schools. This continuous multiprofession conversation has contributed a great deal to growing and supporting this emerging field.

Although CTL researches, develops, and tests many different contemplative educational tools, their largest program is called CARE for Teachers, and focuses on professional development.

CARE for Teachers

CARE stands for Cultivating Awareness and Resilience in Education. Through a unique program that nurtures and promotes K–12 teachers' inner resources (including awareness, presence, compassion, reflection, and inspiration), teachers are able to manage their stress more effectively while simultaneously revitalizing their teaching lives. The program teaches basic mindfulness activities, reflection, and emotional regulation; teachers are then shown how to use these skills under the more stressful and challenging circumstances they might encounter in schools.

In essence, what teachers learn through this program are numerous emotional awareness and regulation skills that empower them to be more calm and mindful inside (and out) of the classroom. Research has shown that the CARE program can help teachers enhance their classroom learning environments, manage their stress in more sustainable ways, and maintain a sense of joy in what they do. Students of CARE participants have benefited enormously from the skills their teachers have learned.

The Garrison Institute offers this program in two different ways: there is a five-day summer retreat at the Garrison Institute itself, or it can be facilitated through four day-long sessions that are spread out over the course of four to five weeks. Coaching via the telephone and Internet is available in between sessions, and is designed to support teachers' real-time practice and implementation of the skills they learn.

To learn more about the CARE for Teachers program and the other programs the Garrison Institute offers, visit the GI website or the CARE for Teachers website *www.garrisoninstitute.org* and *www.care4teachers.org*.

APPENDIX

Glossary

Adolescent

A person at the developmental stage between preadolescence and young adulthood encompassing the years between thirteen and twenty. Adolescents are characterized by full physical and motor development and growing independence and autonomy from their parents. Adolescents are typically deeply invested in their social lives and in resolving questions of identity. Neurodevelopment in adolescence centers on the growth of myelin and the development of the prefrontal cortex, a region involved in coordinating information from across the brain and used in advanced cognitive functions such as understanding relationships of cause and effect, risk assessment, and impulse control.

Agency

An individual's sense of his own ability to affect his environment and actualize his will.

Anthropomorphism

The application of human characteristics (often emotions) to nonhuman entities such as animals, rocks, plants, natural phenomena, etc. To say that a storm is furious or that the bunny looked sad is to anthropomorphize the storm and the bunny. Children anthropomorphize as a way of relating to and understanding other beings; it is an important part of their pretend play, particularly when learning empathy.

Axon

An extension of the cell body of a neuron that connects the neuron to other cells. Axons can be quite short or very long (up to two meters in humans) depending on the specific type of nerve cell that they are a part of. Generally speaking, axons transmit a signal from that cell to other cells while dendrites receive connections from other axons.

Behavior

The observable actions or reactions of humans, animals, or other entities under any given circumstances. In terms of human behavior, it is how one acts or conducts oneself alone, in front of others, or toward others.

Bodily-Kinesthetic Intelligence

A form of intelligence under Dr. Gardner's Theory of Multiple Intelligences that describes people who are action-oriented and love to move. People with this intelligence are described as being very engaged with their bodies, and often have excellent balance and coordination. Also known as "body-smarts."

Cerebellum

The "little brain," located at the back of the skull and below the cortex, the cerebellum is largely responsible for coordinating conscious commands received from the cortex with sensory data from the body received through the spinal cord. The cerebellum is directly involved in balance and equilibrium, timing and coordination.

Child

A child is a young human between three and seven years old.

Child Development

The science of understanding children through the development of their bodies, minds, and social relationships as they progress through life. It is a study of the subtle and overt changes in children as they age, the factors that influence these changes, and how these changes manifest in the child's daily life. There are three overlapping domains of development: physical, cognitive, and social-emotional, each of which is influenced by numerous other factors.

Cognition

Conscious thought. In the brain, cognition occurs in the cerebral cortex, particularly the frontal lobe and prefrontal cortex.

Cognitive Skills

The skills used in the processing of thoughts, both abstract and concrete. This includes things such as memory, attention, comprehension, learning, and language skills.

Cooperative Play

Play in which two or more children interact and work together to define and achieve a mutual goal. In terms of a child's developmental progression, cooperative play comes after parallel play.

Dendrites

The branch-like extensions of a nerve cell that receive connections from other nerves.

Developmental Stages

A model for understanding how humans develop from birth. Although these stages are often broken into different age ranges, developmental stages are not solid or discrete categories; instead, developmental stages are grouped together based on the age ranges in which humans tend to reach certain physical, cognitive, and social-emotional milestones. It should be noted that people around the world define these stages differently depending on the culture they are in. Ultimately, each child is unique and follows her own unique course of development.

Dialogic Reading

A style of reading with young children that promotes interaction between the child and the adult through asking questions and talking about a story. Dialogic reading typically follows a PEER sequence (Prompt, Evaluate, Expand, Repeat) that initiates a dialogue, expands a child's knowledge by giving the adult a chance to add new details and vocabulary, and finally reinforces the learning by repeating important information. Over the course of multiple readings, the role of storyteller shifts to the child and the role of active listener shifts to the adult.

Empathy

The ability to access and share in the emotional experiences of others; vicariously experiencing another person or being's physical or emotional state. Empathy is an important social-emotional skill for children to acquire, as it helps them relate to and connect with other people and beings. This aids in a child's ability to think about the experiences and needs of others, as well as developing the mental flexibility to see things from different perspectives. This skill helps children begin shifting away from their developmentally appropriate selfishness to taking others into consideration.

External Locus of Control

Behavior enacted in response to an instruction or command from another person, usually an authority figure such as a parent or teacher. Typically, this is behavior that cannot be relied upon in the absence of the authority figure or other mechanisms of enforcement.

Fine Motor Skills

The small muscle movements of body parts including the hands, wrists, fingers, feet, toes, lips, and tongue. This includes actions such as pinching, lacing, tying, buttoning, articulating words clearly, and more. Fine motor skills begin to develop after gross motor skills.

Frontal Lobe

The forwardmost portion of the cerebral cortex involved in conscious control of movement, thought, and executive function. The frontal lobe includes the prefrontal cortex.

Gross Motor Skills

The large muscle movements of body parts including the arms, legs, and entire body. These skills include actions such as walking, running, jumping, crawling, swinging, and more. Gross motor skills develop before fine motor skills.

Infant

A young human between birth and walking.

Intelligence

According to Dr. Gardner's Theory of Multiple Intelligences, intelligence is measured by an individual's ability to creatively solve problems, learn and integrate new information, and offer something of value in a culture.

Intentional and Interactive Reading Curriculum (IIRC)

This particular reading curriculum uses dialogic reading as a foundation, and builds upon it by using a combination of CROWD questions, interactive reading techniques, and related games or activities as a means of teaching particular social-emotional skills and values to children.

Internal Locus of Control

Behavior enacted based on an internally generated impulse. Because this behavior arises from an inner desire of the person enacting the behavior, it can be expected to occur regardless of the presence of demand or threat from an authority figure.

Interpersonal

Pertaining to the relationships between people.

Interpersonal Intelligence

A form of intelligence under Dr. Gardner's Theory of Multiple Intelligences that describes people who are good at "reading" other people's emotions and understanding their motivations and desires. They are skilled at working and communicating with others, which gives them an advantage when it comes to mediation and conflict resolution. People with strong interpersonal skills have a knack for finding balanced compromises. They are good at interacting with, relating to, and getting along with others, and can become effective leaders. Also known as a "people-smarts."

Intrapersonal

What exists or happens within one's own self or mind.

Intrapersonal Intelligence

A form of intelligence under Dr. Gardner's Theory of Multiple Intelligences that describes people who have a strong awareness of their own thoughts, feelings, ideas, motivations, and goals. They are skilled at identifying their own strengths and weaknesses, enjoy planning and setting goals, and often need time to be alone to process their experiences and/or for creative expression. Also known as a "self-smarts."

Kinesthetic Intelligence

See "Bodily-Kinesthetic Intelligence."

Limbic System

A group of connected brain structures in the cerebrum responsible for the processing of memory and emotion. The limbic system includes the hippocampus, amygdalae, fornix, septum, and anterior thalmic nuclei.

Linguistic Intelligence

A form of intelligence under Dr. Gardner's Theory of Multiple Intelligences that describes people who have the capacity to use language to express what is on their mind, and to understand other people. Those with a strong linguistic intelligence often think in words instead of pictures, and have highly developed auditory skills. They are effective communicators who enjoy growing their vocabularies and using language as their canvas of expression, and often enjoy reading, writing, listening, and public speaking. Also known as "word-smarts."

Locus of Control

This theoretical construct describes where a person perceives control in their life to be located. Having an *internal* locus of control describes a person who believes that he himself is in control and has the authority to make decisions and effect change; having an *external* locus of control describes a person who believes that someone else or other people are in control, and only they have the authority to make decisions and effect change. It is another way to describe a person who is empowered, or a person who believes that somebody else or other people have power over him.

Logical-Mathematical Intelligence

A form of intelligence under Dr. Gardner's Theory of Multiple Intelligences that describes people who are good at reasoning, recognizing patterns, analyzing, and solving problems. They are conceptual thinkers who have a knack for precision, investigation, and scientific processes. They enjoy exploring and discussing abstract ideas, and have an affinity for the logic of math and numbers. Also known as "logic-smarts."

Mathematical Intelligence

See "Logical-Mathematical Intelligence."

Meditation

A varied set of practices that engage conscious attention, either in open or highly focused contexts.

Mindfulness

The practice of paying attention to one's internal environment (one's thoughts, emotions, and physical sensations) and external environment (the physical and emotional state of other people, beings, and the state of one's surroundings) without passing judgment; the practice of noticing these elements and taking this information into consideration before and while acting; paying attention.

Modeling

Teaching behaviors to others through example, whether positive or negative. For example, parents model behaviors to their children constantly; what a parent does, how he speaks, moves, acts, and reacts to various circumstances is modeling said behaviors to any nearby children.

Musical Intelligence

A form of intelligence under Dr. Gardner's Theory of Multiple Intelligences that describes people who are particularly attuned to patterns, rhythms, melodies, and song. These skills can help people with a strong musical intelligence to identify various patterns, learn new information, have powerful and impactful writing skills, be especially aware of and able to identify sounds in their environment and/or to be skilled at playing musical instruments. Also known as "music-smarts."

Myelin

A layer of fat that develops along the length of nerve axons and accelerates the chemo-electrical signal transmitted by that nerve.

Naturalist Intelligence

A form of intelligence under Dr. Gardner's Theory of Multiple Intelligences that describes people who enjoy being in the outdoors, exploring, and learning about flora, fauna, and biology. They are shrewd observers of their environment who can pick up on subtle changes, and are skilled at collecting, categorizing, and cataloging information. They love being in and learning about the natural world, and tend to be interested in activities like camping, hiking, and/or gardening. Also known as "nature-smarts."

Nature

Contextualized by the conversation about the impact of nature versus nurture on a child's development, nature refers to the genetic "hard-wiring" that each child is born with. Nature is not considered to be changeable.

Neuron

A nerve cell. The brain, spinal cord, and nervous system are all composed primarily of this type of cell.

Nurture

Contextualized by the conversation about the impact of nature versus nurture on a child's development, nurture refers to the ever-changing environment in which a child grows, and how each child shapes and is shaped by said environment. Nurture is where parents have the greatest influence over their child's development.

Occipital Lobe

The rearmost portion of the cerebrum, largely responsible for processing information perceived with the eyes.

Parallel Play

Play in which one child plays alongside other children with limited (if any) interactions. This is typical of toddlers and young children, and is a healthy step toward more social play. In terms of a child's developmental progression, parallel play precedes cooperative play.

Parietal Lobe

A complex region of the brain that lies on the top of the cerebrum behind the frontal lobe and above both the temporal and occipital lobe. It is largely responsible for processing sensory inputs from the body and visual-spatial relationships.

Preadolescent

A preadolescent is a young human between eight and twelve years old.

Prefrontal Cortex

Sometimes referred to as the PFC, it is part of the frontal lobe, and lies directly above the eyeballs. This part of the brain is the region most closely associated with risk assessment, understanding causal relationships, and conscious choice. It is also heavily involved in coordinating and integrating information received from other parts of the brain. The prefrontal cortex is one of the last parts of the brain to develop and continues to change significantly through the late twenties.

Reaction

Taking emotionally based action(s) without making a conscious choice or having any intentionality behind the action; not taking any aspects of a particular situation into consideration beforehand. Reactions are usually triggered and driven by the rising of strong emotions and often lead us to do things we later regret. Contrasted with "Response."

Response

Action(s) derived from a conscious and intentional choice, despite the arising of a potentially different emotional reaction. Responses are based on the consideration of various factors, as contrasted with "Reaction," which is purely habitual or emotionally driven.

Skillfulness

Carrying out a task or behavior with care, consideration, and attention to not only the task at hand but how it may be perceived and interpreted by others and with regard to the possible consequences of that course of action.

Social-Emotional Development

The development of a child's intrapersonal and interpersonal skills. This includes how a child experiences, expresses, and manages her own emotions, as well as her ability to establish healthy, mutual, and balanced relationships with others.

Socioeconomic Status (SES)

A combined economic and sociological measure of a person or family's position in relation to others, based upon the factors of income, education, and occupation. In blunt terms, it is a measure of social class.

Spatial Intelligence

A form of intelligence under Dr. Gardner's Theory of Multiple Intelligences that describes people who are skilled at visualization. They can re-create visual experiences of people, places, and objects that are no longer physically present, and usually manipulate what they see in their mind's eye. People with a strong spatial intelligence can typically give directions, follow directions, and read maps accurately. Not all people who are spatially intelligent are artists; however, most artists possess this intelligence. Also known as "picture-smarts."

Sympathetic joy

Experiencing joy or happiness in response to seeing another person experience joy. In sympathetic joy, the happiness that is experienced is not based on any effect directly received by the person experiencing it; rather, it is in direct response to the happiness of others.

Temporal Lobe

The bottommost portion of the cerebrum, primarily responsible for the processing of auditory information and semantics.

Theory of Multiple Intelligences

A theory proposed by Dr. Howard Gardner in 1983, contending that intelligence is measured by an individual's ability to creatively solve problems, learn and integrate new information, and offer something of value in a culture. To date, Dr. Gardner has identified eight different intelligences: linguistic (word-smart), logical-mathematical (logic-smart), spatial (picture-smart), bodily-kinesthetic (body-smart), musical (music-smart), interpersonal (people-smart), intrapersonal (self-smart), and naturalist (nature-smart). According to this theory, everyone is born with all eight of these intelligences, and individuals are more naturally inclined to some over others; the question is in what combination of strength and to what degree.

Toddler
A young human between the early walking stage and three years old.

Vicarious Reinforcement
When a person observes another's actions and the consequences of those actions, and learns from the experience. This happens regularly with toddlers and children and can occur through everyday interactions, storytelling, and dramatic play.

Index

We Have EVERYTHING® on Anything!

With more than 19 million copies sold, the Everything® series has become one of America's favorite resources for solving problems, learning new skills, and organizing lives. Our brand is not only recognizable—it's also welcomed.

The series is a hand-in-hand partner for people who are ready to tackle new subjects—like you!

For more information on the Everything® series, please visit *www.adamsmedia.com*

The Everything® list spans a wide range of subjects, with more than 500 titles covering 25 different categories:

Business	History	Reference
Careers	Home Improvement	Religion
Children's Storybooks	Everything Kids	Self-Help
Computers	Languages	Sports & Fitness
Cooking	Music	Travel
Crafts and Hobbies	New Age	Wedding
Education/Schools	Parenting	Writing
Games and Puzzles	Personal Finance	
Health	Pets	